# "Due Process" DENIED

### Corruption in Cape May County and at the Board of Medical Examiners in the state of New Jersey

An autobiography of Dr. John Costino, a licensed New Jersey physician, his battle with the corrupt weaponized justice system in Cape May County, and the political, malignant, legal tyranny at the Board of Medical Examiners in Trenton, NJ.

## Dr. John G. Costino

Copyright © 2022  John G Costino

All rights reserved. No part of this book may be reproduced in any form or by any electronic or mechanical means, including information storage and retrieval systems, without permission in writing from the publisher, except by reviewers, who may quote brief passages in a review.

Printed in the United States of Amercia

Published by John G. Costino

# Dedication

This work is dedicated to my wife, my children,
my grandchildren, my family, my friends and patients who have
supported me throughtout this disgraceful ordeal. It is also dedicated to
the physicians of tomorrow as they continue to serve those
in need of medical care.

# PREFACE

All my life I've wanted to do something unequivocal. I considered graduation from college in 1966 to be special, followed by my marriage and children which were certainly special, followed by my graduation from medical school in 1971. I've been a physician for fifty years now and I am certain, unequivocally that it remains the conduct of my life documented through the past thirteen years recorded in this text to be unequivocal.

"Life is a storm, one day basking in the sun, and the next thrown upon the rocks. The quality of a man's character is manifest by what he does when he's thrown upon the rocks."

The contents of this book contain my general philosophy of my work as a physician with certain anecdotal topics salient to me and to most physicians. I have been a clinician since 1971, with a formidable experience in medicine. I have treated thousands of patients, their injuries, their diseases and their secondary and tertiary psychological ramifications.

The last thirteen years of my life have been spent dealing with the legal community of Cape May County, prosecutors and detectives, deputy attorneys at the Board of Medical Examiners (BME), Drug Enforcement Agency characters (DEA), United States Postal supervisors and personnel, and political judges. Many of my statements in this text may seem harsh to you; they are!!!

# "Due Process" Denied

**My statements in this writing represent only my opinions, and mine alone.** They are based upon the facts in my criminal case, and the events that transpired at the Board of Medical Examiners in Trenton, New Jersey. My comments regarding certain prosecutors, certain deputy attorneys and judges are based solely upon my experience in my criminal case in Cape May County, and my civil case at the Board of Medical Examiners, and the Office of Administrative Law (OAL), from 2007 to 2013. Furthermore, from 2013 to 2020 I filed a number of civil lawsuits against multiple individuals involved in my case. All the material in this writing remains a matter of public record. The reader may at any time search the Cape May County record as well as the New Jersey Board of Medical Examiners record to reassure themselves of the accuracy of my critical statements regarding certain prosecutors, detectives, deputy attorneys, judges and other characters involved in my **grueling, burdensome** thirteen year experience.

My statements and criticism relates to only those involved in my experience with Cape May County, and the New Jersey Board of Medical Examiners, and the justice system, criminal as well as civil courts. Currently, the former Cape May County Prosecutor, Robert Taylor, is now retired, and Sandra Dick, the former Chief Deputy Attorney at the Board of Medical Examiners is also retired. My critical remarks and factual statements in this record relate to only those individuals involved in my multiple legal experiences from September of 2007 to January of 2020.

The legal tyranny that I experienced in Cape May County, and at the Board of Medical Examiners in Trenton, and in the civil court system, relates only to those individuals clearly defined in this text. Please understand that my background as a clinician since 1971 has given me a stable platform to evaluate the personalities involved in my Cape May County criminal case, and my civil case at the Board of Medical Examiners and at the Office of Administrative Law (OAL). Although I have never had the opportunity to examine certain individuals who represent the principals in my thirteen year sojourn except for the three undercover law enforcement officers, I have made a critical evaluation of every individual criticized here in one way or another, based upon their briefs and oral arguments, with judges

# Preface

and their final decisions. My experience with these characters includes multiple detective depositions under oath, testimony in open court by various prosecutors and deputy attorneys, and their written statements and rulings made by certain judges. **I've had a firsthand opportunity to evaluate their lies and gross misrepresentations orally in open court, and in their legal briefs.**

I have evaluated all the players involved in this travesty of justice, and my clinical opinions are based upon facts, and hard evidence in an effort to **expose the corruption and conspiracies** which are clearly enumerated, in my case.

In my opinion, many prosecutors are narcissistic, with associated personality disorders, and certain ones express delusional manifestations, along with their egomania, secondary to the absolute control that they exert over the general population, with abusive power, and specifically at the Board of Medical Examiners with their absolute abuse of power, and legal tyranny.

I apologize for the redundancy of certain topics which are factual and important in my experience. Redundancy was necessary in order for the reader to grasp the immutable issues that my attorneys and I identified and brought to the surface. You may find at times my critique of certain judges in this New Jersey system to be negative or unfair believe me, in my opinion, they deserve my criticism. The motivation of certain judges in my experience was purely political, and flies in the face of factual evidence. Certain judges simply rule contrary to the law. Certain judges, in my opinion are simply **fundamentally dishonest**, with a **cognitive bias** and **prejudice** in their attempt **to criminalize my practice of medicine for political expediency.**

As United States citizens, we all have a constitutional right to a **jury of our peers.** A dishonest political judge can and does circumvent that constitutional right whether a civil case in Superior Court, Federal Court, or Administrative Law Court. The reader should understand that I have been the victim of these unjust rulings from the bench, which were **subversive,** and **disgraceful to me as a physician in the state of New Jersey.**

# "Due Process" Denied

Lastly, please excuse my analytical approach in this writing. **It is not a love story, and there is no fluff expressed.** I have attempted to keep boredom to a minimum however the circumstances and factual accounts of the events in my case will be difficult for you to believe. You may think that I am exaggerating, however, what I have written is true and a matter of public record. My language is plain, to the point, and based upon absolute evidence, not supposition.

My background is that of an objective examiner and physician, and I attribute my abilities and my intuition to both of my parents, who were the love of my life!!!

Being strong-minded and somewhat courageous, helps you to understand the frightening power and corruption of the justice system.

# Contents

| | |
|---|---|
| Invictus by William Ernest Henley | pg. XII |
| A Brief Introduction | pg. XIII |
| A Piece of My Mind | pg. XXII |
| Individuals Associated with My Case | pg. XXXIII |

| | | | |
|---|---|---|---|
| Chapter 1 | pg. 1 | Chapter 16 | pg. 188 |
| Chapter 2 | pg. 41 | Chapter 17 | pg. 194 |
| Chapter 3 | pg. 48 | Chapter 18 | pg. 215 |
| Chapter 4 | pg. 56 | Chapter 19 | pg. 231 |
| Chapter 5 | pg. 61 | Chapter 20 | pg. 199 |
| Chapter 6 | pg. 66 | Chapter 21 | pg. 211 |
| Chapter 7 | pg. 69 | Chapter 22 | pg. 222 |
| Chapter 8 | pg. 75 | Chapter 23 | pg. 230 |
| Chapter 9 | pg. 81 | Chapter 24 | pg. 241 |
| Chapter 10 | pg. 90 | Chapter 25 | pg. 248 |
| Chapter 11 | pg. 97 | Chapter 26 | pg. 253 |
| Chapter 12 | pg. 113 | Chapter 27 | pg. 256 |
| Chapter 13 | pg. 130 | Chapter 28 | pg. 259 |
| Chapter 14 | pg. 139 | Appendix | pg. 262 |
| Chapter 15 | pg. 149 | | |

# INVICTUS

By William Ernest Henley
(A memorable evocation of Victorian stoicism)

Out of the night that covers me,
Black as the pit from pole to pole,
I thank whatever gods may be
For my unconquerable soul.

In the fell clutch of circumstance
I have not winced nor cried aloud.
Under the bludgeonings of chance
My head is bloody, but unbowed.

Beyond this place of wrath and tears
Looms but the horror of the shade,
And yet the menace of the years
Finds, and shall find, me unafraid.

It matters not how strait the gate,
How charged with punishments the scroll.
I am the master of my fate:
I am the captain of my soul.

# A Brief Introduction

"Find a way to serve the many for service to many leads to greatness."

I was born in July of 1944, the first of six children. After my father's service in the United States Army, he began his career as a carpenter, and my dear mother raised all six children with authority and compassion in a rather frugal setting in Camden, New Jersey. I went to grammar school at St. Joseph's in East Camden, and high school at Camden Catholic High School, where in my senior year I was elected Student Council President.

I graduated high school in 1962 and then began a four-year career at Rutgers University, and graduated in June of 1966 with a major in biology and chemistry and a minor in psychology. In the fall of 1966 I began a brief teaching career at Camden Catholic High School in biology, general science, and chemistry. Following my one year tenure as a high school teacher, I began a four year career at Philadelphia College of Osteopathic Medicine, and in 1971, I graduated with a degree in medicine. Following my graduation at Philadelphia College of Osteopathic Medicine, I entered an internship program at Cooper Medical Center in Camden, NJ, and in June of 1972, I began a career in emergency medicine. From 1972 to 1976, I worked full-time as an emergency room physician. During this period of time I also accepted a position with the State of New Jersey as a medical examiner in the Dept. of Labor and Industry, Division of Workers Compensation. I examined patients for the state of New Jersey in the compensation court in the cities of Camden, Trenton, Atlantic City and Bridgeton. In the summer of 1976 I left emergency medicine, and began a primary, solo, general practice in Cape

# A Brief Introduction

May County. I am a patient advocate with kindness and compassion in an effort to improve the health and wellbeing of all my patients. Most physicians strive for **high ideals and intellectual excellence** in their daily practice to treat and care for their patient population. Along with my wife, Barbara, who is a registered nurse, and a certified Physician's assistant, I have exhausted every bit of energy devoted to patient care in an effort to improve the lives and the health of all of our patients.

I am certified in General Medicine, Sports Medicine, Quality Assurance, and Utilization Review. I am a Fellow in the American Osteopathic College of Rheumatology, the American Academy of Pain Management, and the American Academy of Sports Physicians. I am also a charter member of the American College of Emergency Physicians. I am certified by the Drug Enforcement Agency (DEA) to prescribe **Suboxone** for use in the treatment of opiate addiction. In addition to my general practice of medicine, sports medicine, and pain management, my office treated many cases of acutely injured patients, and workers compensation injured patients. In 2007 my office was the only pain Management office in the city of North Wildwood, and there was only one other Pain Management physician in the entire county of Cape May. I treated patients for pain management in my practice, and received referrals from a number of other practitioners to treat their pain management patients. My certification by examination with the Drug Enforcement Agency permitted me to treat individuals with opioid, heroin, and other types of oral and injection opioid addiction.

I began the treatment of opioid addiction in 2003 following a certifying examination by the DEA. My treatment of opioid addition grew rapidly from 2003 to September of 2007 when the moronic prosecutor of Cape May County had me arrested. I had great success in treating patients with opioid addiction as my office was very unique with regard to these patients. A patient so afflicted was able to enter my office and receive treatment in a very reasonable period of time. Additionally, injured patients whether Workers Compensation or other kinds of injury were also able to receive same day care in my office on an emergency basis. My patients appreciated the fact that they were able to present to my office on an emergency basis with a particular problem, and received treatment. My elderly patients, of which there were many, also felt very comfortable in my office as I was able to treat a variety of internal medical issues including hypertensive vascular disease, diabetes mellitus, cardiac issues, and various types of other medical, and minor surgical problems. My wife Barbara and I were proud of the medical service we were able to render to the people of Cape May County.

The reasonable and dedicated physician must leave herd mentality behind, trust his intellect, when treating legitimate pain management, and drug and alcohol rehabilitation, within the framework of the law. He must concentrate on the patient's welfare, and shine a light so bright that it cannot be ignored.

Patients so afflicted require sincere and consistent physiologic and psychological treatment. The physician must ignore the ignorance of society, and the insufficiency of the justice department *"war on drugs"*, and concentrate on the significance of these pathologies.

The physician must focus his knowledge and experience in treating all diseases with intelligent care, and concern, regarding the patient's welfare. Based upon his experience, he must concern himself with evaluation, diagnosis, and a treatment process. Following the herd mentality under most circumstances limits the physician's individuality, and creativity, in the treatment of significant disease processes.

# A Brief Introduction

JOHN G. COSTINO, D.O., F.A.O.C. Rh.  
404 SURF AVENUE  
N. WILDWOOD, NEW JERSEY 08260  
(609) 522-8358

PAIN MANAGEMENT  
GENERAL & REHABILITATION MEDICINE  
OCCUPATIONAL MEDICINE  
EMERGENCY & SPORTS MEDICINE

## CURRICULUM VITAE

Dr. Costino was born the first child of six children on July 22, 1944 to Alfretta and John Costino. He was born in Camden, NJ at West Jersey Hospital and lived in Camden for the first eighteen years of his life. Dr. Costino attended Camden Catholic High School and in 1961 was elected student council president of the high school in his senior year. He graduated from Camden Catholic High School in 1962.

*Pre-Medical:* **Rutgers University,** Camden, NJ 1962-1966, degree in Biochemistry and a minor in Psychology. After graduation, taught high school at **Camden Catholic High School** from 1966-1967. Taught biology and chemistry, and was an assistant football and track coach.

*Medical Education* **Philadelphia College of Osteopathic Medicine,** Philadelphia, PA 1967-1971

*Internships:* **Cooper Medical Center,** Camden, NJ 1971-1972

*Emergency Medicine:* **Millville Hospital,** 1972-1974  
**Kessler Memorial Hospital,** 1975-1976

Medical Examiner: **State of New Jersey,** Department of Labor and Industry, Division of Workman's Compensation, 1972-1976

As medical examiner, Dr. Costino examined thousands of patients in the Compensation Court of Trenton, New Jersey, Camden, New Jersey, Bridgeton, New Jersey and Atlantic City, New Jersey for four years. His duties consisted of examination of injured patients and evaluation of their orthopedic or neurologic injury and an evaluation as far as partial permanent disability was concerned relative to that injury.

In 1976, Dr. Costino left emergency medicine and also relinquished his appointment with the Department of Labor and Industry, Division of Workman's Compensation for the State of New Jersey.

*Private Practice:* Wildwood, New Jersey, 1976 – Present  
**General & Rehabilitative Medicine, Occupational Medicine, Minor Surgery, Emergency & Sports Medicine, Pain Management, Addiction Management, Independent Medical Evaluations.**

*Medical Director:* **Millville Hospital,** Emergency Medicine, 1972-1974  
**Kessler Memorial Hospital,** Emergency Medicine, 1975-1976  
**Atlantis Hotel Casino,** November 1984 - May 1989  
**Harrah's Marina Hotel Casino,** October 1984 – October 1985  
**Harrah's Trump Plaza Hotel Casino,** October 1984 - October 1985  
**Claridge Hotel Casino,** December 1984 – December 1985

# "Due Process" Denied

JOHN G. COSTINO, D.O., F.A.O.C. Rh.                CURRICULUM VITAE

(continues)

*Appointments/ Elective Office:*
**Burdette Tomlin Memorial Hospital,** Cape May Court House, NJ, 1976 - Present.
**Vice President, Cape May County Osteopathic Medical Society,** 1988 - Present.
**Professional Review Organization (PRO) of New Jersey,** Board Member, Board of Trustees, 1984 – 1995
**President of the American Osteopathic College of Rheumatology,** November 1991 – 1997
**Program Chairman, American Osteopathic College of Rheumatology,** 1997 -1998, and again in 2006 – 2007
**President Elect of the American Osteopathic College of Rheumatology,** Present
**Alumni Board of Directors, Philadelphia College of Osteopathic Medicine,** 1993 – 2002, President of the Alumni Board, 2001 to 2002

*Certifications/ Diplomat:*
**American College of Emergency Physicians,** Charter Member, 1972 - Board Eligible Emergency Medicine 1977
**American Osteopathic Board of General Medicine,** Certifying Examination, November 1984 -1992
**Fellow of the American Osteopathic College of Rheumatology,** November 1985
**American Board of Quality Assurance and Utilization Review Physicians,** Diplomat by certifying examination on March 27, 1994 from the National Board of Medical Examiners
**American Academy of Pain Management,** Diplomat, October 1991 - Present
**American Academy of Sports Physicians,** Special Competency in Sports Medicine, Certifying Examination, February 1992
**Advance Cardiac Life Support,** Certifying Examination, April 1986, Re-certified 1992
**Forensic Examiner,** Diplomat and Board Certified, The American College of Forensic Examiners, February 1996 – Present
**American Osteopathic College of Rheumatology,** Certificate of proficiency in Rheumatology, March 15, 2003
**Certified by Examination by DEA for Addiction Management**

*Society Participation:*
American Osteopathic Association
American Osteopathic College of Rheumatology
New York Academy of Science
American College of Occupational and Environmental Medicine
American Academy of Pain Management
American Osteopathic Academy of Sports Medicine
New Jersey Osteopathic Association

# An Introduction to my Medical Practice
"I am not burdened by paradox or hypocrisy."

*I chose to live by choice, not by chance. To be motivated, not manipulated. To make changes, not excuses. I chose self-esteem to listen to my inner voice and not the random opinions of others. I chose to do the things others will not, so I can do the things that others cannot. I chose to excel, not just compete.*
-Unknown

My medical practice is varied. I practice general internal medicine caring for patients who are diabetic, hypertensive, with heart disease, but also treat injured patients, workers compensation injuries, and perform minor surgery. I specialized in emergency medicine for approximately four years in the early 1970s, and during those four years in emergency medicine, I cared for a varied patient population. In the emergency room of a hospital, most treatment consists of accident injuries, or medical emergencies. Motor vehicle accidents, and accidents on the job comprise most of the trauma treated. With heart disease, whether myocardial infarction, or acute congestive heart failure, with or without rhythm disturbance, a close second. In the summer of 1976 I began a solo medical practice in North Wildwood, and treated a wide variety of patient issues. Thousands of my patients have been trauma victims referred by family, friends, acquaintances, and also referred by orthopedic and neurological specialists for pain management. All of my pain management patients must sign my **"pain management agreement"**, which is an agreement between doctor and patient, and outlines the responsibility of each. Every prescription written by me is reflected in the patient's medical chart. Concerning Class II products, a copy of the prescription is maintained in the patient's medical chart, and there is certainly a patient medical record for every patient in my practice.

In the early 1970's, as stated previously, I was employed by the State of New Jersey in the Department of Labor and Industry, Division of Worker's

## "Due Process" Denied

Compensation, where I examined thousands of injured patients for the New Jersey Compensation Court system. In 1976, in my private practice of medicine, I continued to do these examinations on the respondent level for the compensation courts in Trenton, Camden, Bridgeton, and Atlantic City. In addition to my worker's compensation respondent examinations, I continued to perform independent, critical examinations for the New Jersey State disability evaluation system for another twenty years through to 1993. Taken together I have examined, both for the workers compensation system in the state of new jersey, and the new jersey state disability system, and have evaluated well over twenty-five thousand patients from 1972 through 2007. I have examined, and have given an estimate of partial permanent disability for approximately 20,000 patients over a period of thirty-five years.

Patients who are injured on the job come under the Workers Compensation statute in the state of New Jersey. Their treatment is controlled by the insurance company provided by their employer. Motor vehicle accident victims are treated by either their individual physician, or a specialist, under the Personal Injury Protection (PIP) laws of the state of New Jersey. Often this coverage is insufficient and both pain management and other diagnostic and or rehabilitative services are limited. Patients who suffer from trauma many times do not receive adequate pain management under the workers compensation, or the PIP insurance laws of the state of New Jersey. Additionally, a patient with a worker's compensation injury will not be covered under their private insurance. These circumstances are part of the legal issues in the state of New Jersey with regard to patient care. Most of these patients need pain management, and seek this treatment from their family physician or a specialist, and become personally responsible for payment of services.

The "state's perception " that an inordinate number of patients paid for certain office visits had a perfectly logical and legitimate explanation which "the state " made no effort to investigate or understand. My treatment of "pain management" many times involves situations in which unfortunately the patient has limited insurance coverage, and as a result, incur out of pocket expenses. Eventually the patient will recover these expenses with their individual lawsuit. Regardless, the bottom line is simply that the patient needs "pain management'. Unfortunately, under the laws in New Jersey there are many patients unable to receive adequate pain management through either their workers compensation or personal injury protection statutes. These patients often need pain management, and must seek this treatment from a private physician, and assume personal responsibility for payment. The state's perception that an inordinate amount of patients pay for treatment has a perfectly logical and legitimate explanation which "the state" makes no effort to **investigate** or **understand.**

**None of the officials who stood so ready and eager to accuse me of crimes and improper behavior** *have ever taken the time to obtain information necessary to fully understand my medical practice*. While claiming that I over prescribe pain medication, these officials have *never* produced accurate documents to prove their claim. As a caveat, and by way of further explanation, my attorney, Glenn Zeitz petitioned both the Drug Enforcement Agency and the County of Cape May's Prosecutor's office to produce these prescriptions which they said I had written illegally. Not withstanding, of course, the fact that law enforcement already knew that there had been **four thefts** from my office by four different individuals, who wrote hundreds of illegal prescriptions, neither agency ever produced a credible record.

The result of Mr. Zeitz's requests is as follows: **Both the DEA and the Prosecutor's Office failed to produce any prescriptions that were illegally written by me.** My attorney received letters from both the DEA and the Prosecutor's office stating, "they could not locate any of these prescriptions." If the illegal prescriptions written by the four thieves *had been identified,* this fact would have clearly proven that *I did not write anything illegal*. This should have occurred but did not, and as a result **Taylor never withdrew his** *false accusations.* Unfortunately, it was simply easier for this moronic Prosecutor, Taylor, and his ignorant detectives to accuse me of a crime, and force me to prove, **over a period of** *five years* that I had done **nothing illegal or improper.**

"Due Process" Denied

The influence of deputy attorney Sandra Dick at the Board of Medical Examiners in Trenton played a significant role in Robert Taylor's misguided and disgraceful criminal indictments. These facts will be well identified throughout this text.

"It isn't what we say that defines our character, it's what we do."

*See DEA letter in Appendix*

## "You have enemies! Good, that means you stood up for something, something in your life."

- Winston Churchill

# A Piece of my Mind:

The Language of Experience

*Some of the following material is taken from multiple journal articles such as Practical Pain Management, New England Journal of Medicine and the Journal of the American Medical Association*

To practice medicine is to experience great moments of joy, valleys of despair, and everything in between. It is both triumphant and a burden. As physicians, we create experiences for our patients. We care for them in sickness, and guide them through the challenging times of illness. "The ways in which we interact, and the environments we create, have an incalculable impact on a patient's ultimate outcome; their piece of mind, their self-confidence, how they heal, and these very same experiences also shape us as physicians. They form the lens, the prism through which we translate our knowledge of physiology and disease into individualized, patient centered care." In no other field are the stakes so consistently soaring as they are in medicine. Not every patient will have a good outcome, and not everyone will be saved. This of course is always the goal. "Experience teaches us to recognize what really matters for people, to sift through the routine and the remarkable, to separate the trivial from the true essence of a patient's needs. To recognize that to best serve our patients we must adapt to them, to learn to see things through their eyes, to work on their terms. Medical school teaches us to speak the universal language of medicine, but our patients really teach us to understand."

We are not "providers", or "practitioners." "We are physicians with a minimum of 11 years of graduate, doctoral, and post graduate residency education." "The other two terms above are fabricated to *homogenize, demoralize, and disincentivize* doctorate, post graduate trained physicians".

"The relationship between patients and physicians is at the core of medical ethics, serving as an anchor for many of the most important debates in this field. Over the past several decades, this relationship has evolved along three interrelated axis. It has been defined in clinical care, research, and in society. Many of the pivotal discussions of these issues have appeared in the pages of multiple journals of medicine."

"The relationship between patients and doctors in the clinical realm has historically been framed in terms of benevolent paternalism. Until about 1960, most codes of medical ethics relied heavily on the Hippocratic tradition, framing the obligations of physicians solely in terms of promoting the welfare of the patient, while remaining silent about patient's rights. "

"The past several decades have seen a tectonic societal shift that has resulted in increasing empowerment of individuals against the authority of government and institutions creating a surge of rights based movements with patient's rights, women's rights, minority group's rights, and consumer's rights, are now at the forefront." Today, patients and physicians are beginning to find a healthier balance of power through the process of shared decision-making. "With this approach, physicians are seen as having expertise and authority over matters of medical science, whereas patients hold sway over questions of values or preferences."

"Although physicians may be experts on the medical facts of a patient's condition, those facts may never be sufficient to specify a course of treatment. Clinical decisions must always include consideration of the values and preferences of patients. The concept of shared decision-making guides the mundane decisions that are made in clinics every day. Physicians present to patients what they see as reasonable medical options, and then help them to incorporate personal values and preferences in order to arrive at decisions that make the most sense for them in terms of both the medical facts and their unique personal perspectives. This approach to engaging patients has other benefits as well, such as promoting their sense of self efficacy and improving their adherence to treatment recommendations."

## A Piece of My Mind

In my opinion, and for your information with regard to opioid rehabilitation, and the treatment of opioid addiction, there are several different pathways available today. Throughout the state of New Jersey and in all counties, there are methadone clinics which have been in existence for more than 30 years.

Methadone is a synthetic Class II narcotic with an extended half-life fraught with serious problems. Because of it's half-life, methadone remains in the body for an extended period of time, with reduced metabolism, and a strong binding to the (MU) receptor in the brain. Methadone is metabolized through the liver's cytochrome p450 2D6 gene (CYP450). This cytochrome system is the common metabolic pathway through the liver for all pharmaceutical products, and all foods and liquids. Unfortunately, there are sweeping variations in the physiology of the human being with respect to the metabolism of pharmaceutical products as well as all foods. Certain patients as a result of their physiology have an inability to effectively metabolize methadone which leads to a greater incidence of methadone toxicity. This toxicity can cause serious cardiac dysrhythmias. Furthermore, treating addiction with methadone is nothing more than substituting one Class 2 narcotic for another without the possibility for improvement or cure. Again, and in my opinion, **Suboxone is a Class IV synthetic product, developed for the treatment and rehabilitation of those patients addicted to opioids, remains the best treatment available today. Suboxone combats opioid dependency by competitive inhibition of all three opioid receptors in the brain, with minimal, if any significant side effects.** There are no significant problems associated with Suboxone, and currently, Suboxone remains, in my opinion, the best product for addiction management and rehabilitation.

## The Forgotten Patients:
Included here are three groups of patients:

1: *Pain management patients*
2: *Addiction management patients*
3: *Medical and Minor Surgical patients*

Unfortunately, many, *many* patients who have benefitted from pain management with opioid medication have been forgotten. Patients who have legitimate chronic pain, who are compliant with their medication, and whose level of functioning has greatly improved as a result of pain management have been forgotten. These patients see their physicians every month, take their prescriptions to the same pharmacy, and are dependent on their medications for pain management. They are not "addicted", but have developed the normal dependence as a result of their treatment program. The current strategies employed by the state of New Jersey and other states in our country have had a significant negative impact on these compliant patients who necessitate, and benefit from their opioid treatment. While opioid misuse and diversion can be a significant problem, in my "pain management practice" the products that were prescribed follow established pain management guidelines, and have been the most effective way to treat chronic pain. Essentially, proper pain management can be the only treatment option that provides significant relief for the patient afflicted with lifelong pain, as a result of injury or chronic disease.

I have practiced pain management as a physician since 1971. In 2003, I sat for the Drug Enforcement Agency examination (DEA) with a group of psychiatrists, and several internists for certification in order to prescribe SUBOXONE for the treatment of opioid dependency and addition. Following successful completion of the DEA course, and examination, my name and office location was placed on the DEA website as notification for individual patients who desired to enter my out patient rehabilitation program for opioid addiction. (Specifically for heroin, fentanyl, and all other oral opioid products).

## A Piece of My Mind

My opioid rehabilitation program which was developed in my North Wildwood office enabled a patient with addiction issues to receive immediate treatment with Suboxone under my direction. Furthermore and in my opinion, this rehab program was extremely successful from 2003 through to December of 2007.

In addition to the product Suboxone, I personally provided specific counseling for the patient along with a very specific schedule for the administration of Suboxone. Within 24 to 48 hours, the addicted patient was free from the significant symptoms of withdraw, and over a period of time, there was significant reduction in the opioid dependency both from a physical as well as psychological standpoint.

My experience in the four years treating opioid addiction whether intravenous heroin, and fentanyl, or with all other oral opioid products, was very satisfying to me as a physician, and this program was highly successful in controlling and eventually eliminating the complicated problem of addiction for the patient, and additionally for the family who also suffers along with the patient. During the four years of my opioid rehabilitation program in my north wildwood office, approximately 225 to 250 patients were successfully treated utilizing Suboxone.

In September of 2007, the Cape May County prosecutor, Taylor, without probable cause orchestrated my arrest. In December of 2007, after months of plotting with Sandra Dick at the Board of Medical Examiners, my medical license was suspended by sitting board members in Trenton. The collusion between Robert Taylor in Cape May County, and Sandra Dick at the BME, I subsequently found out had been going on for approximately eighteen months, prior to my arrest in September of 2007.

As a result of my suspension in December of 2007, all of my pain management patients, my opioid addiction patients, as well as my medical and surgical patients, were abandoned by the Board of Medical Examiners in Trenton. Essentially, the State of New Jersey, through Robert Taylor and Sandra Dick, **without probable cause**, terminated my ability to practice medicine, and abruptly abandoned all of my patients when they suspended my medical license!!!

# "Due Process" Denied

The physician, with whom these patients depended and relied upon, for the management of their chronic pain, or their opioid addiction, or for the management of the many medical and minor surgical issues treated in my office on a routine basis, was essentially lost to all of them.

My pain management patients found it difficult to continue with another pain management physician, since there was only one other physician qualified in Cape May County to practice pain management. Many of these patients had to travel great distances in order to find a physician who would treat their chronic pain. My opioid addictive patients had to travel either to Atlantic County or Cumberland County, for Suboxone treatment in their effort to secure a physician certified to treat their addiction with Suboxone. Unfortunately, many of these individuals returned to illegal sources for their addiction, and some returned to I.V. heroin.

My medical patients were dispersed to a variety of physicians in Cape May County for treatment of their diabetes, hypertensive disease, coronary disease, and the various other medical issues that were treated in my office.

Sadly, several of my patients died within the following 24 months of their abandonment by the New Jersey BME, from overdose of street drugs. Unfortunately, certain prior patients were unable to continue their opioid rehabilitation program as a result of multiple various circumstances.

The function of the Board of Medical Examiners in Trenton should be to protect the public. This Board produced just the opposite effect, as the BME was the proximate cause of multiple further disease in many patients, and death in some of my good, honest and successful citizens of the State of New Jersey.

I am outlining these issues in print, at this point in the text, to announce to the public in general, and specifically to the physician community, and politicians, the level of dishonesty and legal tyranny, that existed in the Cape May County Prosecutor's Office and at the Board of Medical Examiners in Trenton, in the year 2007, and beyond.

A Piece of My Mind

The justice system in the state of New Jersey is more polluted than the situation in Washington D.C. Collectively, the Cape May County Prosecutor's Office, and the Board of Medical Examiners in Trenton have destroyed many, many lives in New Jersey. Today, we are witnessing the neglect, insanity, and stupidity of the political leadership of our country, at the southwest border on a daily basis. The criminal cartels have been, and continue to smuggle thousands of kilograms of **heroin, fentanyl, methamphetamine, and marijuana,** across our border, unimpeded, to infect the citizens of our cities.

This illegal Cartel industry has been flourishing for the past fifty years, and currently has been given *carte blanche* at our borders. Heroin, fentanyl, and methamphetamine, kill approximately 75,000 – 100,000 people in this country alone, per year. The trafficking across our unstable border that we are experiencing today will continue to multiply unless action is taken. Essentially, the death rate of our citizens involved with illegal drugs is controlled by the criminal cartels.

The "War on Drugs" has produced profiteers on both sides of the law.

The suppression of pain management by physicians registered and licensed to practice medicine and surgery in the state of New Jersey, is counterproductive. This suppression of pain management physicians specifically by the Board of medical Examiners in Trenton has led greatly to an increased use of illegal drugs whether oral opioid products obtained over the internet, or I.V. heroin, and fentanyl, across the border by the criminal cartels. Pain management must be treated by qualified licensed physicians in the state of New Jersey unimpeded.

The suppression of reasonable and acceptable tenants of pain management by licensed physicians has created the tremendous influx of illegal cartel **heroin and fentanyl,** which has led to the significant increase in the deaths of our citizens, over the past fifteen to twenty years. These deaths from overdose will not only continue, but will become more intense until these illegal mechanisms and cartels have been terminated. What bears repeating is the following:

"Due Process" Denied

**"The "war on drugs" has produced profiteers on *both sides of the law*."**

The current political atmosphere in Washington D.C. relative to our southwest border is clearly creating a conduit for death in our citizen population.

I was a young man in college when John F. Kennedy was the president of the United States in 1963. Nikita Khrushchev was the Supreme Leader of Russia in 1963. I remember his address to the citizens of the United States as though they were spoken yesterday regarding United States democracy.

**"We won't need a war to defeat Democracy in the U. S., the decay of the United States will come from within.**
-Nikita Khrushchev

**Fentanyl and Heroin ⇨ from China ⇨**
**⇨ to Central and South America ⇨**
**⇨ to Mexico through *our borders* by the criminal cartels and into the United States…to kill American citizens.**

A Piece of My Mind

# The "War On Drugs," A Disgrace to America

"It's easy to stand in the crowd, but it takes courage to stand alone."

"Nothing brings you peace but yourself."

*"The physician must retain faith that he will prevail in the end regardless of the difficulties, but at the same time he must confront the most brutal facts of the current reality. For every hill I've had to climb, for all the blood and sweat and grime, for blinding storms and burning heat, my heart sings but a grateful song, these were the things that made me strong."*
-Unknown

In my opinion, the "war on drugs" is simply a euphemism to conceal the disgraceful behavior of certain dirty county prosecutors, DEA agents, detectives, and politicians in our society today. The "war on drugs" illustrates the hypocrisy and legal tyranny of the corrupt justice system. Fifty to sixty years of worldwide drug related violence in the United States clearly identifies the fact that drug prohibitions, and the "war on drugs", has enriched organized crime and has been the cause of significant <u>disease</u> and <u>death</u>. Hundreds of thousands of people are dead as a result of illicit drugs along with thousands of people with diseases such as HIV, Hepatitis B, Hepatitis C, and other types of communicable and venereal diseases. **The "war on drugs" has produced profiteers on both sides of the law.**

Thousands of young people have been incarcerated over the past fifty years which has destroyed their lives and their ambitions at a cost of billions of dollars to fund this "war on drugs". Troubled and addicted individuals need addiction treatment, not jail. Physicians who provide such treatment need freedom from the overburdening and criminalizing system currently employed by county prosecutors like Robert Taylor, and disgraceful detectives like George Hallett. These creatures are ignorant of the law, and simply desire to criminalize the practice of medicine.

**Pain management** must be confined to the physician and his patient without government intervention or interruption. Patients suffer needlessly from chronic pain because physicians fear the justice system which has been criminalizing the practice of pain management in medicine for the past thirty years. County, state, and federal agencies have been depriving thousands of patients from good medical care, and adequate pain management from sincere, ethical physicians. Please do not confuse pain management within the confines of good medical treatment with the ongoing heroin and fentanyl epidemic which has plagued the county of Cape May, the state of new Jersey, and the rest of the country for the past 50 – 60 years. Heroin and fentanyl are both Class I drugs. They are illegal in New Jersey and across the United States. Incidentally, marijuana is also a Class 1 drug, however as you are well aware, marijuana is now legal in many states both for medical issues as well as recreation. Whether or not this is a mistake in judgment by our intellectuals, only time will tell.

**In my opinion,** the Drug Enforcement Agency (DEA) has become a mismanaged governmental agency. The DEA has been compromised by criminal elements. The DEA embodies everything that's wrong with the failed "war on drugs". The DEA systematically blocks scientific research, formulates and promotes lies and misconceptions relating to pain management. In my opinion, the DEA absolutely violates our civil liberties by secretly spying on virtually all law-abiding citizens.

The textbook <u>Goodman and Gillman</u>, that all physicians must read in medical school, states the following:

**…"focus on minimizing pain for the patient"…**

## A Piece of My Mind

I am a charter member of the American College of Emergency Physicians in 1972. The treatment of acute pain in the emergency room in the hospital is paramount. I spent four and one half years, full-time in emergency medicine, prior to establishing my general medical practice in North Wildwood in 1976. In the emergency department, it's primarily *acute pain* that must be controlled. In an established office practice, the treatment of pain is *both acute and chronic*. Chronic pain from whatever pathologic source, can be and many times is, **forever.** The physician must be intelligent, knowledgeable, strong-minded and courageous, when he accepts the mantle of pain management physician.

# Individuals Associated with My Case

**My Defense Attorneys:**

    **Edwin Jacobs** - Defense attorney, criminal case
    **Glenn Zeitz** – Defense attorney, criminal case
    **Jordan Zeitz** - Defense attorney, criminal case
    **John Tumelty** - Defense attorney, criminal case

**My Experts at the Board of Medical Examiners and Office of Administrative Law Civil Trial:**

    **Dr. Richard Jermyn:**
    Pain Management & Medical Report Expert

    **Glenda Hamilton:**
    Billing and Coding of Medical Recrods Expert

    **Detective Joseph Landis:**
    Cape May County Detective, The only honest detective in my case

**A list of prosecutors, detectives, and other characters in my criminal case:**

    **Robert Taylor,** Prosecutor of Cape May County
    **Tonya Anderson**, Police officer in Little Egg Harbor Township
    **George Hallett,** Detective in the Cape May County Prosecutor's office
    **Lynn Frame,** Lt. Detective in the Cape May County Prosecutor's office
    **Megan Hoerner,** Cape May County Assistant Prosecutor
    **Matthew Weintraub**, Cape May County Assistant Prosecutor
    **Tina Kell,** Cape May County Assistant Prosecutor
    **Tricia Kalita,** Detective Cape May County, NJ
    **Paul Worell,** Detective Cape May County, NJ
    **Edwin Jacobs,** Defense attorney in Atlantic County, NJ
    **Allen Lands,** Disgraceful attorney in Pleasantville, NJ
    **Tom Prevoznic,** Drug Enforcement Agent
    **Alex Sylvester,** US Postal Service Employee
    **Michele Stankiewicz,** US Postal Service Employee

**Superior Court Appellate Judges for the State of New Jersey**
**"The Three Blind Mice"**
- Dorthea Wefing
- Edith Payne
- Linda Baxter

**Judges involved with my case:**

**Raymond Batten,** Superior Court Judge, Cape May County
**Todd Miller**, Administrative Law Judge (ALJ) (OAL)
**Bruce Gorman,** Administrative Law Judge (ALJ) (OAL)
**Michael Donio,** Atlantic County Superior Court
**Christopher Gibson,** Superior Court Judge, Cape May County
**Joseph Rodriguez**, Federal Judge, Camden, New Jersey
**Albert Garofolo,** Superior Court Judge, Cape May County

**Third Circuit Judges: Court of Appeals:**

Thomas M. Hardiman
Joseph A. Greenaway Jr.
Stephanos Bibas - a "nightmare of a judge"

**Board of Medical Examiners (BME):**

**Sandra Y. Dick:**
(Sandra Y. Ben-Asher)
Deputy Attorney General

**David Puteska:**
Deputy Attorney General

**William Carducci:**
Investigator

**William Roeder:**
Executive Director

"Due Process"
DENIED

# "The Man in the Arena"

by President Theodore Roosevelt
(born in 1858 died 1919)

The poorest way to face life is to face it with a sneer.
There are many men who feel a kind of twisted pride in cynicism;
there are many who confine themselves to
criticism of the way others do what they themselves
dare not even attempt.
There is no more unhealthy being, no man less worthy of respect,
than he who either really holds, or feigns to hold,
an attitude of sneering disbelief toward all that is great
and lofty, whether in achievement or in that noble effort which,
even if it fails, comes to second achievement.

It is not the critic who counts;
Not the man who points out how the strong man stumbles,
or where the doer of deeds could have done them better.
The credit belongs to the man who is actually in the arena,
whose face is marred by dust and sweat and blood;
Who strives valiantly; Who errs, who comes short again
and again, because there is no effort without error
and shortcoming; but who does actually strive to do the deeds;
who knows great enthusiasms, the great devotions;
who spends himself in a worthy cause; who at best knows
in the end the triumph of high achievement, and who at the worst,
if he fails, at least fails while daring greatly,
so that his place shall never be with those cold and timid souls
who neither know victory nor defeat.

# A Man's Character Is His Fate

"There is only one way to avoid criticism: do nothing,
say nothing, and be nothing."
- Aristotle

"Most men live in quiet desperation."
- Henry David Thoreau

"I ask not for a light burden, but for broad shoulders."
- Unknown


I am a physician and an objective scientist with a great deal of experience. I have been a physician since 1971. I spent five years in emergency medicine, and thirty-five years in the general practice of medicine. I have been maligned and denigrated by the extraordinary force of the corrupt justice system in Cape May County, orchestrated by the dystopian Chief Prosecutor, Robert Taylor. I've been the victim of the criminalization of medicine in Cape May County. This criminalization of medicine began in the late 1970's, and has progressed unimpeded through to the present time with the justice system, and the Board of Medical Examiners. The moving dictatorship in Cape May County was primarily the work of Robert Taylor. Initially, Taylor was a simple politician, a real estate attorney, who decided one day that he wanted to be the prosecutor in Cape May County. He was eventually confirmed by the then sitting governor, Jim McGreevy. Robert Taylor was a real estate attorney with little knowledge, if any, of criminal law, and certainly no knowledge of medical law in the state of New Jersey. The county prosecutor has more power over the general public than the governor. The governor of New Jersey is elected by the people; however, the county prosecutor is **appointed** by local politicians and then confirmed by the sitting governor. Robert Taylor was the chairman of the Democratic party in Cape May County with little knowledge, if any, of criminal law, and certainly no knowledge of **medicine or medical law** in the state of New Jersey. Taylor became the totalitarian dictator of the county of Cape May through the weaponized justice system that we have today. The legal tyranny which I will describe begins with dishonest prosecutors and detectives, who lie, some commit perjury under oath, and **who commit prosecutorial misconduct with impunity.**

**I was indicted on five separate occasions by five separate grand juries between 2008 and 2012 in Cape May County**. All five were criminal indictments against myself, and when I failed to conform to any of Taylor's ignorant pleadings, Taylor added my wife to two of these criminal indictments. Certain Cape May County detectives along with assistant prosecutors, who, in my opinion knowingly, willfully, and maliciously committed prosecutorial misconduct, completed all five indictments with fabricated testimony.

My *civil liberties* were abandoned, and my *constitutional protections* were ignored through Taylor's theory of collectivism, and **fascist behavior**.

There are two kinds of people in our society, those with power, and those without. George Orwell, Joseph Heller, and Machiavelli wrote excellent texts to this issue. There is a great deal of overlap in our society between those who are protected and those who are unprotected. **The protected people make public policy, and the unprotected have to live with it.** The protected are generally the accomplished, the wealthy, secure, and successful, and those who are employed in city, county, state, and federal government. Additionally, politicians and the liberal media are also protected, and as a result of their protection, they can print or say pretty much anything they desire with impunity. They compose false narratives, simply because they are insulated from the ramifications of their own hypocrisy, and from the effects of their own illegitimate decisions. Those that are protected are protected form much of the roughness of the world. This is the society that we live in today. While I am not the only victim of this malicious legal tyranny, the history of my prosecution, and the attempted prosecution of my wife Barbara will be an eye opener for most rational people in Cape May County, in the state of New

## Chapter 1 - A Man's Character Is His Fate

Jersey, and specifically in the physician community. I'd like now to mention a few additional facts that you should know and understand, as these facts will become more apparent as you go forward in this text.

In the state of New Jersey, we desperately need legal reform because no one is safe anymore. Prosecutors have complete control with the administration of legal tyranny over the citizen population. Specifically over the taxpayers that fund the system. The fact is that **prosecutors in the state of New Jersey are politically appointed** and **not elected** by the people. The natural aristocracy of talent and ethical quality should determine the position of the chief law enforcement officer of the county, not the most politically affluent. Political personalities with little or no common sense, but with a zest for **hypocrisy** and **deception should never hold the position of county prosecutor**. All prosecutors are NOT pathological liars with personality disorders; they are NOT all dishonest narcissistic egomaniacs. Many attorneys are very honest, ethical individuals who begin their careers in the county prosecutors office for a period of time in order to become familiar with the system, and eventually commence a private practice to defend individuals who have been falsely charged and certainly are innocent.

Fast-forward to the grand jury system where 16 to 25 normal, average citizens are subject to a one sided, and usually flawed dissertation by the prosecutor and his witness, usually the prosecutor's detective. At the grand jury, the Machiavellian principle is at its highest level, "the end justifies the means," not "truth or justice". The old saying persists to this day, more now then in the past: **"the prosecutor can and will indict a ham sandwich".**

Not all prosecutors are pathological liars with a personality disorder; only certain prosecutors hold that special position. The grand jury is controlled by the prosecutor. The grand jury must be compelled to hear both sides of any case, not simply the prosecutor's version. Furthermore, under the constitution of New Jersey as well as the United States, **exculpatory evidence** must be given to the grand jury, and if withheld, which of course is a common practice by Taylor's prosecutors, the charges **must be dismissed**. Prosecutors **must be** compelled to deliver the truthful and accurate accounting of the facts of the case **without lies, deception, and perjury.** The dignity of the people must be respected. The corruption and contamination of the current grand jury system must be eliminated. The grand jury system necessitates a **complete reformation** to guarantee truth and justice as outlined in our constitution.

Most county prosecutors overestimate the limits of their knowledge of medicine, medical law, and medical practice. Most lawyers and judges fall into the same category of ignorance regarding **the practice of medicine**. In my case, none of the five prosecutors, especially the chief prosecutor, Taylor, had any knowledge whatsoever of medical law in the state of New Jersey regarding the prescription of controlled substances. After five years of criminal court harassment, my attorney, John Tumelty, finally gave the medical law of the state of New Jersey to the presiding judge Raymond Batten, and also to the prosecutors in Cape May County.

In the state of NJ, regarding the practice of medicine, and the prescription of certain controlled substances, ie: Class II, III, IV, V products are under the case law "**State v Vaccaro**". This case law is a 1976 appellate published decision (142 NJ SUPER). "**Vaccaro**" can be found in any law library, and the following is a brief synopsis:

*"Vaccaro" states in part under Drugs and Narcotics Page 168 : that physician's license and registration authorizes him to dispense controlled dangerous substances, but under this statute he is **"immune"** from criminal liability when he dispenses same in **good faith** in the course of his professional practice only".*
*"A physician who is honest and ethical dispenses these drugs in a good faith effort to treat and cure patients has no fear of the criminal sanctions of the statute."*
*"A physician's license and registration authorizes him to dispense controlled dangerous products, but the statute makes it clear that he is **"immune"** from criminal liability when he dispenses same in good faith in the course of his professional practice only."* *"Furthermore, and when the statute circumscribes the limits of his exemption from it's criminal consequences by the utilization of the term* **"GOOD FAITH"***, he knows, that is, the physician knows full well what is meant*

*and how he must comport himself". "There is nothing vague or ambiguous about the requirement that the legal dispensing of drugs by a physician must be carried out in good faith in the course of his professional practice only." "It is a standard which is clear and understandable to the mind of any reasonable physician, and is therefore beyond constitutional attack."*

*"**Vaccaro**" is the law in the state of New Jersey, and has been the law with regard to controlled products since 1976."*

I told my lawyers, and all of the moronic prosecutors and detectives in my case in Cape May County that this law existed. One would think that a superior court judge, and the chief prosecutor and all of his assistants, and the detectives in the county, **should have at least researched the law** so that they may have some understanding of the facts. **All the prosecutors and the detectives were simply ignorant of the law and formulated a case against me that *did not exist*.**

# "The Justice System is Composed Mostly of Inadequate Personalities with Evil Intent."

- Friedrich Wilhelm Nietzsche

Why do incompetent people think they are competent? Stating that you know something when you really don't know, and convince yourself that something is true even if in reality it's the opposite, is a definitive sign of **cognitive bias** and **ignorance**. Why do stupid people think they are genius? Are stupid people too stupid to realize how stupid they really are?

> "I know nothing except the fact of my ignorance".
> - Plato, 400 BC

> "Real knowledge is to know the extent of one's ignorance".
> - Confucius, 500 BC

> "Ignorance more frequently begets confidence then does knowledge."
> - Charles Darwin, the mid-1800's

> "The painful things about our time is that those that feel certainty are stupid, and those with any imagination and understanding are filled with doubt and indecision."
> - Bertrand Russell, the mid-1900's

> "Beware of false knowledge, it is more dangerous than ignorance".
> - George Bernard Shaw, the mid-1900's

**Incompetent people** tend to overestimate their skill level and performance. They also fail to recognize actual skill in others, and they are poor at seeing how extreme their incompetence really is. Incompetent people judge themselves as having a higher rank than they actually do. They generally overestimate their actual ability. Confident people on the other hand, possess humility, and are filled with doubt and indecision. Confident people control their assessment of themselves and others. Why then do stupid people think they're so smart? Those with the least ability tend to rate themselves above average or superior to their peers, and are unable to admit their faults. It is a glowing example of **inaccurate self-perception,** and the surrender of rational thought and judgment, and a good example of **willful ignorance.**

Unfortunately, Cape May County was replete with incompetent detectives and prosecutors during the entire time of my prosecution in my criminal case. Cape May County may have improved as a result of my prosecution, and my vindication and acquittal on the medical facts. In my opinion, certain stupid, ignorant, and incompetent individuals in the justice system and law enforcement in the state of New Jersey, and especially in Cape May County suffer from personality disorders.

**Personality disorders** are an enduring pattern of inner experience and behavior that deviates from the individual's culture. They are *pervasive, and inflexible*, and they begin usually in adolescence or in early adulthood. They may become stable over time, but eventually are the cause of stress and some level of psychological impairment.

*Narcissistic behavior* includes fantasies of power and success along with a grandiosity with feelings of being special, with a sense of entitlement, and of course arrogance. Narcissism and incompetence consistently go hand-in-hand.

*Paranoid behavior* includes suspiciousness and distrusting of others along with perpetual distortion and misinterpretation of another's statements.

*Antisocial behavior* includes irresponsible acts of commission and omission, with a lack of remorse violating social norms, with aggressiveness, and particularly lying and perjury.

*Obsessive-compulsive behavior* includes rigidity and stubbornness with a sense of perfectionism, and over conscientiousness especially when misplaced.

Narcissistic and cynical prosecutors and certain detectives suffer from the **Dunning Kruger effect**. They tend to overestimate their knowledge and expertise in a particular subject, and often assume that others around them have an inferior knowledge regarding that subject. Scholars on the other hand, regarding certain issues, tend to underestimate their knowledge, and assume others to be as equally informed as them. Why do stupid people think they're geniuses? Why do stupid people think that they know everything about medicine and medical practice and actually **more than you do as a physician?** There was a *cognitive bias*, and an *anchoring effect* in the Cape May County Prosecutor's Office with certain lawyers and detectives. Low ability individuals suffer from a *superiority complex* assessing their abilities as much higher than what they really are.

**Dunning and Krueger attributed this bias to a "metacognitive inability"**. People with reduced ability are unable to recognize their significant ineptitude, and they evaluate their ability inaccurately. People with higher abilities underestimate their relative competence, and unfortunately sometimes attribute this competence to others erroneously. This miscalculation of incompetence stems from errors regarding themselves. *Incompetent* people fail to recognize their true **lack of skill**. They fail to recognize the extent of their *inadequacy,* and they fail to accurately gauge the skill of others. Skilled people attribute better characteristics to others erroneously, whereas lower skilled people overestimate their ability in a general fashion.

There's a great deal of narcissism and egomania in lower skilled individuals contributing to the **Dunning Kruger effect**. Narcissistic egomaniacs elevate their moral nature and moral character over others. Their self-perception is in reality a self-deception, as many are essentially *incompetent*. Unfortunately, many incompetent prosecutors and detectives think they are amazing, and rank themselves among the highest. They regard themselves much above others when they really possess the *least ability.*

The *anchoring concept* fit very nicely with certain prosecutors and detectives in Cape May County. They have an arbitrary anchor in their head, regarding an issue, and then begin to perceive this as reality. This then becomes a *perceptual bias,* however perception is not necessarily reality, especially when evaluating the *practice of medicine* from a distance.

**"Unfortunately the lack of common sense, and poor judgment influence dangerous law enforcement agencies."**

Many stupid and ignorant prosecutors and detectives in society suffer from a *cognitive dissonance,* an inconsistency of thought process, and a very durable lack of critical thinking. The *anchoring theory* may be their initial thought, but then they must work very hard to prove it correct. The anchoring affect influences their first thought process, and then, they must labor diligently to convince themselves. This poor judgment of most issues has a significant negative affect on our society.

**"These false convictions are more dangerous enemies of truth, then lies".**

## "Distrust all in whom the impulse to punish is powerful"
- Frederick Wilhelm Nietzsche

Why do so many incompetent men and women become leaders in our communities, and leaders in our government? Our society has an innate inability to distinguish between confidence and competence. Most incompetent people have poor intuition and no common sense. Many are found in the prosecutor's office, prime example Robert Taylor, and certain other assistant prosecutors as well as certain detectives. A good example, George Hallett, in Cape May County.

The **anchoring bias** is exactly opposite of the scientific method. Certain prosecutors and detectives are prone to biases that lead to errors contributing to a pattern that is both incorrect and incongruent. Most are terrible at evaluating evidence and are biased relative to the interpretation of evidence as they skew evidence to further their own theories. Prosecutors make judgments on intuition and poor evaluation of the evidence under consideration that has actually been filtered and altered by *confirmation bias* suggested by others.

"**Heuristic thinking**" in addition to *stupidity, ignorance, and narcissism,* play an important role in generating rules of thumb. Heuristic philosophy has the potential for making inaccurate decisions of importance. Many prosecutorial decisions are made based upon both **stupidity** and **ignorance**. These decisions are *pernicious, destructive, and devastating* to the communities and the people that live in them.

Unfortunately, **malicious prosecution** of a **corrupt** and **fraudulent** nature has occurred in Cape May County, which was both *vicious and unlawful*. The **hypocrisy** of certain public officials, prosecutors, and certain detectives was selective and political in nature. In my opinion, these *venomous and noxious* individuals are reinforced and protected by government.

Furthermore, certain prosecutors and detectives are **prolific liars, perjurers,** and essentially "**criminals of the justice system**", and in my opinion, they are **unprincipled, treacherous, corrupt, and deplorable.**

In our society today, these unelected, corrupt individuals manipulate the laws to their advantage, and in my case, were completely ignorant of the laws regarding the practice of medicine. Under the veil of the justice system, the collusion between Robert Taylor's prosecutor's office, and Sandra Dick's Board of Medical Examiners, were able to prosecute a crime that did not exist, injure my family, my medical practice, and my life's work. Through their **malicious prosecution**, these corrupt public officials were able to steal my world. Overt acts were performed by both the Cape May County Prosecutor's office, and at the Board of Medical Examiners in Trenton, to **negate** "due process", and **defraud** my family, my medical practice and myself.

As you continue along in this text, you will see the corruption unfold. This *prosecution* of both my wife, and myself knowingly, willfully, and maliciously by the Cape May County Prosecutor and the Board of Medical Examiners, has gone unpunished because of their intrinsic immunity. Both the Board of Medical Examiners and the Cape May County prosecutors department define perfectly the **molestation of conscience, and incompetence.**

## The proofs of everything in this text are a matter of public record!!!

In my criminal case in Cape May County, and the civil issues at the Board of Medical Examiners and at the Office of Administrative Law, I have found the following:

Certain county prosecutors, detectives, deputy attorneys in Trenton, certain judges, DEA officials, and U.S. postal officials, **are guilty of multiple infractions of law.**

I have had first-hand experience dealing with these disgraceful human beings, their lies, their perjury under oath, and their misrepresentations in oral arguments, in their briefs both at superior court, and at the administrative law court, and in civil court.

I have spent five years in criminal court, and eight years in civil court, with various members of the corrupt justice and law enforcement system with characters who **misrepresent facts,** and verbalize **false statements**. Their depositions are **full of lies, and perjury under oath,** along with **trial transcripts replete with absolute false testimony**. The reader will clearly see the narcissism in certain individuals, their **fantasies of my guilt, their sense of entitlement, and their lack of empathy for my abandoned patients.** You will also see the **paranoia** of certain individuals as well as frank **arrogance, suspiciousness, distrust, and perceptual distortion of the facts** clearly evident **in their briefs and oral arguments**. Finally you will see the Machiavellian principal in full force which is

**"power and control" not "truth or justice",** in these deliberations. The paradox of incompetence and hypocrisy with certain members of the corrupt justice system and law enforcement precipitated the **prosecutorial misconduct** performed **knowingly, willfully, and maliciously** in my case. The **misrepresentation** of the facts and flagrant **perjury under oath** committed by certain characters **in law enforcement was unconscionable.** None of these characters were aware of the medical case law in the state of New Jersey published in 1976, as an appellate published decision: **"State v Vaccaro"**

This case law clearly outlines the prescription for the practice of medicine with regard to the dispensing of classified pharmaceutical products. This fact, along with many other facts in my case, underscores both the **incompetence, and ignorance of law enforcement in the corrupt justice system of Cape May County, and the corrupt Board of Medical Examiners. In my candid opinion, these facts underscore the willful misconduct, knowingly and maliciously conducted and perpetrated by the various members of this corrupt justice system.**

> **"The truth is incontrovertible,**
> **malice may attack it,**
> **and ignorance may derided it,**
> **but in the end there it is!!!"**
> - Winston Churchill

# "The Emotional Intelligence is the Essence of Mental Toughness"

"The greater the difficulty, the more glory in surmounting it. Skillful pilots gain their reputation from storms and tempests."
- Epictetus

My general philosophy in treating patients sent to my office for pain management is as follows: I believe in prescribing less, not more medication and I will place a drug addicted patient on Suboxone in an effort to clear them from their opioid addiction. I often deal with patients who have been taking an assortment of pain medications, and I treat them by eliminating and reducing most of their medication. I am conscientious of the addictive nature of opioids and narcotics in general, and vigorously counsel against their over-usage.

**Detective Landis**, the first undercover officer sent by Taylor's prosecutor's department attempted to **entrap** me in December 2005. He presented to my office as a heroin addict. He demanded narcotics in an effort to satisfy his heroin addiction. I admonished him initially, and explained to him that in no way would I prescribe any narcotics for him. I explained fully to him the benefits of Suboxone as a treatment modality to rid himself of his heroin addiction. Of course at the time of his visit I thought he was a genuine patient addicted to heroin and obviously in need of treatment, and certainly not an **undercover agent** from the prosecutors office. My concern for this patient was only for his welfare as an addict, and my effort was to reduce his addiction to zero with Suboxone. At first he was extremely resistant to me for any type of treatment that I suggested. However, after a period of time and with a good degree of dialogue I was able to convince him to begin this program of **Suboxone**. I gave him a prescription for Suboxone, and wrote out for him a program as to exactly how he was to take this medication.

Detective Landis was discharged from my office with a prescription for Suboxone, and a written outline by me as to how he should take his medication. He returned to the prosecutor's office and wrote an excellent report regarding his office visit with me, which reflected the positive nature of his visit, in addition to the prescription for Suboxone, and the outline for it's administration. **This report written by detective Landis was kept hidden in the prosecutor's office from me, my attorney, the grand jury, and the Board of Medical Examiners for three years before receiving it in discovery.** Detective Landis's sequestered report did not in any way support Taylor's assertion that I was over prescribing pain medication. This **"exculpatory evidence" was withheld by the prosecutor from my attorney and myself, from the grand jury, and from the Board of Medical Examiners for three years.** By the time we discovered the fact that Landis was indeed an undercover officer, and that he wrote a report, which was extremely positive, neither the grand jury, nor the Board of Medical Examiners, had any knowledge regarding his office visit. When we finally received this information, in 2008, in discovery, I was in the midst of multiple law enforcement issues concerning my criminal case, and very close to the administrative law hearing, orchestrated by DAG Sandra Dick at the Board of Medical Examiners. By this point in time my license to practice medicine had been suspended by the BME in December of 2007.

Chief prosecutor Robert Taylor, detective George Hallett, and Assistant Prosecutor Megan Hoerner, were well aware of Detective Landis' visit to my office, and the glowing report that he wrote regarding his office visit. Taylor, Hallett, and Hoerner withheld this information not only from Judge Batten and the grand jury that indicted me, but this was also withheld from the Board of Medical Examiners who suspended my medical license **without "due process" in December of 2007.**

The next two undercover operatives sent to my office were **Tonya Anderson, a.k.a. Tonya Smith (UCI),** and **Margarita Abbattiscianni, a.k.a. Maggie Ortiz**

**(UCII)**. At the time of her arrival, Undercover One (UCI) was a Class II police officer employed by Egg Harbor Township, and Undercover Two (UCII) was an officer with the Drug Enforcement Agency, (DEA).

Both of these females were part of the second **"objective due process entrapment"** scheme perpetrated by the Cape May County Prosecutor, Robert Taylor. Both pretended to be dancers in the Atlantic City area, and both stated to me that they were taking medication, **Percocet**, following their night of dancing for their pain. They both said that they received their pain medication from one of their girlfriends, also a dancer in Atlantic City. When they entered my office, as normal patients, both were wired with recording devices by the DEA.

**Tonya Anderson** a.k.a. Tonya Smith, a.k.a. Undercover One entered my office as a patient on April 12, 2007. Her serendipitous recording clearly states that she wanted to establish herself as a patient in my office, get a physical, and talk about a couple of prescriptions. She stated that she worked as a dancer in Atlantic City, and was taking **Percocet** following her night of dancing. She stated that she worked long hours, and was on her feet all night, and had difficulty sleeping, and took this medication following her night of dancing. She wanted to establish herself as a **pain management patient**, and expressed her ability to return to my office on a regular basis as a pain management patient. Anderson signed my **"Pain Management Agreement"** which clearly states several rules and regulations relative to the medication prescribed, and her obligation to this office and to myself as her physician.

At the time of her initial visit I observed her mannerisms, her language, her movement of both upper and lower extremities, the condition of her skin, her eye movements, her gait and disposition. Physical examination revealed her pupils to be equal and her extraocular muscles intact bilaterally. Her extremities revealed normal movement and her ambulatory gate was also normal. She was able to move her head, neck, thoracic and lumbar region without discomfort, and she was able to bend at the waist without restriction. After all, she is an exotic dancer, a young 29-year-old female in good health. Her heart sounds demonstrated a regular rate and rhythm, with no evidence of murmurs, rubs, or gallops. Her lung sounds demonstrated a few rhonchi bilaterally as she was a smoker. Her blood pressure and pulse were normal. In general, her physical examination remained stable.

As a physician who does pain management, and addiction therapy, I am well aware of what goes on in our society with regard to illicit drugs. I am very aware that people buy a variety of narcotics from Internet sources, and have them delivered directly to their home address. During my initial office visit with Anderson, my opinion of her was that she was an honest individual working hard, who wanted to establish herself with a pain management physician in order to obtain a legal prescription, for a legitimate problem. There was at no time during this initial, or any subsequent visits, any indication of *addiction* or *drug seeking behavior* with Anderson. The recordings of each and every visit to my office clearly demonstrate these facts.

During her follow-up visits Anderson related to me that she was doing well, taking one Percocet at night following her full-time work as a dancer, up and down the stage, with acrobatics on the pole as an exotic dancer. She did completely adhere to my doctor / patient relationship as per my "**Pain Management Agreement**", and there was never any indication of *addiction, diversion, or aberrant behavior.*

My presumptive diagnosis of Anderson was an *"acute and chronic strain and sprain of her thoracolumbar spine"*. This means strain and sprain of the muscles, ligaments, and tendons of the posterior aspect of the trunk and extremities. This presumptive diagnosis is well-established with an individual who works as an exotic dancer, a person who slides up and down on a pole, and runs around the stage for 8 to 10 hours a night. This type of work taxes the muscles of both upper and lower extremities as well as the posterior thorax and lumbar regions. This presumptive diagnosis is reasonable, and as close to accurate as possible considering the work that Anderson did on a routine basis. Her physical examination was stable, sitting in my air-conditioned office following her night of dancing, and following the fact that she had already taken Percocet after her work the night before, and had gotten a good night's sleep prior to her presenting in my office, for her afternoon visit. **Based upon a reasonable degree of medical certainty, and my clinical judgment following her initial visit, I wrote a prescription for Percocet 7.5 mg #30 to be taken one each night following her work as a dancer.**

The second female, **Margarita Abbattiscianni**, a.k.a. Maggie Ortiz, a.k.a Undercover II was given the fictitious name of Maggie Ortiz by the prosecutor. She first presented to my office on August 3, 2007. She arrived with her friend Anderson and I was told that they both danced at the same venue in Atlantic City. My question to Ortiz was, "what was her problem?" Her answer was, "**it's just the *pain* and I'm up all night long hours to six a.m.**". Ortiz stated to me that she was taking medication following her night of dancing. Her medical history was negligible, and her physical examination was also stable in that she was also a young female, an exotic dancer, essentially in good health.

Examination of Margarita Abbattiscianni revealed her pupils to be equal and the extraocular muscles intact bilaterally. The movements of her arms and legs were stable, and she was able to flex normally at the waist. Heart sounds demonstrated a regular rate and rhythm, with no evidence for murmurs, rubs or gallops. Her lung sounds were essentially clear, and her blood pressure and pulse were also normal. Her physical examination was essentially stable. Based upon the work that she performed, and the fact that she clearly stated to me that she had **pain** and discomfort following her night of dancing, and that she was already taking medication for this problem, *without any evidence of addiction, diversion, or abnormal behavior.* **It was my conclusion based upon a reasonable degree of medical certainty along with my clinical judgment that Ortiz necessitated continued medication following her night of dancing relating specifically to her symptoms and her work activity. I wrote a prescription for Margarita Abbattiscianni, a.k.a. Ortiz, for Percocet tablets #30 to be taken, one following her night of dancing.**

The **Physicians Desk Reference** (PDR) clearly states that the clinical value of the medication **Percocet** is **analgesia and sedation**. Anderson specifically told me that she was already taking Percocet following her night of dancing, and it was certainly my impression based on her work as an exotic dancer that she should continue with this medication, as there were no contra-indications. Following my initial visit with Anderson and Abbattiscianni it was my decision, based upon a reasonable degree of medical certainty, and upon my clinical judgment, to continue both patients with one Percocet per night following their work-night of dancing.

Over the next 5 1/2 months, I saw Anderson, a.k.a. Tonya Smith, a.k.a. Undercover I, a total of seven visits, and Abbattiscianni, a.k.a. Margarita Ortiz, a.k.a. Undercover II, for two visits. During that period of five and one half months, I maintained complete control of the prescription medication for both Undercover I and Undercover II. Based upon my medical judgment, prescribing Percocet to both patients following their night of dancing was an excellent clinical decision and an acceptable alternative to Xanax, Valium, or other hypnotic drugs also proven to be addictive. Anderson clearly related to me that she had been taking Percocet, and doing well with this medication, and Abbattiscianni also gave me a similar history of pain medication following her work as a dancer.

My **"Pain Management Agreement"** is a requirement for all patients enrolled in a treatment program for chronic pain. This "Pain Management Agreement" clearly indicates that the patient is suffering from **pain**, and is taking pain medication for this purpose. Furthermore, once the patient signs this agreement they indicate that they are willing to abide by all of the tenets of this agreement.

*See the "Pain Management Agreement" and* the PDR
reference *in the appendix*

The Cape May County Prosecutor, Robert Taylor, created **"objective due process entrapment,"** by sending these undercover officers into my office for treatment. Both females fabricated their job descriptions, their activities, and their existing medication use. Despite these deceptions, I provided appropriate professional treatment for both, as my goal was to prevent these patients from continued self-medication, that they received illegally from their girlfriends. Their work as exotic dancers produced clear symptoms of discomfort and pain that are well treated with one Percocet at night for both analgesia and sedation. I gave both voluminous instructions, and there was *never* any indication of *addiction, diversion, or aberrant behavior,* in either patient, and both stated to me that their ability to function at work was enhanced as a result of my treatment program. All of this information as stated above is documented in the **transcript recordings** taken from the serendipitous recorders carried by each undercover at each office visit. I fulfilled every medical regulation, and every law in the state of New Jersey with regard to my treatment program of these two undercover females similar to my treatment program for Detective Landis, the first undercover patient in December of 2005. I followed the case law in New Jersey which is "**State v Vaccaro**", the 1976 published appellate decision.

"State v Vaccaro" states in part "**The physician is immune from criminal prosecution if he is in his office, practicing medicine, in good faith only**". That is exactly what I did *then* and what I've always done since I began my medical practice.

The following is an excerpt from the book, the *Entrapment Defense* by Paul Marcus:

> "The doctrine of entrapment rest rather on a fundamental role of public policy, what stage of the proceedings the facts brought to it's attention, proof of entrapment, at any stage of the case requires the court (the judge) to stop the prosecution, direct that the indictment be quashed, and the defendant, set at liberty. The power and the duty to act shall remain with the court and not with a jury."

It is clear that the Cape May County Prosecutor Robert Taylor, and his underlings, **engaged in "objective due process entrapment"**. **The criminal proceeding against me should have been brought to an end at once by Judge Raymond Batten**. This judge abdicated his responsibility to fulfill his duty to quash the indictment, and set me at liberty. Unfortunately, Judge Batten demonstrated, in my opinion, a **cognitive bias**, and was **prejudiced** against my pain management practice and me. **I was the victim of the incompetent and prejudiced justice system of Cape May County.**

# Look Behind the Facade to See the Treachery in the Events to Follow

"Be grateful for adversity for it forces the human spirit to grow.
For surely the human character is formed not in the absence of difficulty but in our response to difficulty."
- Jim Rohm

The initial allegation against me was titled prescribing excessive pain medication. By history my practice came to the attention of the prosecutor's office in 2005 when a **faulty computer generated report** indicated that my office prescribed excessive amounts of addictive pain medication.

This faulty report was uncertified by either the Drug Enforcement Agency, or the Cape May County Prosecutor's office, and was nothing more than an outline in copy, of my patient's visits with their medication prescribed for a period of four years. This included 1. My general medical patients 2. My workers compensation injured patients 3. My personal injury protection patients 4. My rehabilitative patients 5. My pain management patients 6. My addiction management program patients using only Suboxone, a Class IV product.

In spite of the ignorance of the facts outlined above, the morons of both, the Cape May County Prosecutor's office and the DEA misfits in South Jersey, titled this report as excessive. The majority of this report was faulty and completely uncertified.

It is no secret that my addiction patients are former drug abusers. Remember, I treat opioid addiction, heroin and oral narcotics. I'm certified to treat these

# Chapter 4 - Look Behind the Facade to See the Treachery in the Events to Follow

patients by the DEA, and as a certified physician listed on the DEA website to treat opioid addiction with Suboxone this product would account for an additional 200 prescriptions which are classified. The fact that Suboxone is a classified product should have been well known to the DEA misfits and this information should have been relayed to the Cape May County Prosecutor's Office. Instead, both the DEA and the CMCPO termed this faulty uncertified report as "excessive"

Eighty-five to ninety percent of those in trouble with opioid narcotics and frankly, addicted to opioids, did very well with my addiction treatment program as this is part of my medical practice. The actual reason that anyone could think that I excessively prescribe pain medication lies in the fact that multiple prescription pads were stolen from my office on four separate occasions between 2004 and 2007. These thefts were committed by three former employees and one patient and **all were reported to law enforcement for prosecution.**

## THEFT #1

The first was committed by an employee, M.M.. In November of 2004, M.M. was employed in my office for approximately seven months. She somehow got the key to my locked cabinet, and stole several prescription pads from my locked cabinet. She then wrote numerous prescriptions for herself and others. Law enforcement interviewed her while she was in jail and of course, she simply lied to these investigators in an attempt to get herself a reduced sentence.

## THEFT #2

The second theft was committed by Katherine Mills who was only employed in my office for **three days**. She was caught calling in prescriptions for herself and her friends, from my office, and frantically fled the office abruptly when this became apparent. She was eventually caught and put in jail for a period of time. This individual **Katherine Mills** is the type of disgraceful human being that Detective Hallett **chose to interview and rely upon to support his search warrant application.** Hallett interviewed her along with another detective, Paul Worrell, and both were **dumb enough to believe the fictitious story of Katherine**

**Mills**. They interviewed her while she was incarcerated and then while she was being transferred from one jail in New Jersey to another jail in Pennsylvania. Not surprisingly, she told both detectives a **pack of lies in an effort to bargain her way to a shorter sentence.** By way of example, Mills claimed to be employed in my office for eight months, as the manager, when in fact she was employed for **a mere three and one half days** training to be an office aide. During those three and a half days she was clever enough to call in multiple prescriptions of opioid derivatives for herself and others. As an "experienced" law enforcement officer, **Hallett** should have examined her story and established the facts, or at least corroborated her story with me in my office. Instead, Hallett blindly accepted her lies and misrepresentations to support his quest for a search warrant against me. Hallett easily could have discovered her lies and properly determined that she was **not credible**, and should not be relied upon with respect to the significant issues regarding my medical office practice. Instead Hallett chose never to contact me relative to this issue. All the lies and fabrications given by Mills to law enforcement were eventually certified as pure nonsense by her own family living in Cape May County and by her employment record in Trenton, New Jersey.

**THEFT #3**

The third theft occurred in March of 2005. I was away from my office at a medical seminar when one of my colleagues who worked in my office along with my wife, Barbara, a registered nurse, noticed the prescription pad had disappeared. A patient stole my prescription pad, and Barbara observed the missing prescription pad within a very short period of time, and the North Wildwood police were immediately notified. The police eventually caught up with this individual, however, the prescription pad was never recovered and the patient was never charged. We later found out that over the next six to eight months this patient wrote multiple prescriptions for opioid derivatives, and sold them in Cape May County, Atlantic County and in Philadelphia.

In December of 2005 following the aforementioned thefts of prescription pads, the Cape May County Prosecutor, Taylor, sent an undercover detective into my office posing as a heroin addict. The intent was for him to obtain an improper

# Chapter 4 - Look Behind the Facade to See the Treachery in the Events to Follow

prescription. **Detective Landis**, entered my office with the claim that he was a heroin addict, and needed an opioid prescription to control his withdraw symptoms. The intent, of course, was to obtain evidence of improper conduct on my part, with regard to prescribing opioid medication. The detective was wearing a transmitting device, and he gave me a story regarding his addiction. After he was done with his dissertation, I gently guided him into the understanding that if he continued his heroin use he would end up either "diseased" or " dead". I told him clearly that I would never prescribe any type of opioid medication to a heroin addict. I convinced him to begin a **Suboxone** program in an effort to treat his heroin addiction. After a period of time I convinced him to enter my Suboxone program, and explained to him exactly how to administer it, and furthermore gave him a return visit appointment to my office for follow-up care. Following this visit, Detective Landis returned to the prosecutor's office and wrote a very favorable report regarding this experience with me. His report reflected no evidence of improperly prescribing opioid medication. His report was a glaring record of the proper method of treating heroine addiction, and the fact that he was extremely satisfied by the treatment that he received in my office. The facts regarding this episode are as follows:

**The Cape May County Prosecutor's office withheld Detective Landis's report from my attorney, Judge Batten, the grand jury, the Board of Medical Examiners and myself for three years**. This discovery should have been given to my attorney in September of 2007, following my arrest. This again outlines the *deceptive and disgraceful* behavior of the Cape May County prosecutor and his underlings.

**THEFT #4**

In March of 2007, D. A. who was employed in my office for 6 months stole prescription pads from my locked cabinet. She worked in my office as a secretary, obtained the key to my locked cabinet, and she and her criminal boyfriend Ryan Conyers proceeded to illegally write more than 150 opioid prescriptions, and sold them throughout South Jersey and the Philadelphia area. D. A. and Ryan Conyers were arrested and eventually prosecuted. Conyers was incarcerated for a two-year period. Ironically, in Conyers Investigation reports, **I was identified as the crime**

Taylor's qualification as Cape May County prosecutor in June 2004 we're not carefully questioned by the Senate Judiciary Committee regarding his appointment. There were several individuals in Cape May County who wrote letters urging the Senate Committee to reject Taylor's candidacy claiming that the prosecutor's office needed a major overhaul, without Taylor. Many individuals distrusted Robert Taylor, and thought him not a good candidate for the position of Chief Law Enforcement Officer. Unfortunately, at the time of Taylor's confirmation, the Cape May County Prosecutor's office had been without a permanent prosecutor for several years. I suspect this was the only reason in spite of the numerous objections regarding Taylor's character, that he was eventually confirmed as county prosecutor.

Prosecutors generally seem to have a high opinion of themselves, a grandiose sense of self-esteem, that they are better than everyone else, and that they are entitled to certain edification. Decent people do not seek this position which requires looking at everyone as dishonest. Prosecutors are generally, and in my opinion, **pathological liars** creating issues, and desperate to file charges filling the gaps with speculation. Typically, they have no problem **lying**, appearing quite cool to such a point that it's almost impossible for them to be truthful on a consistent basis, just as the various assistant prosecutors in Cape May County, in my case, who demonstrated a lack of *remorse, shame*, or *guilt* during my entire prosecution. Prosecutors have no problem with this thought process, because everyone is **evil** except themselves. "The end always justifies the means," remains their mantra, and they let nothing stand in their way. Such people posses shallow emotions and in reality are incapable of knowing or understanding the truth. A good leader possesses *competence, humility, and integrity*. Certain men and women are deceived regarding their talents, and possess an inability to distinguish between confidence and competence. They are basically unaware of their limitations. *Taylor,* of course, is the prime example of this inability.

Taylor is simply a political hack who worked as a real estate attorney, and through the chicanery of **politics** was appointed by the sitting governor as prosecutor of Cape May County. Prior to his appointment as Cape May County

Prosecutor Taylor was the chairman of the Democratic Party in Cape May County. Following his initial term as prosecutor, Taylor was then supported exclusively by Senator Vandrew, then a democrat for his second term as county prosecutor. Taylor, **in my opinion,** remains a **paranoid, narcissistic, egomaniac,** not well versed at all in criminal law, but represented a powerful element in the corrupt justice system of Cape May County. **In my opinion,** Taylor was preoccupied with a *pervasive distrust, and unjustified suspicion* of others particularly those *more successful* in the community than *himself*. Furthermore, in my opinion, Taylor suffers from a **delusional personality disorder** who utilized his prosecutorial power to displace his **underlying insufficiency.** Additionally, Taylor was unduly influenced by one of his detectives, **Marie Hayes**, to arrest me without evidence or any reasonable suspicion of illegal activity.

**I offer some examples of Taylor's insufficiency:**

- *In 2006,* Taylor indicted a New Jersey State Trooper named Robert Higbee and charged this officer with vehicular homicide. Taylor presented unsound data to the grand jury, and the trial resulted in a full acquittal of Trooper Higbee.

- *In 2007* Taylor charged an Ohio physician Dr. George Carty with the murder of a Lower Township, NJ man in 1982. Dr. Carty was burdened with a bail of $500,000, and was incarcerated for three years. Dr. Carty's case was eventually dismissed by a Cape May County Superior Court judge for lack of evidence.

- *In March 2011*, the mayor of the city of Wildwood, Gary DeMarzo was also falsely charged and arrested by Mr. Taylor, and eventually all of the allegations leading to his arrest were found to be blatantly false. The presiding Superior Court judge opined that the state's failure to present all relevant evidence resulted in a grand jury proceeding that was fundamentally unfair. In April 2012 the Superior Court judge dismissed the indictment against Mr. DeMarzo.

Taylor colluded with Sandra Dick at the Board of Medical Examiners in Trenton, New Jersey to arrest me in September 2007. In my opinion, Taylor, along with Sandra Dick at the BME formulated a political plan to arrest me. This eventually led to the suspension of my medical license shortly thereafter by the BME. Following my suspension, I was indicted in February 2008 which was fundamentally flawed, with **malicious abuse of process**, and **prosecutorial misconduct**, followed by a five-year criminal case that I had to endure. **Detective George Hallett** gave **false and egregious testimony** to the grand jury, withheld **exculpatory evidence** from the grand jury, and blatantly **lied** to the grand jury under oath. My criminal trial was eventually convened in November 2012, after I rejected five pleadings offered by Taylor. **I was acquitted of all 26 criminal counts in November 2012 by a jury of my peers in Cape May County in less than two hours.**

Taylor, in my opinion, is guilty of **malicious abuse of power**, and **malicious use of process,** when he arrested both my wife, a registered nurse, and myself with false and egregious criminal counts. I was actually indicted by Taylor on five separate occasions and my wife Barbara was included on two of those indictments. The only reason Taylor indicted my wife was his attempt to entice me to take one of his disgraceful pleadings. **I rejected all five of Taylor's pleadings, and eventually the two indictments against my wife and myself were dismissed by Superior Court Judge Batten for prosecutorial misconduct.** The remaining indictments were won at trial with the superior guidance of my defense attorney John Tumelty. Taylor and his assistant prosecutors, along with his stupid detectives had **zero understanding of the facts in my criminal case**, and absolutely no understanding of my medical practice, or the medical law in the state of New Jersey. **Furthermore, the influence generated by his detective Marie Hayes, was without any factual basis, and certainly without any evidence, merit or ethics.**

**To summarize:**
We desperately need legal reform in the state of New Jersey because no one is safe any longer. The decision to indict an individual **should not** belong only to

the county prosecutor. At the grand jury presentment, the individual charged should have the opportunity to defend himself. **All evidence** must be produced at the grand jury, not just the tainted, one-sided prosecutor's version. The people alone should indict, and if evidence is **exculpatory,** it must be presented to the grand jury intact. In my case, **a plethora of exculpatory evidence was withheld by assistant prosecutor Megan Hoerner and her detective/witness, George Hallett. When this occurs, the prosecutor and detective should be sentenced to the same penalty sought against the wrongfully accused**.

The absolute decision to indict must be taken away from **dishonest prosecutors and detectives**. These dishonest prosecutors and detectives injure many innocent people **intentionally** with the blessing of government. There is no difference in character between **lying prosecutors, detectives, or criminals.** The dignity of the people and the laws of the state *must be respected* or the society falls apart. There is a great need for oversight in this current process. This **corruption** unfortunately, is everywhere in our government, not just in Cape May County… **just look at Washington, D.C.**

## "Power and Control is the Objective Not Truth or Justice"
-Machiavelli

**The next creature to introduce:
George Hallett – Cape May County Detective**

**George Hallett** was a detective in the Cape May County Prosecutor's office and in my opinion, suffers from a disorder of both **cognition** and **affect**. His abilities as a detective are extremely poor. He is, in my opinion, a superb **liar** and **confabulator**, as he deliberately misinterpreted evidence, and superimposed his own opinions upon his altered evidence. As an example, which Hallett placed in his search warrant application, **Hallett** and one of his colleagues **interviewed the criminal named Kathy Mills** while transferring her from one jail to another. **Hallett simply believed all her lies and distortions** relative to my medical practice, and her work therein. **Mills told Hallett** and his partner, Paul Worrell, that she worked in my office for **nine months**, and was the **office supervisor**.

**The facts are that she worked in my office for approximately three and a half days and left abruptly because, as a criminal, she was phoning in illegal opioid prescriptions for herself and her friends.** Mills was caught red-handed by one of my employees, and abruptly ran out of the office and was never seen again. **Hallett never bothered to investigate any of her fictitious stories but absorbed all that she said as fact.** In my opinion, Hallett is either **incapable**

## Chapter 6 - "Power and Control is the Objective, Not Truth and Justice"

as a detective of distinguishing fact from fiction, or he **knowingly, willfully and maliciously** abandoned all responsibilities as a law-enforcement officer, and purposefully utilized this **false information for his search warrant application to obtain an indictment**. Either way, Hallett is simply a **disgrace.**

Hallett wrote his search warrant application utilizing multiple lies and misrepresentations, and presented this flawed document to Judge Batten to sign. Hallett's search warrant was full of **deception, distortion, and dishonesty**. This search warrant *excluded* **multiple significant "exculpatory evidence"** regarding my treatment of the two female undercover law enforcement people as well as my **"Pain Management Agreement"** signed by Tonya Anderson, the star actress. Hallett also eliminated the **four thefts** clearly identified by my office to law enforcement. **His entire thesis regarding this search warrant application was false, and he knowingly, willfully and maliciously provided this false information to Judge Batten**.

On February 18, 2008 Hallett was the only witness at the initial grand jury presentment with Assistant Prosecutor Megan Hoerner. Hallett committed **perjury under oath** by giving false evidence with malice of intent, as he **lied** to the grand jury at multiple periods in this presentment. Hallett **willfully lied** regarding undercover Maggie Ortiz, who clearly stated to me that she had **pain** and was "up all night dancing till six in the morning". Hallett **lied** to the grand jury by inferencing that they were unable to find a medical file for undercover Maggie Ortiz. Both he and Assistant Prosecutor Hoerner, at the time of the grand jury presentation, had complete knowledge that there was a medical file for this patient Maggie Ortiz.

He went further at this grand jury presentation by stating "that since no medical chart was located for Maggie Ortiz, **Dr. Costino therefore was charging money for the office visit without producing a medical record**". In addition to all of the *lies, misrepresentations,* and frank *perjury* that Hallett committed at the grand jury presentation, he additionally omitted significant **exculpatory evidence** which, had this evidence been presented to the grand jury, I would have been exonerated.

Hallett had absolutely no working knowledge of my medical practice, or the medical law in New Jersey and was simply ignorant of these issues. There was never any evidence for **"probable cause"** either in his search warrant application, or at the grand jury presentment. I will outline all of these issues clearly and succinctly later in the text.

Neither Robert Taylor, Megan Hoerner, nor George Hallett, had any knowledge of the medical law in the state of New Jersey specificity "**State v Vaccaro**". They had no knowledge of my medical practice, or the practical functioning of my medical office. There was essentially **no common sense** employed by any of these law-enforcement people regarding my practice of medicine.

This indictment **should have been dismissed** by Judge Batten because the grand jury testimony was laden with **deliberate material misrepresentations, omissions, false factual, and false legal statements, suppressed evidence, prejudice and grossly misleading information.** The indictment should have been dismissed because the **presentation was patently unfair, and violated my "due process" rights. Judge Batten refused to dismiss this indictment.** This refusal represents an abomination of justice.

In my opinion, Judge Batten was **biased,** and **prejudiced** against me, and my practice of "*pain management*". Furthermore, **his friendship with county prosecutor Robert Taylor, his longtime buddy, compromised this decision.**

# "The Justice System is Composed Mostly of Inadequate Personalities with Evil Intent"

-Friedrich Wilhelm Nietzsche

**The next two disgraceful creatures in my criminal case are: Tonya Anderson and David Puteska**

**Tonya Anderson a.k.a. Tonya Smith, a.k.a Undercover I,** was the first female undercover officer to enter my practice in their investigation. In my opinion, Anderson suffers from a **borderline personality disorder,** with a pervasive pattern of **instability of self-image**. Anderson underwent two separate breast implant surgical procedures prior to her appearance in my office in April of 2007. She exhibits basic **impulsivity**, and is a **prolific liar**. Anderson committed **perjury** under oath at the administrative law hearing (OAL), in December of 2008 into January of 2009. Her inability to pass her physical training testing during her recruit training is primary evidence of her physical problems, contributing to her basic insecurities. **Robert Taylor** chose this individual in 2007 as his **primary state witness and the first female undercover officer in my criminal prosecution.**

On January 6, 2009, my attorney Glenn Zeitz petitioned Captain Richard Buzbee of Little Egg Harbor Township Police Department for medical records, and performance records, of Tonya Anderson when she was a recruit at the Ocean County Police Academy Training Center (OCPA) in 2005. These records were very important for the determination of Anderson's physical conditioning at the time of her training at OCPA, and they provided a reasonable inference relative to her past medical history. Issues regarding her spine and extremities would be significant because she posed as an undercover officer, disguised as an exotic dancer in Atlantic City for the Cape May County Prosecutors office. I have in my possession the OCPA performance records of Tonya Anderson, and they are voluminous, I will summarize for you her performance at the Academy.

On September 8, 2005 Anderson **failed** her pre-test physical training requirement, and as a result she was disqualified for certification for Ocean County. Her report states "Recruit Anderson's pretest fitness level is **below** OCPA minimum standards presently disqualifying her from county certification".

On November 28, 2005 Anderson again **failed** her physical training requirement: "Recruit Anderson's mid-test fitness level is below OCPA's minimum standards presently disqualifying her from county certification".

On January 13, 2006 Ocean County Police Academy generated a physical fitness program basic class report reflecting Anderson's overall performance on the physical fitness requirements, and it states the following:

> " Recruit Anderson obtained a post test physical ability score of 188 out of a possible 500 equal to a rating of "FAIL". Recruit Anderson's physical fitness ranking in this class is 63 out of 63.
> Furthermore, recruit Anderson's fitness level is below the OCPA minimal standards disqualifying her for county certification ".

In spite of the fact that Anderson performed so poorly regarding her fitness level for county certification, Anderson was hired as a Class II officer for the city of Egg Harbor Township. The morons at The Cape May County Prosecutor's Office actually borrowed her from Egg Harbor Township to pose as an undercover exotic dancer. She was the primary undercover individual in this illegal **"due process entrapment"** fiasco in their effort to **"entrap"** me in my medical office.

# Chapter 7

Anderson is an **abject liar**, and **perjurer** with her certifications and with her testimony under oath at the administrative law hearing in 2008, and 2009. **Anderson was treating with a local chiropractor, Dr. Joseph O'Rourke, for pain and discomfort in her spine and extremities, during the exact same time while acting as an undercover cop for Cape May County, while treating in my office for pain management.**

Anderson signed her initial false certification on September 19, 2008 at the Board of Medical Examiners in Trenton. My attorney, Glenn Zeitz, eventually discovered that she lied and perjured herself on her first certification orchestrated by Deputy Attorney General **David Puteska** at the Board of Medical Examiners (BME). Both Anderson and DAG **Puteska** were fully aware at the time of her certification that it was **false.**

At the administrative hearing in December 2008 and January of 2009, Anderson, the **state's star witness**, committed **perjury** under oath. **In my opinion**, she was told by **Sandra Dick** and **David Puteska** that she would be protected from prosecution at the BME for her perjury. Anderson categorically denied ever having pain or discomfort in her spine or extremities, and failed to reveal any of her chiropractic treatments for these issues at this administrative law hearing or at her office visits with me. DAG Puteska was well aware that Anderson had received treatment from Dr. O'Rourke by the time of the OAL hearing. Puteska was well aware that she had received prior treatment from her chiropractor, even though she denied all of the above to everyone else. Puteska composed Anderson's first certification, where she denies all treatment to her spine and extremities. Anderson's medical records from Dr. O'Rourke's office specifically in July of 2007 while she was treating in my office, clearly states that **she had "pain"** and discomfort in her **cervical, thoracic and lumbar regions** in addition to her **right shoulder,** with **sleep disturbance** extending over the prior **four years**.

In my opinion, these records along with various other court hearings and documents which were produced, identify that Deputy Attorney David Puteska colluded with Deputy Attorney Sandra Dick, and Tony Anderson to fabricate a false narrative, and permit Anderson to commit **perjury**, under oath, not only on her certifications, but also under oath at the administrative law hearing in December of 2008 and January of 2009. As a result of Anderson's **perjury** at the OAL hearing my medical license remained suspended and eventually revoked for a period of time.

**David Puteska** is a **deputy attorney assigned to the Board of Medical Examiners**. He was the **underling of Deputy Attorney Sandra Dick**, who **controlled the Board of Medical Examiners**.

Deputy Attorney Puteska and Anderson were joined at the hip and were both essentially under the control of Chief Deputy Attorney **Sandra Dick**. David Puteska and Sandra Dick were the state's attorneys at the initial Board of Medical Examiners hearing in December of 2007, when the Board suspended my medical license. This activity was in concert with Cape May County Prosecutor Robert Taylor.

David Puteska stated to the Board that I "did not" perform a legitimate physical examination of Anderson. Furthermore, Puteska stated that I "admitted" falsifying patient's records. These statements, of course, are *absolutely false,* as my medical records of Anderson and of all my patients were complete when Taylor's minions serendipitously confiscated them from my office in September of 2007. My medical records expert, **Glenda Hamilton**, examined all of my medical records, associated with this case, and found them to be **better than average**, at the Administrative Law Hearing, and at my criminal trial in 2012. There was never any falsifying of patient records or of any other issues regarding this case. I have never been accused by any insurance company, or by Medicare or Medicaid, the federal insurance industry, of any discrepancy. At the administrative law hearing, my experts, **Glenda Hamilton** and **Dr. Richard Jermyn** testified that my medical records were better than average, and fulfilled all the necessary requirements of New Jersey law.

In my opinion, both David Puteska and Sandra Dick with their **impaired intellect**, and **corrupt intent** did not possess any knowledge of the utilization of a **template** in medical record keeping. Furthermore, in my opinion, they had no knowledge of the intricacies of the physical examination, and did not possess critical knowledge of the various aspects of the physical examination by a physician.

Additionally, Puteska certainly had no knowledge of the **CPT coding system** that must be utilized in a physician's office for the insurance companies to recognize both diagnosis and treatment. **Puteska, in my opinion, is nothing more than a prevaricator of the truth**, who did the bidding of Sandra Dick, and orchestrated and authored Anderson's **first false certification.** Furthermore, in my opinion, both **Puteska and Dick** had knowledge that Anderson had been treating with a chiropractor for multiple issues during the time that she was treating with me, and they certainly had this information prior to the administrative law hearing in December of 2008 and January of 2009, **but refused to disclose this "exculpatory evidence"**.

The disgraceful New Jersey Board of Medical Examiners, along with their chief deputy Sandra Dick, suspended my medical license in December 2007 with the claim that they were "**protecting the public**." This ordeal began in September 2007 when the **corrupt** County Prosecutor Taylor colluded with Sandra Dick, to have me arrested. Following my arrest in September of 2007, I was subjected to an incomprehensible series of accusations with multiple criminal charges. **The Cape May County prosecutor, Taylor, and several of his detectives along with DAG Sandra Dick and David Puteska created multiple factually inaccurate charges with multiple false statements regarding my practice of medicine.** Factually inaccurate statements regarding my medical practice also appeared in the disgraceful **search warrant application** authored by George Hallett, and signed by Judge Batten. The grossly false and inaccurate charges for proceeding against me were **fabricated** by the officials employed at the Cape May County prosecutors office, and the Board of Medical Examiners, typical of the *faulty investigation* and the *prejudice, distortion, and deceit,* with which it was it was conducted.

The Board of Medical Examiners essentially denied me "**due process**" of law under the constitution of both New Jersey and the United States at the first Board hearing in December 2007, and also at the administrative law hearing in

"Due Process" Denied

December 2008 and January of 2009. It is truly unbelievable to me that these characters that work for the government are so **dishonest**. Not only do **they lie and deceive with impunity,** but are also absolved *without reprisal* and with *no oversight* by the attorney general of the state of New Jersey. "**Due process**" is inextricably rooted in the constitution of the United States of America. Taylor and his gang of morons, along with Sandra Dick and David Puteska at the BME, failed in their duty to provide me "**due process**", and in doing so have **failed themselves, their oath, and the public trust.**

# The Drama Is In The Details

"We fall, we break, but them we rise, we heal, we overcome. Courage is not having the strength to go on. Courage is going on when your strength has been challenged."
- Theodore Roosevelt

Through the molecular labyrinth of **lies and deception,** the Cape May County Prosecutor **Taylor,** and DAG **Sandra Dick** at the Board of Medical Examiners prosecuted my case.

It all began in the middle of 2005, when the Cape May County Prosecutors Office received erroneous information from the Drug Enforcement Agency (DEA), regarding prescription data sheets. This data was not based upon any type of scientific analysis, however Taylor accepted it as fact. On December 13, 2005 **Detective Joseph Landis** from the Cape May County Prosecutor's Office - Narcotics Task Force, was sent to my office as an undercover agent posing as a patient addicted to heroin. He attempted to obtain a fraudulent prescription from me for pain medication. Detective Landis was wearing a wire connected to a transmitting device. Following this visit and after I begin a treatment program for him with Suboxone, Landis returned to the prosecutors office, and wrote an excellent report outlining his experience with me. At the end of his report Detective Landis clearly stated that based upon his investigation, **he was unaware of any individuals who received controlled substances illegally from my office at any time in the past.**

On January 24, 2007, a meeting was conducted by members of the following governmental agencies: the Drug Enforcement Agency, the United States Postal

Service, Cape May County Prosecutors Office, Little Egg Harbor Township Police Department. The purpose of this meeting was to commence a second proactive undercover investigation into whether or not I had been illegally prescribing opioid medications. The possibility that I was engaging in insurance fraud was also discussed. During this meeting the decision was made to engage a female Class II police officer from Egg Harbor Township to pose as a patient and to serendipitously record her office visits with me. At this meeting it was noted that Dr. Costino had been a physician in good standing in the state of New Jersey with registration and license to prescribe medication for the past 35 years. Furthermore, Dr. Costino had not had any lawsuits by any patient either for medical malpractice, or any lawsuits concerning medications that were prescribed throughout those 35 years.

On April 12, 2007, **Anderson** reported to the Cape May County Prosecutor's Office where she received the following items: a digital recorder, a fictitious health insurance card with her fictitious name Tonya Smith, a fictitious home address, a prepaid cellular telephone, a fictitious date of birth, a fictitious social security number, fictitious employment information, and a fictitious telephone number.

After receiving all this information, she presented to my office for her first visit. **Anderson** provided my staff with all of this fictitious information, and she completed new patient forms, and falsely told my staff that she was simply here in my office for a physical examination. A medical chart was established for Anderson, and when I eventually entered the examination room, she advised me that she was a dancer in Atlantic City, was on her feet all day, and half the night, and worked at least for five to six nights a week. She clearly stated to me that she was taking **Percocet** after her night of dancing because it helped her to get the rest that she needed in order to get up and do the same work the next day. Anderson further stated that Percocet worked for her. I of course had multiple questions for this individual, as she denied being addicted to Percocet, or any other type of medication, and I asked her further questions regarding the work that she did as an exotic dancer on the stage, up and down the pole, with twisting and turning et cetera, et cetera. Anderson related to me that she danced seven to eight hours per

# Chapter 8 - The Drama Is In The Deatails

night, sometimes until four o'clock in the morning, and never took her medication, Percocet, for recreation. Anderson never stated that any of the inferences that I raised concerning her medical condition were either incorrect or otherwise baseless. Her statements relative to her employment together with her acknowledgment that my inferences about her medical condition were correct, were clearly intended to be **unfairly** and **unconstitutionally** done in an effort to induce me into prescribing her medication. At the end of her first visit, I believed this individual to be honest and sincere, and I had no reason to suspect any underlying nefarious activity. I certainly believed that she worked hard as a dancer, and I relied upon her history that she had issues with her physiology relative to the exhausting work of exotic dancing. **Remember, Anderson clearly said to me that she was taking Percocet only on the nights that she danced.** She admitted that she received this medication from one of her girlfriends, another dancer.

**Percocet** is an excellent product for both analgesia and sedation, and certainly is an appropriate medication for an individual performing this type of vigorous work, instead of drinking alcohol all night.

This young lady was a 28-year-old female who performed exotic dancing eight hours a night up, and down the stage, twisting and turning, up and down the pole, and taxing the muscles of the cervical, thoracic and lumbar regions, and both upper and lower extremities. These muscles, tendons and ligaments, are subject to micro tears in the tissue which in medical terminology are called **cumulative trauma disorders.** Following my initial conversation with Anderson, I did my reasonable induction physical examination, and gave her directions regarding the medication that I would prescribe for her. I wrote her a prescription for Percocet, 30 pills, to be taken once per night following her dancing shift. **This statement was clear on her written prescription.** I placed this information in her medical chart along with a copy of this prescription for further reference.

On May 2, 2007 **Anderson** returned to my office for follow-up visit, and at that time she stated to me that the Percocet was helping her, and acknowledged that she only took this medication following her night of dancing. She said to me that she was sore, and the medication was working for her, relative to her work as a dancer. Conversational exchange took place between Anderson and I, and this confirmed for me that she was doing well with regard to the medication, and not having any problems regarding this medication. There was certainly *no evidence of addiction, or aberrant behavior* with this patient.

On June 7, 2007 Anderson arrived in my office, and upon her arrival, she was given my **"Pain Management Agreement"** to read carefully, and sign and date this agreement. My **"Pain Management Agreement"** in summary prohibited a patient from sharing medications with others, or using other physicians for pain management. Additionally, it provides information relative to the use of pain medication for pain only, and confirms that the patient is taking her medication for **"pain only"**. A copy of this agreement is given to the patient, and the original is placed in her medical record. During this visit she was clear relative to the fact that she was dancing every night, and "things were picking up because they were now in the summer months". Anderson complained to me at this visit that the 7.5 mg Percocet that I originally prescribed for her was wearing off too soon. I explained to her that this is not an unusual complaint, because patients do become habituated to this type of medication. I increased the dosage of Percocet to 10 mg, to be taken one per night following her dancing activity. Again Anderson was clear and concise regarding this medication and never gave me any indication of addiction, and her behavior was very stable in my office.

On July 13, 2007 Anderson again presented it to my office, and stated to me that she was very, very active with her dancing activity. Similar to the previous visit, she clearly intended to **unfairly** and **unconstitutionally** induce me to continue to prescribe medication for her with regard to her work as a dancer. I certainly believed everything she said to me, because she seemed to be honest and forthright, and was taking her medication as prescribed following her night of dancing. Additionally, at every visit I examined her heart and lungs, blood pressure weight station and gait, and general demeanor on a routine basis. Her physical examination was relatively stable at each visit. Anderson never said to me that she lost her medication, and never gave me any excuses relative to the

## Chapter 8 - The Drama Is In The Deatails

medication that I prescribed. I continued her on Percocet, 30 pills, to be taken one per night following her dancing activity.

On August 3, 2007 Anderson returned to my office and brought along with her, a second exotic dancer, a friend, Margarita Abbattiscianni, with the fictitious name Maggie Ortiz. After finalizing the office visit with Anderson, I asked Maggie Ortiz what was her problem. Ortiz stated to me clearly that she had "**pain and works all night sometimes until six in the morning**". Remember, Maggie Ortiz a.k.a Undercover II, is a DEA officer and her real name is Margarita Abbattiscianni. Ortiz attributed her pain and discomfort to dancing eight or ten hours at night with similar ramifications stated above with regard to Anderson, a.k.a Tonya Smith, a.k.a Undercover I. Ortiz was a 30-year-old female, in good condition as a dancer. At this visit with Ortiz, I asked her my normal questions and her story was similar to Anderson's. Ortiz however was much clearer regarding her pain and discomfort secondary to her dancing activity. I examined Ortiz in my normal fashion, heart, lungs, spine and extremities, blood pressure, weight and demeanor. My examination of Maggie Ortiz was essentially stable. My examinations of both of these females were stable at all of their office visits, as I would expect them to be, since they are dancers in very good physical condition.

The serendipitous transcript recordings of both Anderson and Ortiz confirm that neither one ever said that the inferences raised by me concerning their condition with regard to their dancing, we're neither incorrect or otherwise baseless. At the time of my office visits with them, I believed both females to be honest and sincere young women working as exotic dancers, doing the kind of work outlined above, on a routine basis 8 to 10 hours per night. Following my examination of both females, I wrote a prescription for Percocet 10 mg, 30 pills to be taken one per night following their dancing activity.

On August 23, 2007 both females return to my office, and at that time they were still "very, very busy", however they said to me that in early September they are "going to take their show on the road" and settle in the state of Florida. "The show" of course relates to exotic dancing, as both clearly stated to me that they were doing well with their medication, taking one each night following their dancing activity. In the middle of my discussions with them at this last visit, an unusual situation developed.

Initially Anderson, and then Ortiz, began to ask me questions relative to **Percocet** versus a second medication, **Oxycontin**. They had additional questions relative to the functioning of both Percocet and Oxycontin as a comparative issue. I gave them information relative to both products, and when they pressed the issue, I **admonished** both, stating clearly that **they do not need Oxycontin,** since this product is intended for more serious painful issues such as a *herniated disc, fractured bones, or more significant metabolic diseases like cancer.* I will admit to you, that at that moment in my office *I was furious* for having to go through this discussion with these two patients. Of course, at this time I still considered them to be reasonably good patients, with questions regarding their medication. I certainly had no knowledge that they were both undercover agents, attempting to **unfairly, and unconstitutionally** induce me into prescribing additional medication to them, principally **Oxycontin**. Up to this point they had been honest and sincere patients and they were essentially leaving my practice to move to Florida. The next time I saw these two females was at the administrative law hearing in December 2008 when they both became witnesses for the state.

# My Arrest

"We fall, we break, but them we rise, we heal, we overcome."

"Fate whispers to the warrior,
'You cannot withstand the storm.'
The warrior whispers back, 'I am the storm."
 - Unknown

On September 14, 2007, I was arrested in my office **by Detective George Hallett** from the Cape May County Prosecutors Office along with a number of other detectives from that office, additional police officers from North Wildwood, as well as DEA officers. There were approximately *28 law enforcement characters* in my office 8:30 in the morning on Friday, September 14, 2007. These cops frightened my office patients, and my medical staff, as you might imagine. My office waiting room was full with patients waiting to see me as their physician.

This was a bona fide law enforcement "**raid**" of my office. Approximately 100 patient medical files were taken from my office by Hallett and his gang, from a list prepared by both **Hallett** and **Assistant Prosecutor Megan Hoerner**. In addition to my medical files that were confiscated, these characters also took my computers, and other things that they deemed necessary to their cause. Following this office **"raid"**, several detectives and police officers began to interrogate my employees. They put me in handcuffs, and escorted me to the North Wildwood Police Department.

**Hallett and Hoerner concocted a patient list in order to confiscate approximately 100 patient record files.** The patient files that were taken from my office were primarily **pain management patient files.** Additionally, they confiscated the medical record of Tonya Smith, a.k.a. Undercover I and Detective Landis but failed to retrieve the record of Maggie Ortiz, a.k.a. Undercover II as you shortly will understand the reasoning for this failure.

**Observe carefully the following:**
Both Detective Hallett and Assistant Prosecutor Hoerner, **in my opinion, intentionally misspelled** the fictitious name of Undercover II, Maggie **Ortiz on the Cape May County Prosecutor's office evidence log.**
*See Evidence Log of confiscated patient files in Appendix*

***They purposely misspelled*** her fictitious last name as *"Artiz"* instead of *"Ortiz"*. When these law enforcement people were **unable to find** any patient by the name of *"Artiz"*, they **refused to allow** my employees to assist them in this endeavor. The end result of course, is the fact that they *never* recovered the Undercover II, **Ortiz**, medical chart that day.

Following my arrest, I was taken to the North Wildwood Police Department, and eventually detective Hallett arrived to interrogate me. I initially demanded some answers regarding my arrest. I forcibly told Hallett that I did not need an attorney, and demanded an explanation as to what prompted this activity. Hallett refused to give me any significant information, but began to ask me a number of questions which I was certainly able to answer without reservation. **I told Hallett clearly that there was a patient medical record for every patient treated in my office. Hallett** *never related to me* **that he was** *unable to locate* **the medical record of Undercover II, Ortiz.**
You'll see why shortly.

Hallett did ask me some ridiculous questions, and as time went on his questioning became more and more absurd. I informed him that in addition to my general medical practice, and minor surgical practice, I did also practice **pain**

## Chapter 9 - My Arrest

**management,** and **addiction management** utilizing **Suboxone. I clearly told Hallett multiple times that there was** *certainly a patient file on every individual treated in my office.* Unable to listen to any more of his **moronic questions,** I was able to post bail, and was released to my home in North Wildwood.

I was referred to a defense lawyer in Atlantic City by the name of Edwin Jacobs by one of my close personal friends. Edwin Jacobs and I then began to initiate my defense against the **illegitimate,** and **fictitious charges** made by Prosecutor Robert Taylor. The initial brief written by my attorney, Jacobs, was done in order to **void** the search warrant application authored by George Hallett. This document was replete with **lies, deception, and misinterpretations,** and was **devoid** of **exculpatory evidence** which would have completely negated the spurious charges against me. Our brief titled "Frank's v Delaware", was argued by Jacobs in Superior Court in front of Judge Raymond Batten. The state's opposition was led by Assistant Prosecutor Megan Hoerner, and following the entire afternoon of argumentation, Judge Batten **denied** my application to dismiss this egregious search warrant, essentially negating my fourth amendment rights.

I related to Edwin Jacobs, on multiple occasions, that my work as a physician followed all of the prescribed medical laws, and medical regulations of the state of New Jersey. I expected this attorney to research and understand these regulations in an effort to prove that my prescribing habits, and the treatment of my patients, conformed perfectly to all of the New Jersey laws and regulations. Unfortunately, Jacobs was, in my opinion, *grossly insufficient,* and also unaware of "State v Vaccaro."

Hallett's search warrant application was a **flawed document**. Hallett intentionally failed to incorporate in his search warrant, the **multiple thefts** that took place in my office **over a three-year period**. He also **eliminated** the fact that Maggie Ortiz, Undercover II, clearly indicated to me, in the record, that she had **pain** as a result of her work as an exotic dancer. Hallett **failed to incorporate the office visit** of **Detective Landis** who posed as a drug addict demanding drugs for his addiction in December 2005. **Detective Landis** was the first undercover agent sent to my office, by the prosecutor, and you are familiar with the excellent outcome. **Hallett failed to include my "Pain Management Agreement"**, signed by Anderson, in his search warrant affidavit. All of my "pain management" patients must sign this **"Pain Management Agreement"**, agreeing to all of the stipulations if they continue to remain in my pain management practice. This **"Pain Management Agreement"** clearly identifies all of the obligations that patients must abide by.

*See "Pain Management Agreement" in Index*

**Instead of incorporating important exculpatory evidence** regarding my medical practice, **Hallett concentrated on a myriad of falsehoods, lies, and confabulatory statements** including the most outrageous statement made by Catherine Mills, the **criminal** who worked in my office for only three and a half days before she was caught phoning in illicit prescriptions to local pharmacies for herself and her friends.

Hallett also failed to include in his search warrant, that both exotic dancers admitted to me prior to their first office visit, that they were taking **Percocet** following their night of dancing, and that they obtained this medication from a girlfriend prior to any office visit with me. Hallett very cleverly omitted this information from his search warrant application which was signed by Judge Batten.

It would be ludicrous to think that an exotic dancer would not incur strains and sprains, types of micro injuries to the muscular structures, ligaments, and tendons of the spine and extremities as a result of their activity which clearly requires some level of pain relief. I drew this as a reasonable conclusion to my office visits with these two females, and made my clinical decisions based upon reasonable medical certainty. I prescribed one pill each night following the night of dancing.

**The Physicians Desk Reference** (PDR 2007 edition, page 1131) clearly specifies that the principal actions of therapeutic value of **Percocet** is *analgesia and sedation*. This medication is taken to ease the obvious strains and sprains that these dancers experience. Rather than taking these circumstances into consideration, as a normal individual would, Hallett, instead, was fixated on the fact that the two females felt fine in my air-conditioned office, after they had taken their

## Chapter 9 - My Arrest

medication, and had a good night's sleep. The two undercover agents completed their work at five or 6 a.m., took their medication, slept for six or seven hours, and eventually presented to my office in the afternoon for examination. This was their history. Had these imposters been actual dancers responding to similar questions, I would have concluded the same result. Their statements would in all likelihood have included complaints of pain and discomfort relative to their work. It is ridiculous for the state, or the Board of Medical Examiners, or anyone else, to suggest anything different.

As important as it was, Hallett also omitted from his search warrant application the **four prescriptions thieves** who wrote hundreds of illegal prescriptions for opioids that were attributed to me **erroneously**. I reviewed all of the prescription data sheets sent to the prosecutor's office by the DEA, which were completely **inaccurate**, and contained **multiple errors**. Hundreds of illegally written prescriptions were created by the four thieves, and are **not recorded** in my office notes or copied in the patient files. Law-enforcement officials in Cape May County were well aware of these **thefts,** however Hallett did not include this information in his search warrant. My attorney, Glenn Zeitz eventually petitioned the Cape May County Prosecutor, Taylor, and the Federal Drug Enforcement Agency (DEA), to provide the actual prescriptions that were illegally written, and attributed to me. **Neither the Cape May County prosecutor, nor the Drug Enforcement Agency,** *ever produced these illegal prescriptions.* **Both agencies claimed that they were never in possession of them, and that they were unable to obtain them, underscoring more** *lies and deception* **by both agencies.**

*See PDR page concerning Percocet and DEA letter in Index*

On the day of my arrest and interrogation by Hallett, I clearly stated to him that all prescriptions written by me for controlled substances are recorded in the patient's medical chart. Furthermore, every patient treated by me has a medical chart in my patient files. Furthermore, **any prescription that is** *not* **noted in the patient's medical chart, was NOT written by me. Neither the DEA nor the prosecutor in Cape May County ever examined the 100 patient medical charts that were seized from my office at the September 14, 2007 raid by law enforcement.**

**Taylor, Hallett or Hoerner *never examined these medical charts*, either because they were incompetent, or lazy.**

## *STUNNING, ISN'T IT!!*

Hallett's search warrant application, was replete with **misinformation, deception,** and outright **lies** written for the purpose of persuading Judge Batten to sign. **Hallett accused me** of a crime, and also accused approximately 100 of my decent and honest patients of crimes. **His search warrant** was nothing more than a **disgraceful document filled with erroneous statements made with reckless disregard for the truth.**

Hallett accused certain patients of mine of using multiple pharmacies for their prescription needs. He accused multiple responsible patients of dishonesty and disregard for the law. Following these erroneous accusations by Hallett, I had all of my pain management patients *complete a certification* in which they denied these absurd allegations, and essentially explained their medical problems on each individual certification along with their pain issues regarding their pain management treatment program. **Despite Hallett's deceptive and false allegations, the patient's certifications bear the truth. All of my patient's certifications were given to the Cape May County prosecutor, and also to the Board of Medical Examiners, prior to my first hearing at the Board.**

**In the most disingenuous and irresponsible manner, Hallett attempted to implicate me and one of my patients in a drug distribution and insurance fraud scheme.**

## Here are the FACTS:

A patient of mine, an electrical contractor by trade, developed a significant problem in his cervical spine with associated severe pain and disability. Following my examination, and MRI evaluation of his cervical spine, a tumor at the C2, C3 level was apparent. I referred this patient for surgical intervention at the University of Pennsylvania. Following his surgery, he continued with cervical pain and subsequently developed two herniated cervical discs. This patient necessitated pain management, and continued care under the care of his surgeon and myself for pain management.

Unfortunately, this patient had multiple problems with his *insurance carrier,* as many, many people do, resulting in his having to pay money for the necessary pain medication prescribed. This patient had several employees and paid in excess of $80,000 per year to insure his family and a few employees. In spite of these enormous premiums in the year 2006, his insurance company would not cover his medications properly. He finally had to file a lawsuit against this insurance company. In the interim, the local ACME pharmacist gave him a great deal of trouble with regard to the medication prescribed, and the fact that he had to pay hard cash for certain prescriptions. This moronic pharmacist actually filed a complaint against this patient, and myself, with law-enforcement, alleging that the patient was buying prescriptions, and selling medication. This irresponsible pharmacist essentially accused this patient with selling his prescriptions for cash. Additionally, this moronic pharmacist implicated me in some sort of fraudulent activity with my patient. **The most important issue, and the real disgrace of course, is neither the county prosecutor Taylor, nor Hallett ever investigated *any facts regarding this case*.** The **reckless and moronic activity** of this ACME pharmacist, and George Hallett, can **never be excused**. I eventually called this female pharmacist and read her the "**riot act**". Eventually this patient had success with his lawsuit, against his insurance carrier, and recovered all of his out-of-pocket expenses. The facts regarding this patient's problems certainly did not get in the way of **Hallett's absurd thought process**.

*Another* example of Hallett's misconceptions is as follows:

I made a house call on a Sunday afternoon to one of my elderly patients, and on the following day, in August of 2007, Monday morning, my office billing employee completed the necessary paperwork for the billing of the house call to **Medicare**. The story got back to Detective Hallett that I was billing Medicare, for a housecall which was never completed. **Hallett,** of course, **never investigated any of these absurdities, but authored** his search warrant application **full of misinformation, deceptive and disgraceful statements, and outright** lies. **Hallett's search warrant application demonstrates the *gross misconduct* which occurred in the Cape May County prosecutor's office.**

Considering all the *false, reckless, incomplete and scurrilous claims* made against me in Hallett's search warrant, and the **poor and improper** investigation performed by Hallett, it simply cannot be demonstrated that there was "**probable cause**" to suggest that I committed any type of drug distribution, or insurance fraud, or any crime whatsoever. **When all of the garbage is weeded out, and the false information examined properly,** it is **crystal clear** that the **Cape May County Prosecutor's Office developed no evidence of any crime.**

Seven transcripts representing the office visits of the two undercover females were **inadequately** described by Hallett in his search warrant. **These transcripts, as a fact matter, establish my excellent representation of a doctor-patient relationship.** These transcripts alone represent excellent treatment of the two female undercover patients in my office. The transcripts **never** established any well-grounded suspicion that a crime was committed. My judgments are fully supportable, and explained in my *certifications* and in the *office transcripts*. Hallett simply never formed an honest basis for "probable cause," or for the issuance of this search warrant application. There is substantial evidence that his affidavit contained numerous **false statements** that were put forth **knowingly, willfully, and maliciously with reckless disregard for the truth simply to further the political gain of Robert Taylor and Sandra Dick**.

The **Fourth Amendment** of the U.S. Constitution requires that an evidentiary hearing be conducted. I demanded this hearing in an effort to establish the truth by a preponderance of evidence that no "probable cause" existed. Following the elimination of all of the false, egregious, and disgraceful information in this affidavit, this search warrant must be voided. This Frank's v Delaware brief was argued by Edwin Jacobs in Superior Court in front of Judge Raymond Batten. Judge Batten **denied my application to dismiss** this *egregious and dishonest s*earch warrant, essentially **disregarding my Fourth Amendment rights**.

## Chapter 9 - My Arrest

> **Fourth Amendment to the U. S. Constitution:**
>
> The right of the people to be secure in their persons, houses, papers, and effects, against unreasonable searches and seizures, shall not be violated, and no warrants shall issue, but upon probable cause, supported by oath or affirmation, and particularly describing the place to be searched, and the persons or things to be seized.

# "Absolute Power Corrupts Absolutely"
- George Orwell

The **Board of Medical Examiners** is, in my opinion, a flawed body of personalities. This Board consists of approximately 20 physicians all of whom are **political appointees**. Appointments to the **BME** are generally for 2 to 3 years with some physicians, however, "**the hard core henchmen**", remain on the Board for **multiple years**. These physicians are *supposed to be* independent individuals who examine *all of the relevant information* regarding another physician *before making a decision relative to his or her medical practice.* These Board members *should have* some experience with the subject matter. They *should have* some experience with **pain management, addiction treatment, billing issues**, and **recordkeeping**, if they are going to make judgments regarding these issues. Additionally, they *should know* something about the practice of medicine, and possess some level of **expertise** in certain **sub-specialties**.

The individuals who control the **Board of Medical Examiners** are the hardcore **deputy attorneys**, who are "**career state employees**", lasting for multiple decades. The absolute control of this **Board** rests in the hands of the deputy attorneys, under the Attorney General in Trenton. These deputies *control all of the activities* of the **Board of Medical Examiners**. The physicians on the Board are essentially **directed** by the deputies with regard to all activities. The prime example is Chief Deputy **Sandra Dick**, that is her real name, **Dick**, who has been in control of the **BME** for approximate 30 years. In addition to **Sandra Dick**,

## Chapter 10 - "Absolute Power Corrupts Absolutely"

there are a number of other deputy attorneys who function under her, with control of the physicians on the Board, and essentially all of the physicians in the state of New Jersey. The Board physicians are appointed through the various counties, as a political plum. These physicians meet once a month in Trenton, New Jersey. The career deputy attorneys however, work five days a week, 52 weeks per year, in Trenton, in a draconian style to maintain complete control of all of the physicians in New Jersey.

DAG **Sandra Dick** maintains absolute influence over these Board physicians. The physicians, *rarely, if ever,* examine *the briefs, and transcripts* offered by defense in a physician's case. The Board physicians simply rely upon **Sandra Dick** and her cohorts to make determinations, and essentially influence the Board physicians, with voting on any particular matter with respect to a physician charged with a violation. **Sandra Dick** and her cohorts compose all of the briefs and documents prepared at the **BME** level. The president of the Board, a physician, simply signs his name to any documents prepared by Deputy Attorney **Sandra Dick**. These deputies, at the Board function as *prosecutor, judge and jury,* in all related matters concerning a particular physician's case.

My initial hearing at the **BME** occurred in December 2007. The hearing was conducted by DAG **Sandra Dick**, and her underling, DAG **David Puteska**. I was summoned to the **Board** for this hearing, based upon a charge from Cape May County Prosecutor **Robert Taylor**. As I subsequently found out, both **Robert Taylor,** and Assistant Prosecutor **Megan Hoerner**, had been in constant contact with **Sandra Dick** for several months prior to my arrest. Essentially this conspiracy between Cape May County Prosecutor **Robert Taylo**r, and Deputy Attorney **Sandra Dick**, had been in play for approximately twelve to fifteen months prior to my arrest in September of 2007, and specifically in an effort to suspend my medical license in December of 2007.

The Cape May County Prosecutor **Robert Taylor** as I have previously mentioned, **withheld** the entire first undercover office visit with **Detective Landis** which occurred in December 2005 for three years. This entire episode with **Detective Landis** was omitted from **Hallett's** search warrant application, *not* **disclosed** to

# "Due Process" Denied

Superior Court Judge Batten for three years, *not* **disclosed** to the physicians of the BME in December of 2007, and *not* **disclosed** to the citizens of the **grand jury** in Cape May County in February of 2008. My attorney Glenn Zeitz received this information regarding the office visit with Detective Landis *probably by mistake,* in October of 2008, in a final discovery package. This information was a shock to both of us since obviously, I had no knowledge that Detective Landis was an undercover agent when I examined and treated him in December of 2005 and placed him on Suboxone to treat his heroin addiction. This first attempt to "entrap" me by Cape May County Prosecutor **Taylor,** failed miserably. **If this discovery had been obtained prior to the initial BME hearing, this information would have clearly identified the fact that my office practice is performed properly with regard to** *Controlled Dangerous Substances.*

The hearing in December 2007, was essentially a **Star Chamber**, a **kangaroo court**, in which the only outcome to be achieved by both **Taylor** and **Sandra Dick** was to **suspend** my medical license simply because I practice "**pain management**". I testified at this hearing clearly and concisely, however the physicians on this board were directed by **Sandra Dick** as *prosecutor, judge and jury,* to suspend my medical license. This **Star Chamber**, comprised of politically appointed physicians, and career deputy attorneys led by Sandra Dick, direct the course of punishment for any *perceived or misrepresented* offense with **impunity**. The suspension of my medical license in December 2007 essentially terminated my ability, to practice medicine, and to earn a living, while dealing with **Taylor**, and preparing a defense for an eventual jury trial in Cape May County, and a civil trial (hearing) at the Office of Administrative Law.

It is **a monumental mistake to think that**
the *physicians* of the Board of Medical Examiners control the
issues and the adjudication of perceived offenses
by a physician summoned to the Board.

# Chapter 10 - "Absolute Power Corrupts Absolutely"

*The facts of the matter are as follows...*

- There are multiple deputy attorneys on this Board, who don't know their **ass** from **third base** regarding **medicine** and the **practice of medicine**, or **pain management.**

- The physician members are political appointees to the Board from the various counties in the state of New Jersey. Some physicians have practices in their hometowns, and a few of them are younger physicians. Most of the physicians on the Board are older, retired physicians, and are also **ignorant of the medical law regarding controlled substances,** ie: "State v Vaccaro".

- *"Vaccaro"* states in part under drugs and narcotics pg 168 of the record, that **"a physician's license and registration authorizes him to dispense controlled substances, but under this statue he is "immune" from criminal liability when he dispenses same in "good faith", in the course of his professional practice only."** *"A physician who is honest and ethical and who dispenses these drugs in a good faith effort to treat and cure patients, has no fear of the criminal sanctions of the statute." "A physician's license and registration* **authorizes** *him to dispense controlled dangerous products." "This statute makes it clear, that he is "**immune**" from criminal liability when he dispenses these products in* **good faith** *in the course of his* **professional practice only.**"

- "Furthermore, and when the statute circumscribes the limits of this exemption from it's criminal consequences by the utilization of the term "**good faith**," he knows, that is, the physician knows full well what is meant, and how he must comport himself." "There is nothing vague or ambiguous about the requirement that the legal dispensing of drugs by the physician must be carried out in "good faith" in the course of his professional practice only."

- "It is a standard which is clear and understandable to the mind of any reasonable physician, and is therefore beyond constitutional attack."

- "State v Vaccaro" is the controlling law in the state of New Jersey regarding controlled prescription products, and it has been the law with regard to these controlled products since 1976.

**When I was summoned to appear before the Board in December of 2007 *none* of these physicians practiced pain management or addiction medicine.** Essentially, all of these deputy attorneys of the Board and physicians of the Board, were ignorant regarding the practice of pain management, and addiction medicine. Furthermore, the deputy attorneys of the BME should have been well versed in the laws of the state of New Jersey regarding the prescribing of controlled substances, mainly opioids, in clinical practice. **I'm speaking specifically of the 1976 appellate published decision, "Vaccaro" which proscribes completely the use of these medications in clinical practice by licensed physicians in their offices.**

**DAG Sandra Dick & DAG David Puteska were either ignorant of the New Jersey law, or they simply refused to acknowledge this 1976 appellate decision "State v Vaccaro" to further their deplorable activity, in order to levy a punishment, a suspension of my medical license, without cause.**

Furthermore, my initial attorney of a few months, Edwin Jacobs, was also ignorant of the New Jersey laws regarding the practice of medicine, specifically **"Vaccaro",** even after I related to him, that I conformed to all of the rules, regulations, and laws of the state of New Jersey in my medical practice.

Additionally, the administrative law judge, Miller, was also ignorant of

"**Vaccaro**", with essentially no research on his part at this Administrative Law hearing. **Miller negated my testimony and the testimony of my experts, who clearly stated the facts regarding the practice of medicine with controlled substances, and ruled against me to satisfy Sandra Dick, and her cohorts, and to further restrict my ability to return to gainful employment in my medical office**.

The suspension of my medical license was done with **malice**, orchestrated through the disgraceful behavior of **Robert Taylor and Sandra Dick**, employing nothing more than **false and erroneous charges** by this **incompetent,** and **vicious county prosecutor,** Taylor. The **BME** suspended my medical license to practice medicine for an indefinite period of time. This was done without "**probable cause**" or "**due process**," and was "**absolutely unconstitutional**". Unfortunately, in December of 2007, I was represented by an *inept attorney*, **Edwin Jacobs**, who had minimal knowledge of the **Board of Medical Examiners** and their corrupt activities.

Jacobs should have taken an immediate "**interlockatory appeal**" to restore my medical license which was suspended without an indictment and certainly without any conviction, and allow me to continue my medical practice until the judicial process was completed. Jacobs neglected my constitutional rights, as I was at the mercy of DAG Sandra Dick at the Board of Medical Examiners, and the prosecutor's office in Cape May County. The suspension of my medical license terminated my medical practice in December of 2007, a successful thirty-five year medical practice in North Wildwood. Following my suspension, I began a five-year ordeal in criminal court in Cape May County, with the **legal tyranny** of the so-called justice system.

"**The best revenge is massive success.**"
- Frank Sinatra

# First Hearing at the Board of Medical Examiners (BME)
### December 17, 2007

## Physician Board Members Present:

| | |
|---|---|
| Dr. Cheema | Dr. Lambert |
| Dr. Ciechanowski | Dr. Lanazow |
| Dr. Criscito | Dr. Mendelowitz |
| Dr. Criss | Dr. Paul |
| Dr. Haddad | Dr. Reichman |
| Dr. Jordan | Dr. Scott |

Dr. Stanley

Dr. Strand

Mr. Wheeler

---

### DAGs Present:
Sandra Y. **Dick**

Mr. David **Puteska**

### BME Executive Director:
Mr. William **Roeder**

# "I Have Prepared My Entire Life For This Evil Tragedy"

*All five grand jury presentations against me were accomplished allowing the prosecutor and the detective witnesses to direct each case with lies, misrepresentations, perjury, and prosecutorial misconduct, knowingly, willfully and maliciously.*

"The intellect tires, the will, never. The brain needs sleep, the will, none. The whole body is nothing but objectified will. The entire nervous system constitutes the antennae of the will. Every action of the body is nothing but the act of the will objectified."
- G. Gordon Liddy

"We conquer by endurance."
-Ernest Shackleton

There are three types of juries in the United States of America:
(1) criminal grand juries, (2) criminal petit juries and (3) circuit jury's. Juries are mentioned in the United States Constitution, Article 3, and in the fifth, sixth, and seventh amendment. The right to a trial by jury is more than 800 years old. The grand jury decides whether or not there is enough evidence "probable cause" that a person has committed a crime. If so, the individual will be indicted. The grand jury has between 16 to 25 members, and its proceedings are not open to the public. The entire issue at the grand jury is controlled by the prosecuting

# "Due Process" Denied

attorney.

The right to a trial by jury in a civil case is addressed by the Seventh Amendment which provides:
In suits of common law, where the value in controversy shall exceed $20, the right of trial by jury shall be preserved, and no fact shall otherwise be re-examined in any court in the United States.

The role of the jury is to provide unbiased views or resolution of evidence presented in a case in a court of law. The jury service system is important to democracy because of the unbiased, impartial viewpoints that cannot be denied from our citizens. Citizens of the jury are selected from a wide cross-section of society for most plaintiffs in a trial by jury. Trial by jury is a better choice for a number of reasons. The standard of proof in a civil case is much lower than in a criminal case. Juries also tend to be much less political and are easier audiences than judges. Trial by jury is a much better choice than a bench trial by a **politically oriented judge**. In a criminal trial the jury verdict must be unanimous, ie: twelve jurors must agree. Jury members must decide for themselves, without direction from the judge, the lawyers, or anyone else how they will proceed in the jury room to reach the verdict.

At the grand jury proceeding, the prosecutor has complete discretion to do and say whatever because the defendant is generally not present. I have had the opportunity to review all of my five grand jury transcripts, and I will share with you the **deceptions** and **misrepresentations** orchestrated by Assistant Prosecutor **Megan Hoerner**, Detective **Hallett,** and others in the prosecutor's office of Cape May County. Assistant Prosecutor **Megan Hoerner**, and Detective **George Hallett** cleverly and deceptively altered many facts in order to indict me in February 2008. **Hallett committed perjury under oath** at this first grand jury proceeding in Cape May County, and Assistant Prosecutor **Hoerner** went right along with it.

Both Hallett and Hoerner participated in the undercover operation of all three law-enforcement officers, **Detective Jason Landis, Tonya Anderson, and Margarita Abbattiscianni.** The two females were termed Undercover I and

## Chapter 11 - "I Have Prepared My Entire Life For This Evil Tragedy"

Undercover II. Both Hallett and Hoerner were intimately involved with these law enforcement individuals, and both knew the correct spelling of their fictitious names, **and there can be no mistake about this fact**. When Hallett and the rest of the law enforcement people entered my office on September 14, 2007 to arrest me, they provided a list of names of patients whose medical records they intended to seize. These patients were principally pain management medical patients who were also accused of multiple infractions, by Hallett. **Hallett or Hoerner**, or both collectively, and very cleverly, misspelled the fictitious name of **Maggie Ortiz, to *"Artiz"***. The prosecutor's log of names stated *"Artiz" instead of Ortiz.* Hallett, did not recover the medical chart of Undercover II, Maggie Ortiz, because the spelling of her name **was altered** either by Hallett or Hoerner, or both. **Hallett** *refused* to allow my staff to assist him and his minions in their effort to obtain the medical chart of **Maggie Ortiz**. The name of Undercover II, was cleverly misspelled, to create the fictitious story that Hallett presented to the grand jury of the **absence** of a medical record for Maggie Ortiz.

### Fast forward to the grand jury proceeding in February 2008:

The first statement by Hallett at the grand jury was with regard to the Drug Enforcement Agency's prescription data records, relating to the charge that I prescribed excessive amounts of medication for pain management patients. Both Hoerner and Hallett **omitted the fact**, and chose **not to disclose** to the grand jury **that I was the victim of four thefts from my office of multiple prescription pads from which multiple illegal prescriptions had been written**. Law enforcement was well aware of these **thefts** from my office, because they were all reported. **This important information was** *completely and deliberately* **withheld from the grand jury.** This omitted **exculpatory evidence** is **extremely important information** to the grand jury, and **would have explained the relevant circumstances of excess prescriptions** on these **invalid** D.E.A. data records.

Both Hoerner and Hallett also *failed to disclose* the office visit of **Detective Landis** in December 2005, which represented an excellent example of my pain management practice.

Another major deliberate act on the part of Hallett and Hoerner as **Hallett committed perjury** at the grand jury with his testimony stating, *"that the field in North Wildwood was owned by Wildwood Catholic high school."* The fact is that this field is owned by the diocese of Camden, and is leased by the city of North Wildwood as a park for its citizens, and **not a School Zone**.

Both Hallett and Horner also failed to disclose to the grand jury that both Undercover I and Undercover II were taking medication in the form of **"Percocet"** prior to ever arriving at my office. They were taking this medication for their pain and discomfort as a result of their exotic dancing activity. These statements are in the official transcripts of both undercover females.

**The *most egregious* and *false testimony* to the grand jury is as follows:**

Hallett testified to the grand jury that he and his cohorts were unable to recover the medical file of Undercover II, Maggie Ortiz. Recall if you will, law enforcement deliberately misspelled **Maggie Ortiz** fictitious name and attempted to recover a patient record under the name of ***"Artiz"***. Obviously, law enforcement, ie: Hallett and his minions, were unable to recover any medical chart on **"Artiz", BECAUSE IT DID NOT EXIST**. Hallett *had prior* knowledge that there was a medical chart on *every* patient that was treated in my office. I related this information to him on the day I was arrested at my initial interrogation with him, and clearly stated to him that *"there was a medical chart on every patient"*. Furthermore, my attorney informed both Hallett and Hoerner that the medical chart on Undercover II was in my **file cabinet** with the rest of my medical records. Furthermore, and to add to their significant corruption, the medical chart of Maggie Ortiz was placed in **evidence** at the Board of Medical Examiner's hearing in December 2007, well before this indictment several months later. Both Hallett and Hoerner had full knowledge of my hearing at the BME in December of 2007. **There was simply no excuse whatsoever for Hallett to commit perjury at the grand jury, or for Hoerner to acquiesce with regard to the medical chart of Maggie Ortiz.**

This was a set up by Hallett or Hoerner or BOTH.

## Chapter 11 - "I Have Prepared My Entire Life For This Evil Tragedy"

**Both Hallett and Hoerner went an additional step further when questioned by one of the jurors who asked the following:**

"Do you mean that Dr. Costino is taking payment in cash without producing a medical chart?"

**The answer from Hallett to the juror was "yes" indicating to the grand jury that I was putting money into my pocket, and *not* producing a medical chart on this patient. This was a blatant lie, and abject perjury on the part of Hallett, and indicated to the grand jury** *that they must indict.* This ordeal represents a blatant example of the **prosecutorial misconduct** of both Hallett and Hoerner, *knowingly, willfully and maliciously* **performed in an effort to obtain their indictment.**

Both Hallett and Hoerner had **full knowledge** that there was a chart on Maggie Ortiz, and they **gave false information** and **perjured testimony** to the grand jury in their effort to indict me. Recall if you will, it all started when *they deliberately misspelled* the Undercover II name on their Cape May County Prosecutor's evidence log, of patient files to be **seized**. This entire fiasco was orchestrated by Hallett or Hoerner, or both with the blessing of Robert Taylor.

*See the Cape May County Prosecutor's Office Evidence Log in Appendix*

The entire presentation to the grand jury was nothing more than a pack of *lies, distortions, and perjury* under oath on the part of Hallett. Both Hallett and Hoerner eliminated significant **exculpatory evidence** at the grand jury presentation. Had this exculpatory evidence listed above been presented properly, as a matter of law, the grand jury would have exonerated me.

This first grand jury orchestrated by Assistant Prosecutor Hoerner and Detective Hallett was performed with prosecutorial misconduct in an effort to obtain their indictment. The following is a partial list of **exculpatory evidence omitted, from this first grand jury presentment:**

## Omissions:

- **Omitted** - the entire medical visit of Detective Landis in December 2005.

- **Omitted** - my "Pain Management Agreement" given and signed by all chronic pain patients and particularly signed by Tonya Anderson, a.k.a Tonya Smith a.k.a. Undercover I.

- **Omitted** - the **four criminal thefts** of my prescription pads with hundreds of illegal prescriptions written by the four thieve which had all been reported to law enforcement.

- **Omitted** - The **false statements** by Hallett regarding Catherine Mills, another prescription criminal who worked in my office for three and one half days but claimed to Hallett and one of his cohorts that she was the office supervisor and worked for 8 months in my office.

- **Omitted** - both undercover females stated to me that they were taking Percocet prior to ever entering my office for treatment.

- **Omitted** - the fact that the prescription data records were completely **flawed** as they included hundreds of prescriptions illegally written by the criminals who stole my prescription pads and wrote **multiple illegal prescriptions** while all **four criminal thefts** were reported to law enforcement.

- **Omitted** - the statement to me by Undercover II, Maggie Ortiz, at her first office visit on August 3, 2007 **"I have pain and up all night 'til 4 a.m."** This statement is taken directly from the original transcript.

**The *most egregious* distortion was the implication by both Hallett and Hoerner that I never produced a medical chart on Maggie Ortiz, and instead accepted payment in cash without creating a medical record. This mechanism of altering the name of Undercover II from Maggie Ortiz to Maggie *Artiz* was done *maliciously, willfully and deceptively* by Hallett or Hoerner or both, in an effort to obtain their indictment.**

## Chapter 11 - "I Have Prepared My Entire Life For This Evil Tragedy"

This disgraceful activity further underscores the depths of deplorable activity of the Cape May County Prosecutor's Office. The lies and deceptions were cleverly calculated by these law enforcement characters in order to ensure a criminal indictment. This *is* another example of the ***subversive and fundamental dishonesty*** of the ***corrupt justice system,*** and **legal tyranny** to further the criminalization of medicine.

This indictment should have been dismissed, based upon the state's prosecutorial misconduct, in presenting **misleading and false evidence** to the grand jury, and failing to provide **exculpatory evidence**.

**"Dismissal of an indictment is appropriate if it is established that a violation substantially influenced the grand jury's decision to indict, or if there is grave doubt that the determination ultimately reached is arrived at fairly and impartially."** When a person's fate is before a grand jury he is constitutionally entitled to have his case considered by an *impartial and unbiased* body capable of deciding the issue of **"probable cause"** on the evidence fairly submitted to it.

**"Further, an indictment may be dismissed upon a palpable showing of fundamental unfairness, or where there is conduct of the prosecutor that amounts to any interference with the grand jury's decision-making function." "The court should not hesitate to dismiss an indictment if the evidence establishes that the conduct of the prosecutor in obtaining the indictment amounted to an intentional subversion of the grand jury process. If the record in the case demonstrates such conduct of that quality, dismissal of the indictment is the only appropriate remedy. Consequently, jurisdiction rests with the court to review the facts of the case at bar and consider defendants motion to dismiss the indictment for prosecutorial misconduct".**

"Moreover, our state constitution envisions a grand jury that protects citizens who are victims of **personal animus, partisanship, or inappropriate zeal** on the part of the prosecutor and or the detective witness. The grand jury cannot be denied access to evidence that is **credible, material**, and so **clearly exculpatory**

## "Due Process" Denied

as to induce a rational grand juror to conclude that the state has **not** made a prima facia case against the accused. If evidence of this character is withheld from the grand jury, the prosecutor in essence presents a **distorted version** of the facts and interferes with the grand jury's decision-making function".

"A prosecutor's interaction with a grand jury and possible misconduct is subject to judicial review. The dismissal of an indictment pose costs upon the prosecution and the public. At a minimum, the government will be required to present its evidence to the grand jury unaffected by **bias** or **prejudice**. The cost of continued unchecked **prosecutorial misconduct** are also substantial. This is particularly so for the grand jury, where the prosecutor operates without the check of a judge, or a trained legal adversary, virtually "**immune** from public scrutiny." The prosecutor's abuse of this special relationship to the grand jury poses an enormous risk to defendants.

"In theory a trial provides the defendant with a full opportunity to contest and disprove the charges against him, in practice, however, **the handing-up of an indictment will often have a devastating personal and professional impact that later dismissal or acquittal can never undo.**" "Where the potential for abuse is so great, **and the consequences of a mistaken indictment so serious, the ethical responsibilities of the prosecutor, and the obligation of the judiciary to protect against even the appearance of unfairness, are correspondingly heightened.**"

*"The New Jersey Supreme Court found that precedence make clear that the court may invoke it's supervisory power to remedy perceived injustices in grand jury proceedings consequently jurisdiction rests with this court to review the facts of this case at bar and consider defendant's motion to dismiss the indictment for prosecutorial misconduct."*

In May 2011, my attorney Glenn Zeitz wrote a brief to dismiss this indictment on the basis of **prosecutorial misconduct**. This indictment should have been dismissed two years earlier. **Hallett's grand jury testimony was laden** with deliberate material misrepresentations, omissions, false factual and false legal statements, suppressed evidence, and unduly prejudicial, and grossly misleading statements, with the elimination of extremely important exculpatory evidence. This entire indictment must be dismissed because the presentation was patently unfair, and violated my "due process" rights.

*It doesn't get any worse than that.*

In view of all of the above, Superior Court Judge Batten *refused to dismiss this indictment.*

"Due Process" Denied

My review of selective, pertinent, lies and perjury in the
Grand Jury presentation by Hallett and lead by Asst. Pros. Megan Hoerner in
superior court on February 19, 2008.

1 : These 9 counts of Distribution of CDS represents a total of 9 prescriptions I wrote, each prescription renedering 30 Tablets of Percocet, a month's worth of medication to be taken one each night following the exotic dancing work.

2: These 9 counts of Distribution of CDS within 1000 feet of School Property represent the identical 9 prescriptions referenced in the first 9 counts. However, the morons in the CMCPO **stated to me that my office is located approximately 1000 feet from school property, they are totally incorrect.** I easily provided proof of their inaccuracy. Furthermore, all of my patients are treated in my office at 404 Surf Ave. There are no patients that receive any treatments, prescriptions or any other type of medication outside of my office. All patients are treated within the walls of my office at 404 Surf Avenue, following the requirement of the law "Vaccaro."

3: The 7 counts of Health Care Claims Fraud represented the fact that UC 1, Tonya Anderson's 7 office visits were billed **to her fictitious Blue Cross and Blue Shield insurance carrier.**

The following images delineate the perjury in the witness testimony at the Grand Jury appearance on February 19, 2008. The witness was Detective George Hallett and the presenter to the grand jury was Assistant Prosecutor Megan Hoerner.
Documents Superior Court of NJ, Cape May County.
Criminal Case Management Case #07001173 ;
Indictment #08-02-001251 ;
July Term 2007, November Session 2007
Pages 10, 11, 15, 16, 26, 29, 30, 33, 34, 35, 36.

# Chapter 11 - "I Have Prepared My Entire Life For This Evil Tragedy"

## My 1st Indictment February 19, 2008

## Detective George Hallett UNDER OATH before the citizens of the Grand Jury. Hallett questioned by Asst. Pros. M. Hoerner

SUPERIOR COURT OF NJ
CAPE MAY COUNTY
CRIMINAL CASE MANAGEMENT
FILED

Date: FEB 19 2008

Case No. 07001173

JULY TERM 2007
NOVEMBER SESSION 2007

SUPERIOR COURT OF NEW JERSEY
CAPE MAY COUNTY
LAW DIVISION
(Criminal)

INDICTMENT NO. CS-00-00135-I

THE STATE OF NEW JERSEY

vs.

JOHN COSTINO,
        Defendant.

Distribution of a Controlled
Dangerous Substance
NJSA 2C:35-5a(1)
NJSA 2C:35-5b(5)
3rd Degree
(9 counts)
Distribution of a Controlled
Dangerous Substance
NJSA 2C:35-5a(1)
NJSA 2C:35-5b(4)
2nd Degree
Distribution of a Controlled
Dangerous Substance within
1,000 feet of School Property
NJSA 2C:35-7
NJSA 2C:35-5a(1)
(9 Counts)
Health Care Claims Fraud
NJSA 2C:21-4.2
NJSA 2C:21-4.3(a)
2nd Degree
(7 Counts)

# "Due Process" Denied

```
15      Q.   All right.  Did you receive information from
16   the DEA after consulting with them regarding
17   prescription data sheets of patients who had been to
18   Doctor Costino?
19      A.   Yes, I did.
20      Q.   Okay.  And did a review of those prescription
21   data sheets indicate that there were an excessive       NO
22   number of prescriptions written by Doctor Costino for
23   pain medications?                           All Legitimate Rx's
24      A.   Yes, it did.   A Lie
```

There were multiple prescription data sheets that I'm sure Hallett never received along with my patient medical charts.

```
3       Q.   Okay.  And in addition, as a result of several
4    complaints from patients regarding inappropriate       Catherine
5    comments, as well as an interview with at least one    Mills
6    ex-employee regarding allegations of inappropriate     False
7    prescription writing and billing, was there an         Statement
8    undercover investigation done?
9       A.   Yes, there was.
```

**Catherine Mills was the criminal** who called in **illegal prescriptions** for her and her girlfriends during the **THREE DAYS** she worked there in my office. She was in jail for a number of months.

```
21      Q.   Okay.  What did he note her chief complaint to
22   be?
23      A.   Neck sprain.          NO  False Statement
```

**Dr. Costino NEVER diagnosed Anderson with a neck sprain.** Her presumptive diagnosis was **THOROCOLUMBAR STRAIN and SPRAIN**.

## Chapter 11 - "I Have Prepared My Entire Life For This Evil Tragedy"

```
 5      Q.   All right.  What did he note in her chart?
 6      A.   He noted in her chart that it was acute cervical
 7   sprain and -- in her chart.
 8      Q.   Okay.  Now did the insurance company pay him
 9   $94.09?
10      A.   That's correct.
11      Q.   All right.  Did the undercover officer ever
12   make any mention on April 12th, 2007 of neck sprain?
13      A.   No.
```

More lies. No neck sprain.

```
 3      Q.   Did the defendant ask the second undercover
 4   officer what was wrong?
 5      A.   Yes, she (sic) did --
 6      Q.   Okay.
 7      A.   -- he did.
 8      Q.   Now is the recording a little bit unclear
 9   here?
10      A.   Yes, it is.
11      Q.   But does she -- Is it clear that she indicates
12   that she's up all night and works long hours?
13      A.   Yes.  That is clear.
```

**Hallett committs perjury here.** The record is clear. The second undercover, ORTIZ, said to me "It's just the pain and up all night til 6 am."

109

```
10      Q.  Okay. Did he then again say to her, I'm sure
11  you get these acute strains and sprains?
12      A.  Yes.
13      Q.  And what was her response to that?
14      A.  I'm pretty flexible. Not much pain.
```

Ortiz additionally admitted to me towards the end of her examination **again that she *DID have pain* and her statement was, "not much pain"**

```
16      Q.  Okay. What about the second undercover's
17  chart? What did it show?
18      A.  It didn't show anything be -- When we executed the
19  search warrant for the -- for files, there was no file
20  for the undercover agent that paid cash.
21      Q.  The second one?
22      A.  The second one, --
23      Q.  Okay.
24      A.  -- yes.
```

More lies by Hallett to Asst. Pros. Hoerner

```
16      Q.  Okay. And again, was there ever a chart found
17  for the second undercover officer?
18      A.  No.
19      Q.  Okay. Now you indicated before that there was
20  a search warrant executed in the defendant's office?
21      A.  That is correct.
22      Q.  And a number of files were seized?
23      A.  That is correct.
24      Q.  And the first undercover officer's file was
25  seized?
```

Prosecutors **DELIBERATELY CHANGED** her last name.   Continued on next page....

# Chapter 11 - "I Have Prepared My Entire Life For This Evil Tragedy"

......Continued

```
 1  A.  That's correct.
 2      Q.  What was interesting about the first
 3  undercover officer's file?
 4  A.  Well, it was a template each -- on each visit.  In
 5  other words, a --
 6      Q.  What do you mean by a template?
 7  A.  Well, a copy of the physical exam is made and then
 8  inserted and used as if it contained the findments
 9  (phonetic) of a physical exam and, you know, on each
10  visit.
11      Q.  So there was almost like a photocopy?
12  A.  Photocopy of -- of the prior visit.  It was pretty
13  much the same thing.
14      Q.  Okay.  And again, was there a file ever found
15  for the second undercover officer?
16  A.  Never.
17      Q.  Okay.
18  A.  No.
19      Q.  Now is Percocet the brand name for Oxycodone?
20  A.  Yes, it is.
```

**THIS is the most CRITICAL lie by Hallett to
the citizens of the Grand Jury.**

```
16  A.  During the -- my interview with Doctor Costino
17  regarding the undercovers, there were certain questions
18  when I would ask him, he wouldn't be able to answer
19  them and he said until he looked in the file and he --
20  he did say that for every patient there is a file.
```

**Here Hallett admitted to the Grand Jury that I told him
there is a file for every patient.**

# "Due Process" Denied

DETECTIVE HALLETT                    Page 36

1  GRAND JUROR: Were any of the visits recorded
2  by the detectives as they happened?
3  THE WITNESS: Yes. Yes, they were re -- These
4  conversations were recorded.
5  BY MS. HOERNER:
6  Q. And are there transcripts for each of the
7  visits?
8  A. Yes, there are.
9  Q. And did you have the occasion to review those
10 transcripts prior to coming in here to testify for --
11 A. Yes, -- *He didn't Read*
12 Q. -- the Grand Jury? *Then well*
13 A. -- I did.
14 PROSECUTOR HOERNER: Good question. Any other
15 questions?
16 GRAND JUROR: There was no file on the -- the
17 second undercov -- cover officer?
18 THE WITNESS: No. There was no medical file
19 that we found at the time we searched the premise and
20 we asked the help if there was, in fact, a file and  *A LIE*
21 they could not locate a file at the doctor's office as
22 well. *(FABRICATED Falsehood) by Hallett + Prosecutor*
23 GRAND JUROR: But she was paying cash?
24 THE WITNESS: She was paying cash. That's
25 correct.

**This is the MOST EGREGIOUS LIE by Hallett to
the Grand Jury WITH Asst. Prosecutor Hoerner's APPROVAL.**

# Prosecutors and Detectives are Exempt from the Consequesnces of Their Own Ideology and Disgraceful Behavior

Through the molecular labyrinth of lies and deception both the Cape May County Prosecutors Office and the Board of Medical Examiners, prosecuted my case for five years.

Following the Cape May County indictment of February 2008, my attorneys Glenn Zeitz, and Jordan Zeitz, continued my criminal defense in Superior Court of Cape May County. During the next few month's preparation was also made to defend my BME case, at the Office of Administrative Law (OAL), in December 2008. This civil trial was coordinated with the Board of Medical Examiners, and Sandra Dick, beginning in December 2008, and ending in January of 2009, a total of four days of hearings. Prior to this OAL civil trial, there were certain specific issues that needed to be addressed with regard to my defense.

First and foremost was the fact that George Hallett, the insufficient detective at the prosecutor's office **lied under oath** to the grand jury in February 2008. The perjurious statements made by Hallett concerning the two undercover females, specifically with regard to Ortiz and her **pain**, had to be remedied. Furthermore, it was clear to both sides that there *was a medical record* completed by me on

## "Due Process" Denied

Undercover II, Ortiz, written at the time of her office examinations. This record initially was not confiscated by George Hallett and his minions because someone in the prosecutor's office deliberately misspelled her last name A-R-T-I-Z instead of O-R-T-I-Z.

Hallett mischaracterized both issues at the grand jury presentation. Glenn Zeitz mandated to the OAL court that these issues must be cleared completely prior to this hearing, in addition to a few other issues.

The second major issue that had to be understood was concerning whether or not the two undercover females had incurred prior injuries, accidents, or other problems which were orthopedic and/or musculoskeletal in origin. Said issues were **never described by either the BME, or the prosecutor's office.** These issues were extremely important, and needed to be brought to the surface, and completely understood prior to the OAL hearing.

By way of further explanation, the initial transcripts of my office visits with both undercover females were sent to my attorney in October of 2007. These transcripts were also sent to the prosecutor's office, and to all other agencies represented in this case. These transcripts were the product of the postal inspector Alex Sylvester, and Michelle Stankiewicz, the actual transcriber. The Postal Inspectors Office was required to transcribe this information from the serendipitous recorders that the undercover females carried with them to my office for their visits. The office visit of August 3, 2007, with Maggie Ortiz, (a.k.a. Undercover II) is one visit specifically in question.

Clearly and unequivocally Ortiz said to me "**I have pain and I'm up all night until 4:00 in the morning.**" This statement was **CLEARLY IDENTIFIED** on the original August 3, 2007 transcript. After reading the transcripts carefully, I identified several omissions from the initial transcripts, which I realized immediately concerning my conversations with the two females. It was clear on the transcript of August 3rd that Maggie Ortiz said to me "that she had **pain** and up all night till 4 a.m. in the morning". There were two other additional omissions from

## Chapter 12 - Prosecutors and Detectives Are Exempt From Consequences

the transcripts that I identified.

This omission of Ortiz relative to her **pain,** from the official transcript, now becomes a potential criminal act. On February 15, 2008, Thomas Prevoznik, the Drug Enforcement Agency supervisor, sent an email to Detective George Hallett at the prosecutor's office stating "there was an error on the transcript of August 3, 2007."

Prevoznik's next email to Hallett stated that Maggie's response to Dr. Costino was **incorrect** on the initial transcript. In addition to this email, Prevoznik also sent to Hallett a second transcript of this August 3rd visit, where the word "**pain**" was *completely removed*. Not only was the word **pain** removed, but this crucial word was also substituted by an additional 29 other words on this second "substituted" transcript. **Essentially what had been done was a complete alteration of the original transcript.** The word "pain" was **eliminated**, and a completely new phrase was fabricated and added to the substituted transcript in its place.

This became an immediate red flag, and of course the question is:

## Who perpetrated this alteration in the original transcript???

This alteration of my medical record represents the *misconduct and disgraceful behavior* of either Thomas Prevoznik, the DEA supervisor, or Alex Sylvester, the postal inspector, or both. These two characters were responsible to safeguard the CD recordings for the transcribing of the office visits. There is an obvious conspiracy going on here to alter the original CD recordings and transcripts, altering the evidence, and eliminating the word **"pain"** from the conversation between Ortiz and myself at her office visit of August 3, 2007. It was clear to my attorneys and I that these deceptive characters of law-enforcement would go to any lengths in an effort to win this case. My attorney Glenn Zeitz immediately notified the administrative law judge (A.L.J.), Bruce Gorman and petitioned for a video deposition of Margarita Abbattiscianni (a.k.a. Maggie Ortiz), to determine the accuracy of the words spoken to me, by Ortiz, at the office visit of August 3, 2007.

On November 7th 2008, a videotaped deposition of Margarita Abbattiscianni was completed. She testified that she had never seen any of the written transcripts prior to her video deposition. Margarita Abbattiscianni was given the initial transcript, and she was able to read the words on the transcript while listening to her voice via the CD recording.

She was questioned under oath by both my attorney Glenn Zeitz and DAG David Puteska at this video deposition. The questions were directed specifically to what was said between her and I at the August 3, 2007 visit. She was questioned as to the accuracy of the initial written transcript, and the fact that she did say, **"I had *pain* and up all night until four in the morning"**. She further stated that this original transcript was **accurate as written**. According to her video deposition, and testimony, it was clear to both Glenn Zeitz, and DAG Puteska, and to myself, that the initial transcript was accurate and furthermore, that someone, either Prevosnik, Sylvester, or Hallett, had **conspired to eliminate the word "pain"** and substitute an additional 29 words on this second altered transcript of August 3, 2007 office visit.

The second item that had to be cleared before the OAL hearing is whether or not either of the two undercover females had endured underlying orthopedic or musculoskeletal issues prior to their appearance in my office for treatment. Glenn Zeitz requested from the BME the medical records for the prior two-year period of both undercover females. **Sandra Dick at the BME refused this petition**. My attorney then immediately notified the Administrative Law **Judge Bruce Gorman** requesting a hearing to obtain these essential medical records of both undercovers. These records were necessary to determine the extent, of any prior injuries whether medical, surgical or orthopedic, that either undercover female may have had, previously undisclosed.

In July of 2008, a motion to compel the production of documents was made by the Administrative Law Judge Bruce Gorman to the Board of Medical Examiners. **His statement to the Board is as follows:**

# Chapter 12 - Prosecutors and Detectives Are Exempt From Consequences

*"This matter comes before me on respondent Dr. John Costino's motion to compel production of documents. The Board of Medical Examiners has sought suspension and or revocation of Dr. Costino's license to practice medicine. This case is based upon the testimony of two undercover law enforcement officers affiliated with the Cape May County Prosecutor's office and known to you as Undercover I and Undercover II. The Board asserts that Costino improperly prescribed a controlled substance for treatment. Costino does not deny prescribing this medication, but asserts that he had good medical cause to do so. Costino along with his attorney Glenn Zeitz served upon the Board a request for production of documents, and any and all medical records of these undercover agents identified in the verified complaint including, but not limited to any and all medical history provided to any medical provider prior, during, and after the relevant time period. Any records evidencing injuries of any kind sustained by either undercover, and any other claims, workers compensation, disability, personal injury insurance details, or any other claims made by either undercover at any time."*

**DAG Sandra Dick**, at the BME, **objected to this stating**:
"This request seeks documents that are neither relevant to the subject matter involved in these proceedings, or reasonably calculated to lead to the discovery of admissible evidence notwithstanding this objection. The BME does not possess any medical records for either undercover, not prepared by Dr. Costino".

**Judge Gorman counters:**
"Dr. Costino argues that his examination of both undercover females caused him to conclude by his best medical judgment, that they required the medication that he prescribed. He now seeks their medical records to ascertain whether their prior histories will assist in confirming his diagnosis."

**The BME counters:**
**"They cannot produce the medical records because they are not in the Board's possession."**

**Judge Gorman's response is as follows:**

117

"Due Process" Denied

*"**The Board of Medical examiners position is without merit**". The Board has heretofore admitted that it's cause turns on Dr Costino's diagnosis of medical conditions of both undercovers. The Board has acknowledged both undercovers will be their primary fact witness. Clearly, the two undercover females are not independent personages, they are law enforcement officers affiliated with Cape May County Prosecutor's office and cooperating fully with the attorney general's office in the prosecution of this case. **The Board's statement that it does not have the records, and it's implication, that it cannot access them, lacks credence.** I know that the county of Cape May is a subdivision of the State of New Jersey and the Cape May County prosecutor answers to the agenda of the attorney general in all matters."*

"Finally, as law enforcement officers, both undercovers have an obligation to provide materials relevant to this case. Accordingly, I am satisfied that the Board has the capacity to access the medical records of both. I am also satisfied that the records are relevant to this case. The medical records of both undercovers may support the diagnosis given. Dr. Costino is entitled to show that his diagnosis was appropriate, and that his prescriptions for the pain medications warranted. Accordingly, Costino's motion to compel these records of both undercovers **must be granted**."

"The Board of Medical Examiners will produce these records within 14 days of the date of this order. I therefore order that respondents compel production of the medical records of both undercover females be granted. "

Accordingly, the Board of Medical Examiners, principally **Sandra Dick**, had no alternative but to obtain the medical records of both undercover females, or present a legal document, a **certification**, stating that none exists. On September 23, 2008, **David Puteska,** acting for the BME **sent two certifications written by him and signed by each undercover,** to Judge Bruce Gorman in the required time period. Unfortunately for me, and again by virtue of **a clever political move** by Sandra Dick, **Judge Bruce Gorman was "removed"** from my case and Todd

# Chapter 12 - Prosecutors and Detectives Are Exempt From Consequences

Miller, a second administrative law judge was assigned.

The Administrative Law hearing before Judge Miller and coordinated with the BME was a four-day affair. The hearing was held on December 4, 2008, January 27, 2009, January 28, 2009, and January 29, 2009. Following this four-day affair, the proposed "findings of fact" and "conclusions of law" were written by DAG Puteska, and given to Judge Miller in March of 2009. Similarly, my attorney Jordan Zeitz submitted our proposed findings of fact and conclusions of law at essentially the same time. On May 14, 2009, OAL Judge Miller submitted his proposed finding of fact and conclusions of law.

I submit to you, that Judge Miller's report was **nothing more than a reiteration of DAG Puteska's "findings of fact" and "conclusions of law"**. After evaluating both Miller and Puteska's submissions to the BME, my attorney Glenn Zeitz then submitted a letter to the BME with a request for oral argument. In addition to this request for oral argument, my attorneys also wrote **voluminous exceptions** to the opinions of both DAG Puteska and Miller, since both of their submissions were **extremely flawed, incongruent, and lacked honesty.** The request for oral argument was, of course, **denied by the Board of Medical Examiners, specifically, Sandra Dick.**

## Examples of Puteska's lies and misrepresentations of this case are as follows. Similar lies and misrepresentations are also mimicked in Judge Miller's report:

- Puteska states that Anderson wanted Percocet "to relax and relieve her stress and anxiety". The office visit transcripts are clear regarding exactly what Anderson said to me, and she *NEVER SAID* **relax, stress, or anxiety.**

- Puteska states that my examination of Anderson was "incomplete", and that all I did was listen to her heart and lungs 'through her clothes, with two breaths thru my stethoscope." **This of course is a blatant lie, and a complete misrepresentation of the facts, enumerated by medical experts.**

- Puteska states that the initial visit of April 12, 2007 was billed at $200. There was *NEVER* **any billing** of any amount of **money, since the billing is done** *specifically* **through the Medicare CPT codes**. The physician really can never understand what Medicare or any insurance company will pay for a specific visit, the **payment is basically uncertain regarding individual CPT codes, and Medicare scrutiny.**

- Puteska states that Costino used a template, in lieu of taking contemporaneous notes to complete the physical examination portion of the office record. He further states that the examination sections were copied with similar notations. **This of course is** *another* **blatant lie,** as anyone examining the record of the office visits would clearly understand that they are not copied from one visit to the next. **The blood pressures are different the pulse record s are different** and the **initial evaluation is much different** than the remaining template records.
An idiot could visualize this.

- Puteska further states that my diagnosis was made without a physical examination of Anderson's spine. Again, **Puteska is clearly misinformed,** as his statement is a **complete misrepresentation of the record**.

- **Both Puteska and Miller** *omitted* **my "Pain Management Agreement" in their briefs.**

- **Anderson signed my "Pain Management Agreement" wherein the agreement states that the patient has pain, and that the patient will abide by all of the rules and regulations stated in this Agreement. The Agreement clearly states that the patient has "pain" and Anderson signed this agreement without objection, acknowledging specifically that she had "pain". Furthermore, that she would abide by all the rules and regulation of the "Pain Management Agreement " was completely omitted.**

# Chapter 12 - Prosecutors and Detectives Are Exempt From Consequences

- Puteska further states that I made a diagnosis of acute and chronic thoracic and lumbar strain and sprain. **He states that my diagnosis was made without examination. This diagnosis was a presumptive diagnosis based upon the patient's presentation, history, my examination, evaluation, and management. My statements are based upon the Medicare mandates for all physicians who practice medicine. I follow these Medicare principles of practice with** *history, evaluation, and management,* **for ALL PATIENT VISITS in my office. There are obviously additional misrepresentations in both Puteska and Miller's reports, as Miller mimics all of the stupidity of Puteska.**

My medical expert, **Dr. Richard Jermyn**, testified at the OAL civil trial: Dr. Jermyn is the founder, and director of the University of Medicine and Dentistry **Pain** Center in Stratford New Jersey. He is the chairperson of the Universities Pain Care Center. He is extremely qualified as a **pain management specialist,** and he was the only pain management specialist that testified at this civil trial (hearing). Dr. Jermyn testified as my defense expert, and his conclusions and testimony relative to my management and treatment of both undercover females is as follows: *taken directly from the trial record*

**Dr. Jermyn**:

*"I believe after reviewing the medical charts and medical transcripts, that Dr. Costino believed he was treating a nociceptive pain problem, which he documented in his medical chart as a thoraco –lumbar strain and sprain. I do believe he felt this to be his primary presumptive diagnosis. As a result, I feel it's appropriate that Percocet be prescribed for this very common diagnosis, and as a first line prescription. " "Further, and I'm going to say it again, I believe Dr. Costino felt that he was treating a nocioceptive pain issue. The prescribing of this medication was certainly appropriate". "Furthermore, the prescription of Percocet is clearly appropriate."*

# "Due Process" Denied

*"If this is his diagnosis, it is absolutely appropriate. Dr. Costino did develop this diagnosis of musculoskeletal strain and sprain, and I feel confident that this medication is appropriate." Dr. Jermyn agreed with me relative to my diagnosis and treatment of both Anderson and Abbattiscianni.*

**A few additional statements are taken directly from Miller and Puteska's reports:**

Both Puteska and Miller state that **Dr. Jermyn** "*made **many erroneous assumptions** relative to Dr. Costino's diagnosis and treatment of these two undercovers.*" **Think about that for one moment...**

This moronic lawyer, Puteska, and this moronic judge, Miller, are completely **disagreeing** with the "**pain management specialist**", who is a **certified physician**, and a "**specialist**" in pain management, which represents his primary medical practice.

## Stunning, isn't it!!

**During this hearing, Judge Miller attempted to rearrange Dr. Jermyn's opinions on several different occasions during his testimony. Miller asked certain questions of Dr. Jermyn:**

**Question:** *"In your personal opinion, is the diagnosis correct as represented in Dr. Costino's diagnostic records? Is the diagnosis acute strain and sprain?"*

**Answer:** *"yes".*

**After further questionable statements by Miller to Dr. Jermyn, Dr. Jermyn responded saying the following:** (*Taken directly from the record*)

"What I did see was a patient who said very clearly that she only requires this medication after working. The doctor specifically told her these medications were for **pain** following the night of dancing, and that is what she was using them for. Dr. Costino also counseled the patient on addiction and spoke to both

## Chapter 12 - Prosecutors and Detectives Are Exempt From Consequences

undercovers that his major concern was addiction, and that they were to take one tablet of Percocet following their night of dancing."

**Dr. Jermyn completely supported my history, evaluation, and management of both undercover females** relative to my office record, and office notes, that he read and understood. **Miller, in all probability never read or understood any of my medical records concerning these two undercover females.**

**Glenda Hamilton** of *Cooper Hospital Medical Center* was my expert defense, fact witness, regarding **medical coding, and medical records.** She testified at the O.A.L. trial, and clearly identified the fact that the medical coding, as well as my contemporaneous medical records were not only appropriate, but also better than average, and very reliable. Judge Miller essentially disregarded Glenda Hamilton's testimony and frankly, I do not believe that he even understood most of her testimony, since it was rather technical.

Furthermore, both David Puteska and Todd Miller, found Dr. Jermyn's testimony, as mentioned above, to be **unreliable**. As stated above in his report, Judge Miller actually stated in the record, that my defense expert, **a pain management expert**, and chairman of the "pain management department" at John F. Kennedy hospital system, was **"unreliable"**. *How ignorant a judge can be?*

Puteska also wrote in his report, that Glenda Hamilton's opinion, **as an expert in medical records and coding**, was **contaminated** by "false records" and "misleading diagnosis". **Puteska is simply another glaring example of just how stupid and ignorant these state employed political creatures can be!!!**

I gave testimony in this OAL civil trial for 4 hours on July 29, 2008, the last day of this **bench trial**. I clearly identified all aspects of my treatment, evaluation, and medical management, regarding both undercover females. I testified to my reasoning regarding my evaluation of these patients, and defended my position as an experienced physician regarding their treatment with "Percocet". I identified to Judge Miller that neither Anderson nor Abbattiscianni were *abusers of drugs, addicted to drugs, or diversion patients*. I examined both patients at every visit, to identify the fact that they were not injecting drugs into their bodies, and had no identifying bruises or wounds that would indicate any type of abuse. Miller of course, simply **disregarded** my testimony, as he also **disregarded** the testimony of *Detective Landis, Dr. Jermyn, and Glenda Hamilton*. I clearly identified the fact to Miller, that I treated both undercover females in the same manner that I treated Detective Landis, as all three were sent to my office to "**entrap" me** into doing something unlawful.

Following both reports of DAG Puteska, and Judge Miller's regarding the findings of fact, and conclusions of law, my attorneys Glenn Zeitz, and Jordan Zeitz, wrote voluminous exceptions to the opinions of both Puteska and Miller. These exceptions written by my attorneys are based upon **facts** of the case, and **facts** included in the testimony given by myself, and my experts.

The written reports of both Puteska and Miller that were sent to the Board of Medical Examiners, **were replete with lies and misrepresentations, and in my opinion demonstrated the fundamentally dishonest character of both Puteska and Miller.** They both represent the **subversive techniques, and the abuse of power**, exhibited by dishonest law enforcement individuals, and the legal tyranny specifically of **Judge Miller, which further characterizes the corrupt political interpretation of the law**.

As a result of the fundamentally **corrupt** reporting of both Puteska and Miller, my attorneys sent their "findings of fact" and "conclusions of law", in addition to their brief regarding the **exceptions** to Todd Miller's report. **In my opinion,** Judge Miller represents a phony, and a prop, for Sandra Dick at the Board of Medical Examiners in their quest to revoke my medical license for five years.

Following the reporting outlined above, the Board of Medical Examiners controlled by Sandra Dick, in a sequestered setting, voted to **reject** reinstating my medical license, thereby preventing my ability to return to medical practice and earn a living. This decision by the BME, and a few henchmen physicians, lead by Sandra dick, represents not only a **cognitive bias**, and **prejudice** against me but also underscores the **conspiracy** between Sandra Dick at the Board, and Robert Taylor at the Cape May County prosecutors office. Glenn Zeitz provided *prima facial* evidence of my innocence in this matter.

Puteska, Miller, Sandra Dick, and Robert Taylor, **in my opinion,** are **corrupt lawyers** demonstrating the **abuse of power** that they possess to control and continue the **legal tyranny** to perpetuate the **criminalization of medicine**.

**Included in Glenn Zeitz's voluminous exceptions to Judge Todd Miller's report to the Board of Medical Examiners is the following:**

1. Dr. Costino's actions **DID NOT** constitute repeated acts of negligence in violation of N.J.S.A 45:1-21(d). The seventh edition of Black's Law dictionary defines the term negligence as the failure to exercise the standard of care that a reasonable prudent person would have exercised in a similar situation.

2. Dr. Costino's actions **DID NOT** constitute professional misconduct in N.J.S.A 45:1-21(e) The seventh edition of Blacks Law dictionary defines the term misconduct the dereliction of duty or unlawful and improper behavior.

3. Dr. Costino's actions **DID NOT** constitute the engagement of acts constituting moral turpitude or conduct relating adversely to activity regulated by the Board in violation of NJSA 45:1-21(f) The seventh edition of Blacks Law Dictionary defines the phrase moral turpitude as "conduct that is contrary to justice, honesty or morality, or conduct that is shameful, wicked, or shocking to the moral sense of the community.

4. Dr. Costino's actions **DID NOT** constitute a failure to comply with the provisions of any act or regulation administered by the Board in violation of NJSA 45:1-21(h)

Licensees shall prepare contemporaneous, permanent professional treatment records and shall maintain records relating to billing made to patients or third party carriers for professional services.

Dr. Costino's medical records reflect:
- The dates of all treatments
- The history
- The findings on appropriate examination
- Diagnosis or medical impression
- Treatment ordered, including specific quantities and strengths of medications including refills if prescribed, administered, or dispensed, and recommended follow-up.

As part of the patient's **history, examination and evaluation**, the practitioner shall:
- Perform an appropriate history and physical examination.
- Make a diagnosis based upon the examination and evaluation of the patient consistent with good medical care.
- Formulate and discuss with the patient a therapeutic plan commenting on risks and benefits of treatment.
- Ensure the availability of the physician for appropriate follow-up care.

NJAC 13:35-7.6(a) provides in relevant part that when prescribing controlled substances the physician shall ensure that a patient's medical history has been taken and the physical and psychological assessment has been performed.

The medical record shall reflect:
- Complete name of the controlled substance
- Dosage strength and quantity of the controlled substance
- Indication for the use of the controlled substance
- Instructions as to the frequency of the use
- Physician shall keep accurate and complete records including any

# Chapter 12 - Prosecutors and Detectives Are Exempt From Consequences

agreement with the patient specifically the "pain management agreement".

In this case, Dr. Costino complied with all the medical laws and regulations listed above in a complete fashion. There was a separate medical record created for Anderson and Abbattiscianni on every date that they received treatment. The medical record contained the **history, examination, evaluation and management of both patients.** The physical examination was clear and concise, and the medication prescribed, (PERCOCET) #30 doses to be taken one at night following the dancing work activity.

**Dr. Costino's actions, and work product was in *complete compliance* with Medical Board and New Jersey State Law and Regulations.**

## *IN CONCLUSION...*
Dr. Costino's actions *DID NOT...*

- constitute the indiscriminate prescribing of CDS – (controlled dangerous substances) in violation of NJSA 45:1-21(m).

- **DID NOT** demonstrate the failure to be of good moral character as required by NJSA 45:9-6.

- **DID NOT** constitute professional misconduct in violation of NJSA 45:1-21(e)

- **DID NOT** constitute the engagement in acts constituting moral turpitude of conduct relating adversely to activity regulated by the Board in violation of NJSA 45:1-21(f)

- **DID NOT** constitute a failure to comply *with any* of the provisions of any act or regulation administered by the board in violation of NJSA 45:1-21(h)

*AND LASTLY...*

- **Dr. Costino's actions *NEVER* demonstrated the failure of him to be of good moral character as required by NJSA 45:9-6**

Chapter 12 - Prosecutors and Detectives Are Exempt From Consequences

# Administrative Law Hearing (OAL)

### State's Witnesses:

1. Little Egg Harbor Class II Police Officer, Tonya Anderson
2. Drug Enforcement Administration Special Agent, Margarita Abbattiscianni
3. Detective George Hallett

### Defense and Expert Witnesses:

**Expert Witnesses:**
1. Officer Joseph Landis
2. Dr. Richard Jermyn (expert on CDS & patient record keeping)
3. Glenda L. Hamilton (expert on billing and coding)
4. Dr. John Costino

**Character Witnesses for Dr. Costino:**
1. **Richard Renza, D.O.,** Colleague, classmate and friend
2. **Dominic Natale,** Childhood friend
3. **Robert Speer, D.O.,** Colleague, classmate and friend
4. **Edward Fox,** Classmate and friend
5. **William Henfey,** Mayor of N. Wildwood
6. **Roman Osadchuk,** Long-time friend
7. **Hon. John Callihan,** Superior Court Judge (Ret.)
8. **Robert Renza, D.O.,** Colleague and friend
9. **Robert Maurer, D.O.,** Colleague and friend

"The Pharisees summoned the man for a second time before them. They said to him, "Tell me what you know of this man for he is a sinner." "That he is a sinner I cannot say, all I can say is once I was blind and now I can see."
- John 9:24-25

"Realize Untrustworthy and Evil People Exist in the World, Stay Mindful, and Take Deliberate Action."
– Marcus Aurelius

At the Board of Medical Examiners hearing in December of 2007 I outlined my medical practice along with the need of pain management and addiction treatment utilizing Suboxone in Cape May County. *"**None** of the **Medical Board physicians practice pain management or addiction treatment**.* I perform this work in the trenches of our society in my office in North Wildwood while some of these board physicians do their work in their ivory towers, and pontificate at their board meetings with the deputy attorneys. The board physicians are charged with protecting the public interest, but in reality, they have **abdicated their responsibility** and in most cases, **their common sense**. They have abandoned the public interest, and my patients in North Wildwood, and Cape May County. **In our society aren't you innocent until proven guilty?** Should your medical license be suspended on a **spurious charge** by a **narcissistic and insufficient county prosecutor?**

## Where is "due process?"

Chapter 13

My medical records are above average. This is not simply my opinion but the opinion of my pain management expert, **Dr. Richard Jermyn,** at the OAL hearing who testified in my behalf, as well as the medical records expert, **Glenda Hamilton** who also testified in my behalf at this administrative law hearing.

**Dr. Jermyn,** a pain management expert, and recognized by the Board of Medical Examiners as an expert in this field, testified that my medical records were " better than most". The BME criticized my medical records, without any justification, and with a **cognitive bias** and **prejudice** against me.

At a minimum the physicians on this Board should have understood the billing mechanism that is performed in a physician's office. Apparently, most of these physicians have little understanding of the coding and billing system performed in the physician's office and the billing service. Certain Board members went along with the deputy attorneys, Sandra Dick and David Puteska and challenged and criticized my standard billing methods.

Physicians in the state of New Jersey must follow the **Federal Medicare Guidelines** with regard to billing. This system consists of **history, examination and management** (HEM) of the patient. My medical records clearly demonstrate that I fulfilled all the criteria to the letter of the law. The BME's judgment demonstrated a poor understanding of the criteria that follow the federal guidelines. They were clearly identified by the billing expert, Glenda Hamilton, at the OAL hearing in January of 2009. Both medical and billing records done in my office were considered very good by Glenda Hamilton who also gave an excellent explanation to the court regarding the HEM system, coding and billing system, that all physicians, except for psychiatrists, utilize in the state of New Jersey.

Another example of the BME's abdication of responsibility and one, most interesting, is their denial to provide the medical records of the two undercover females. This was finally decided on appeal to the administrative law **judge, Bruce Gorman,** who clearly stated **"these medical records were relevant and important to Dr. Costino's treatment of the two undercover females."** It took an administrative law judge order for Deputy Attorney David Puteska to finally provide a certification by both UC1 and UC2. Prior to the OAL civil trial, **Anderson certified that she *did not* have any medical problems relating to her cervical, thoracic or lumbar spine.** This, of course, **turned out to be *completely false*.** Her certification was written by DAG Puteska, and signed by Tonya Anderson, a.k.a. Tonya Smith, on Sept 19, 2008 prior to the OAL civil trial. At the OAL trial, **Anderson was placed under oath, and she committed absolute perjury throughout her entire testimony.**

Six months later, in July of 2009, as a result of an order from Judge Raymond Batten in superior court of Cape May County, the truth was revealed by way of medical records from **SeaPort Chiropractic Center** where Anderson received treatment by Dr. Joseph O'Rourke on July 26, 2007 while also being treated in my office and having signed my "Pain Management Agreement".

On July 26, 2007, Anderson described her major complaints to Dr. O'Rourke as being pain in her upper back, her neck, her right shoulder, and lumbar region. Her pain " comes and goes" and she has had this pain for the past four years.

Dr. O'Rourke made a diagnosis of "subluxation of her cervical spine, subluxation of her thoracic region, thoracic spine, and subluxation of her lumbar region, along with lumbar muscle spasm and associated pain in all of these areas." These statements are taken directly from Dr. O'Rourke's office records. Specific findings by Dr. O'Rourke, as stated in her medical record is, "cervical sharp pain, radiating and constant, thoracic sharp pain, radiating and constant, and lumbar pain intermittent". Following the *"in camera"* inspection of Dr. O'Rourke's records by Judge Raymond Batten, Glenn Zeitz, and Megan Hoerner, the Assistant Prosecutor of Cape May County, Horner, insisted that Anderson sign *a second* certification stating the following:

**"Pursuant to Judge Raymond Batten's order dated May 5, 2009, I hereby certify that from the time period of August 23, 2005 through and including August 23, 2007, I went to SeaPort**

Chapter 13

**Chiropractic Center on one occasion. I hereby certify the following statements made by me are true and I am aware that if any of the forgoing statements made by me are willfully false I am subject to punishment."** This was signed by Tonya Anderson. *See both certifications by Anderson in Appendix*

*On July 20, 2009, Glenn Zeitz wrote to DAG Puteska at the Board of Medical Examiners:*

**"I am now in receipt of newly discovered evidence which I believe is relevant material that has the potential to effect the outcome of the case against Dr. Costino.** This evidence should have been turned over to me prior to the Administrative Law hearing in December of 2008, pursuant to an order of the Board. This evidence is critical to this matter and involves **false swearing and perjury** by your star witness, Tonya Anderson."

In my opinion, DAG Puteska conspired with Tonya Anderson under the direction of DAG Sandra Dick to create this entire farce. Puteska knew that Anderson had received treatment prior to the OAL hearing. Puteska had her sign "the first false certification", and she was advised that the Board of Medical Examiners would not punish her for her **perjury** with either her **false certification** or with her **false testimony** at the administrative law hearing. This represents the depths of deception at the Board of Medical Examiners orchestrated by DAG Sandra Dick and facilitated by Puteska in their effort to find me culpable, and therefore subject to their level of punishment.

*Mr. Zeitz wrote the following in his brief to the Board of Medical Examiners:*
*"It is well recognized that a false certification can subject the affiant to criminal offenses of perjury and false swearing. In this case,* ***undercover agent Anderson was willing to commit both false swearing and perjury under the guidance of Puteska and Dick to advance the prosecution of Dr. Costino."***

In August of 2009, Mr. Zeitz sent another letter to DAG Puteska with a

# "Due Process" Denied

copy to Executive director Roeder. Glenn Zeitz petitioned for a hearing regarding this new and important information relevant to Anderson's **perjury** with her **false certification**, and her **false testimony** at the AOL trial, and the fact that she had been **lying for approximately two years**. Puteska responded to Glenn Zeitz stating that the **Board denied oral argument and denied a hearing regarding this issue.**

*Glenn Zeitz then wrote a second letter dated September 3, 2009, to Mr. Roeder with a copy to Judge Todd Miller, Sandra Dick, and David Puteska stating the following*:

"Since the original suspension of Dr. Costino's medical license in December of 2007, the Board of Medical Examiners has acted in an **arbitrary** and **capricious** manner, and with **a complete *abuse of discretion* in the treatment of Dr. Costino's rights.**" "The Board has now been presented with uncontradicted proof that the Attorney General's office, and it's star witness, Tonya Anderson have **flagrantly violated the Board order to a fair determination of this matter.** The star witness for the prosecution, **Tonya Anderson** has engaged in **false swearing, perjury, and contempt** of the Board's order requiring the production of relevant material records to respondent and his counsel. "

"*The only conclusion that can be drawn from the sudden decision not to have oral argument is that the Board of Medical Examiners **does not want to have a formal record**, and **transcript** created regarding the misconduct of the Board of Medical Examiners prosecution and it's star witness. This harkens back to the days of the "**Star Chamber**" and evidences the continuing "**due process**" **violations** that have occurred since the inception of this prosecution.*"

"*It is obvious to me that the Board has engaged in a "cover up" of the misconduct in this case and is attempting to "conceal" from certain physician members of the Board the true level and depth of the misconduct in this matter.*" "Once again I request oral argument so that a complete record of what has *occurred in this case can be created and so that in a later appeal to the appellate division may contain a proper record of what has occurred in this case. "*

Clearly, there has been **NO OVERSIGHT** by the Attorney Generals' office regarding the "misconduct" of Anderson, Puteska or Sandra Dick in this matter.

When you see all of the facts presented, you've got to ask the following questions regarding law enforcement:

Where have the leaders gone?

Where are the creative communicators?

Where are the people of character, courage conviction and common sense?

( I may be a sucker for alliteration but I think you get the point!!! )

---

**A few more salient questions regarding the issues outlined above:**

1. What motivated Anderson to lie on her first certification dated September 19, 2008 and completely omit her treatment with Dr. O'Rourke on July 26, 2007 midway during the time that she was under my care for **"pain management"?**

2. Why *did she lie* under oath on the witness stand at the administrative law hearing?

3. Why did Anderson *lie* and jeopardize her career regarding these medical records.

4. The BME was under a judge's order to produce Anderson's medical records. The responsibility to carry out this order was given to DAG Puteska and Sandra Dick. What role did they play in Anderson's deception? Is this a major conspiracy **between the three of them?**

> 5. What role did Assistant Prosecutor Megan Hoerner play in this escapade?
>
> 6. What conversations actually transpired between **Anderson, Hoerner, Puteska, and Dick** during the time period between Judge Batten's order in May of 2009 and the receipt of the medical records of Tonya Anderson to Judge Batten on July 17, 2009, from Dr. O'Rourke's office?
>
> 7. How did Megan Hoerner discover that Tonya Anderson received treatment with Dr. O'Rourke on July 26, 2007?

Obviously Anderson had no choice but to admit the truth sometime between Judge Batten's order and the receipt of her medical records on July 17, 2009. Anderson waited until July 20, 2009 to sign her second certification. She had no choice but to "*come clean*" and at least admit a partial truth on her second certification in July of 2009, written by Assistant Prosecutor, Megan Hoerner.

Based upon Dr. O'Rourke's medical records of Tonya Anderson, she has had pain with reference to her spine and extremities for the past **four** years.

*See Dr. O'Rourke's Patient Record of Anderson in Appendix*

If my treatment of Anderson was so deficient as to warrant a suspension of my medical license in December of 2007, **why does Dr O'Rourke's diagnosis mimic my diagnosis?** Anderson's medical records by Dr. O'Rourke exonerate me. This is obviously the reason why Anderson lied, and why Puteska and Dick **conspired** with her. **The medical records were withheld from both the administrative law court as well as the superior court in Cape May County for two years**. The only conclusion that one must make is that the conspirators,

**Anderson, Puteska and Dick** withheld these facts to enable them to suspend my medical license. This action represents absolute **misconduct knowingly**, **willingly** and **maliciously** performed by officer **Anderson** and DAGs **Puteska and Dick**. I am now well aware that there was a continued dialog between **Puteska, Dick and Horner** with respect to Anderson over this relevant period of time. The only possible way to enable the truth of the matter to surface is to subject each one, **Anderson, Puteska, Dick and Hoerner** to an evidentiary hearing. **The evidentiary hearing** *was denied*, and was *never conducted for obvious reasons.*

The pain and discomfort that Anderson exhibited in Dr. O'Rourke's office is manifest, and understood, when one considers her poor physical abilities record during **her police training as a recruit**. She essentially failed all of her physical abilities during her police academy training. This correlates with Dr O'Rourke's medical records and my evaluation of Anderson.

A hearing was scheduled in September of 2009 at the Board of Medical Examiners to examine these issues. Two weeks prior to this hearing, DAG Sandra Dick and her cohorts **cancelled** the hearing. Glenn Zeitz then wrote to the NJ State Attorney General in Trenton, and the attorney general eventually **commanded** Sandra Dick at the BME to hold this hearing.

The hearing took place in October of 2009, and Mr. Zeitz clearly presented all of these salient issues to the physician Board members, and to the deputy attorneys in attendance. Mr. Zeitz petitioned for a **remand** of my case to a second administrative law judge, to elucidate all of the issues concerning the **perjury** of Tonya Anderson, the **state's star witness.**

Although several physicians on the board voted in my favor, to conduct a second administrative law hearing for the stated reasons, **Sandra Dick in her closed session was able to convince the majority of these physicians to deny a remand. A second administrative law hearing was *never granted.***

The BME **failed** in their *duty and responsibility* to ensure that I receive "**due process**" and **failed** to restore my medical license. The responsibility for these "due process" violations falls directly on the politically appointed physicians of the New Jersey State Board of Medical Examiners and of course, on the career deputy attorneys who perpetrated this entire **fraud**. Anderson, Dick and Puteska acted in a *concerted, corrupt and fraudulent manner,* committed **misconduct knowingly, willfully and maliciously,** and all are **ethically compromised**, but have never received punishment for their **corruption**.

The administrative law judge, Miller, was appraised of these important facts, and should have intervened in the process, realizing that during the OAL hearing in December of 2008, Anderson's **perjury** was accepted by Judge Miller as truthful testimony. Sandra Dick controls the physicians of the Board of Medical Examiners, and the DAGs beneath her. Puteska wrote Anderson's **first false certification**, and had her sign it. **In my candid opinion, Puteska and Dick were well aware that there would be no consequence to anyone following the production of this perjured certification.**

# The Eighth Commandment of the Lord: "Do Not Bear False Witness Against Thy Neighbor"

On September 10, 2008, prior to the OAL civil trial hearing with Judge Miller, the Board of Medical Examiners heard oral argument on the attorney general's request for "interlocutory review" of an order from the OAL Judge Gorman requiring the disclosure of medical records relating to the two female undercover agents. During this hearing Glenn Zeitz argues that "not seeing anything in the investigative files of any kind that someone from the Board went out and examined the two undercovers and determined if they were 100% healthy people. That there was absolutely nothing wrong with either one of them." Even though both said that they did not have any medical problems of any kind, there is no substitution for actual records which would clearly confirm the above. There is no substitution for accurate records especially when you're dealing with law-enforcement personnel. There is a legitimate basis for the production of these records, and for a judge to conduct an "*in camera*" inspection of same. You know later on in life, it turns out that you find out how many times you read in the newspaper, for example, about a case where something surfaces later and it turns out that something was withheld by law-enforcement."

**"Would you at least let your freedom or your license rest on law enforcement officers stating 100% that they would not mislead anyone?"**

Remember, on September 19th 2008, prior to the OAL civil trial, DAG Puteska wrote Anderson's first certification and had her sign it:

**"That from the time period of April 12, 2006 through and including August 23, 2007 I did not have any medical problems relating to the cervical, thoracic or lumbar spine, and that if the foregoing statements made by me are untrue, and willfully false, I am subject to punishment".**

On December 4, 2008 Anderson was placed under oath before Judge Todd Miller, and testified at this OAL trial in this manner:

| | |
|---|---|
| Question: | "When you were sent to Dr. Costino on April 12, 2007 did you have any back or neck injuries?" |
| Answer: | "No." |
| Question: | "Did you have any back or neck pain or discomfort?" |
| Answer: | "No." |
| Question: | "During the visit were you asked about any back or neck pain?" |
| Answer: | "Yes." |
| Question: | "What was your response?" |
| Answer: | "That I had none." |
| Question: | "Did you at any time during your physical with Dr. Costino on April 12 mention any problems with your neck ort back?" |
| Answer: | "No." |
| Question: | "What do you consider your neck and your back?" |
| Answer: | The witness then touching her neck and upper back region and lower back region told the court that she |

## Chapter 14 - The Eighth Commandment of the Lord

Answer: understood what neck and back and mid-back regions were. Anderson then suggested that her thoracic spine is actually from where your cervical spine ends down to your lower back where the lumbar spine begins.

It was clear to Miller, that Anderson knew full well where her neck, her back, her thoracic and lumbar regions were located. She, however, **denied** any history of any type of pain or discomfort, or any issue whatsoever, with regard with to her cervical, thoracic or lumbar spine.

Fast forward to July 20, 2009, seven months after this OAL civil trial, when Anderson then submitted her second certification to Superior Court Judge Raymond Batten of Cape May County, written by Assistant Prosecutor Hoerner. Her second certification stated the following:

**"That from the time period between August 23, 2005 through and including August 23, 2007, I went to Seaport Chiropractic Center on one occasion. During this period of time I also went to Dr. William Glen for annual physicals."**

This second certification was partially true. Nowhere in this certification did Anderson mention any relevant information concerning her complaints, or her treatment recommended by Dr. O'Rourke regarding the office visit at Seaport Chiropractic Center. Anderson never mentioned any findings of Dr. O'Rourke at this visit in July 2007 when she was in a *treatment program with me for "pain management."*

Anderson's second certification was written by Assistant Prosecutor Megan Hoerner relating to the order by Superior Court Judge Raymond Batten. My attorney, Glenn Zeitz, needed to be certain that these undercover patients did or did not have any prior history, difficulty, or pathology in their cervical, thoracic, or lumbar regions. Glenn Zeitz and I ***did not*** believe Anderson's first certification of September of 2008, and I felt certain that DAG David Puteska and DAG Sandra Dick conspired with Anderson to commit **perjury** with her first certification, prior to the OAL civil trial. Glenn Zeitz in his wisdom petitioned Judge Batten in Superior Court in Cape May County to have Anderson and Abbattiscianni submit past medical records regarding any type of injury, accident, or pathology during the relevant time period. As a result of Judge Batten's order, Assistant Prosecutor Megan Hoerner along with Anderson produced her second certification outlined above. On July 29, 2009 Glen Zeitz, together with Megan Hoerner and Judge Batten, reviewed *"in camera"* Anderson's chiropractic records which were produced on July 26, 2007, by Dr. O'Rourke's office, and were essentially unknown to Judge Batten, my attorney Glenn Zeitz and myself, until July 29, 2009, two years later.

Anderson did attend Dr. O'Rourke's office at Seaport Chiropractic Center multiple times prior to July 26, 2007. On that date, July 26, 2007, between two office visits with me for **"pain management"**, she experienced so much *pain and discomfort* that she felt it necessary to see her chiropractor for treatment. At that visit of July 26, 2007, Anderson complained to Dr. O'Rourke of having *pain and discomfort* in her cervical region, her right shoulder and her lumber spine. She further stated to him that "sleep" worsens her condition, and that her "pain comes and goes", and interferes with her daily routine and with her ability to sleep comfortably. Anderson also complained of sharp intermittent, and at times consistent pain in her spinal regions. Dr. O'Rourke made a diagnosis as follows:
- Subluxation of the cervical region
- Subluxation of the thoracic region
- Muscle spasm in the thoracic and lumbar region
- **"Pain"** in all three areas of her spine

Objective findings by Dr O'Rourke:
- Paravertebral muscle spasm in the cervical thoracic and lumbar region with associated decreased range of motion in all areas of her spine with a relatively normal gait.

# Chapter 14 - The Eighth Commandment of the Lord

On July 30, 2009 Glenn Zeitz sent correspondence to Deputy Attorney Puteska advising him "I am now in receipt of newly discovered evidence which I believe is relevant material. This relevant material has the potential to affect the outcome of the case against Dr. Costino". "This evidence should have been turned over to me prior to the administrative hearing pursuant to an order of the Board of Medical Examiners in 2008. This evidence is critical to this matter, and involves **false swearing and perjury** by your **star witness** Tonya Anderson".

Glenn Zeitz then filed a motion to reopen the record and have further proceedings before a second administrative law judge to evaluate Dr. O'Rourke's medical records and obtain additional testimony from additional witnesses regarding same". "A failure by the Board to at least review and consider new medical evidence **wrongly withheld** specifically after a Board order by Judge Gorman, goes to the heart of the case against Dr. Costino, and is clearly **an abuse of discretion.**" "David Puteska and Sandra Dick," Mr. Zeitz stated, "as officers of the court, you have an obligation to correct this deficiency and to further investigate **false swearing, and perjury**, to ensure that proceedings before this Board adhere to the principals of procedural **"due process".**

"Anderson's medical records are clearly material because they support Dr. Costino's defense. Since his diagnosis of thoracic and lumbar strain and sprain, causing her pain, was based on subjective findings which were corroborated by Dr. O'Rourke, they relate directly to the focal issue of the OAL trial. The focal issue is Anderson's medical condition during each visit, as these records would **impeach, and powerfully undermine Anderson's** credibility which the trial court Judge Miller, has in essence found to be without reproach."

This of course refers to the OAL civil trail with Judge Todd Miller. Miller's statement in his brief identifies Anderson's credibility was found to be **"without reproach."** "With respect to altering the outcome, the existence of such history, injury, or condition of Anderson has the capacity to alter the Board's finding on whether Dr. Costino's medical decision making was appropriate. There can be no doubt that a different physician, namely Dr. O'Rourke, made the same or similar findings of Dr. Costino concerning Anderson's medical condition during the relevant time period. This certainly would alter the outcome of this case."

"A **remand** is therefore necessary so that a proper record can be created concerning the circumstances surrounding Anderson's certifications, her previous, **false sworn testimony**, the recent disclosure of her medical records at superior court in Cape May County that totally contradicts her testimony, and other issues relating to same, and why there was a **flagrant violation** of the Board's order for the production of her medical records."

"Furthermore, in this case, a different judge should be assigned **to conduct the remand** since the assigned trial court judge, Miller, has exhibited a **bias**, along with other *disqualifying factors* regarding Dr. Costino. Dr. Costino respectfully requests that the Board delay issuing of a final decision." A "**remand**" in this matter to the Office of Administrative Law to supplement the record based on newly discovered material, and relevant evidence is necessary. The Office of Administrative Law should reassign the "**remand**" to a different judge to allow Dr. Costino to present witnesses regarding the medical records of Anderson that were eventually turned over in **flagrant violation of this boards previous order."**

**On September 9, 2009 at the Richard Hughes Justice Complex in Trenton, a hearing was held, open to the public and called to order by chairperson, Dr. Jordan for the open disciplinary matters. The Board members present were as follows:**
Dr. Peter Nussbaum, Dr. Paul Mendelowitz, Dr. Paul Jordan, Kevin Walsh, Dr. Katherine Lambert, Dr. Stewart Berkowitz, Dr. Ilays Rajput, Dr. Steven Lomazow, Mr. Dan Weiss, Dr. Peter Iannuzzi, Dr. George Scott and Dr. Sindy M. Paul. Deputy attorneys present: Dick, Puteska, Levine, Wefing, Ehrenkrantz and Executive Director: William Roeder.

Glenn Zeitz began this hearing by reminding the Board members that he had previously petitioned the BME for an order from Judge Gorman in order to obtain the medical records of the two undercover females. Mr. Zeitz then went through the history of the Board's **initial refusal to render the undercovers medical**

## Chapter 14 - The Eighth Commandment of the Lord

**records.** Mr. Zeitz then reminded these Board members that there were two "certifications" by Anderson, the *first completely false,* and the *second partially true*. He further noted his suspicious relative to the voracity of Anderson and other law enforcement officials relating to my case. Mr. Zeitz argued that I was **prejudiced** because he never had the opportunity to question or to cross examine Anderson regarding **the truth**. Furthermore, he *did not have the opportunity* to submit Anderson's true record to the Administrative Law Court. This **prejudice and injustice** demands a "**remand**" to a second administrative law judge to obtain a fair and impartial hearing *on the facts in light of the newly discovered evidence.*

When questioned by certain Board members regarding this "**remand**", Mr. Zeitz explained to them that it was necessary to cross-examine Anderson because she claimed that her "*pain comes and goes*". Mr. Zeitz would attempt to establish a period of time that she experienced pain, and whether or not these time periods coincided with Dr. Costino's office visits as the prescribing of medication is certainly appropriate treatment for her symptoms regarding intermittent pain in the thoracic and or lumbar regions.

In his closing statement, Mr. Zeitz petitioned the Board to "**remand**" my case to a second Administrative Law judge so that I may have a fair trial. He wanted the opportunity to argue **the failure** to produce an accurate record prejudiced Dr. Costino. He wanted the right to cross-examine Anderson and believed that he had the right to seek a **contempt charge against Anderson.** Furthermore, that the attorney general should refer this issue to the county prosecutor for further proceedings in consideration of Anderson's **false swearing and perjury**. He further argued that the only remedy was to "remand" this case to a second administrative law judge.

Following this hearing, the Board of Medical Examiners moved into their executive session so that Sandra Dick could influence her Board members to disregard the testimony of Mr. Zeitz's, and the facts of the case which have heretofore had been undisclosed, and to deny me this "remand" to a second Administrative Law judge, and OAL civil trial.

DAG Sandra Dick eventually completed her executive session, and her influence over the Board and returned the Board to their open session, and announced the following:

## "The BME has reaffirmed its prior decision of revocation of Dr. Costino's medical license for a five year period extending from December 2007 through December 2012."

The Board *did not honor* our request to *"remand"* my case to a second Administrative Law Judge **for an honest and unbiased proceeding.** Although several members of the Board were honest and did vote positively to allow my request for a "remand", Sandra Dick was able to convince the majority of **these disgraceful physicians, and deputies**, to vote against this "remand". By denying the "remand", this Board also denied Glenn Zeitz the opportunity to question Anderson regarding her **dishonesty, and perjury**, regarding her **false certifications, her false testimony, and perjury** at the initial Administrative hearing in December of 2008 and January of 2009.

DAG Dick did not want revealed under oath the critical and factual relationship between her, David Puteska, and Anderson regarding their **illegal activity**. If indeed Anderson had told the truth from the start, it would have been clear to any reasonable Board member that my prescription of minimal medication (one Percocet following each night of dancing) for this patient regarding her **pain and discomfort** in conjunction with her work as an exotic dancer was appropriate and legal. **This medication, in my opinion, and within a reasonable degree of medical certainty was necessary for both patients.**

Anderson's past medical history clearly identifies problems with her cervical, thoracic and lumbar regions in addition to other issues regarding her physiology. **A "remand", and a second OAL civil trial would have implicated Sandra Dick, and David Puteska committing numerous fraudulent crimes regarding my case.** In fact, Dick, Puteska, Anderson, and certain Board members

## Chapter 14 - The Eighth Commandment of the Lord

simply **did not want the truth, or the facts** revealed to the Cape May County Prosecutor's Office or to the public in general.

**Following this denial to remand my case, Mr. Zeitz filed an appeal to the New Jersey superior court of appeals in an effort to possibly receive "due process" and finally "justice".**

**This timely appeal to the NJ Superior court of appeals was filed in January of 2010. It was eventually heard by a three judge panel who I term the "Three Blind Mice," Dorothea Wefing, Edith Payne, and Linda Baxter.**

**Two months later their appellate decision was rendered:**

## Appeal denied!!!

**This three judge panel, of appellate creatures denied me a remand, a return to the office of Administrative Law, civil court with a second OAL judge to elucidate the perjury and certain other issues of the BME's failure. Following this denial, I then filed a separate, formal set of briefs to the Supreme Court of the state of New Jersey.**

**This Supreme Court filing became a major endeavor to the highest court in New Jersey within a specified period of time by my attorneys Glenn Zeitz and Jordan Zeist.**

**Within a short period of time, and after following all the proper dictums regarding this Supreme Court appeal, we received the following:**

## The Supreme Court of the State of New Jersey has refused to hear your case.

**In other words... F. U. Dr. Costino**

## "Remand Hearing"
### at the Board of Medical Examiners (BME)
### September 9, 2009
### Board Memebers Present:

Dr. Peter Nussbaum
Dr. Paul Mendelowitz
Dr. Paul Jordan (chairman)
Dr. Katherine Lambert
Dr. Stewart Berkowitz
Dr. Ilays Rajput
Dr. Steven Lomazow
Dr. Peter Iannuzzi
Dr. George Scott
Dr. Sindy Paul
Mr. Kevin Walsh (Board Member at Large)
Mr. Dan Weiss (Board Memeber at Large)

### Deputy Attorneys Present

Sandra Y. Dick, DAG
(Sandra Ben-Asher)
Mr. David Puteska, DAG
Levine
Wefing
Ehrenkrantz

### BME Executive Director:

Mr. William Roeder

# Preliminary Statement of the Case

**This preliminary statement of the case was filed by Jordan Zeitz as an appeal to the Superior Court of Appeals before Judges Dorothea Wefing, Edith K. Payne, and Linda Baxter.** (The Three Blind Mice)

## A. Nature of the Case

This is an appeal of the New Jersey State Board of Medical Examiners (The Board) affirming the Office of Administrative Law (OAL) Initial Decision of May 14, 2009. (Initial Decision) which found that appellant John G. Costino, D.O. (Dr. Costino) had committed the allegations contained in Counts I & II of the verified complaint filed on December 5, 2007 (Verified Complaint) thereby warranting a revocation of Dr. Costino's medical license for five years. The issues in this case are:

(1) whether the Board **abused it's discretion by denying Dr. Costino's request for a remand back to the OAL** for the limited purpose of confronting the key prosecution witness against Dr. Costino, and calling said witness's chiropractor as a defense witness **based on the post trial discovery** –i.e. after the OAL had issued the initial decision but before the Board had issued the Final Decision – of evidence previously subject to a Board order that the prosecution witness, **Anderson had committed false swearing and perjury when she certified and later testified that she had no problems with her neck, back, or spine while**

under Dr. Costino's care which the witness knew to be false and which would have materially supported Dr. Costino's defense that the **witness was suffering neck and back pain warranting the prescription of Percocet;**

(2) Whether the Board abused it's discretion by finding Dr. Costino had committed the allegations contained in the Verified Complaint since such a finding was not based on competent, credible, and substantial evidence; and

(3) whether a **license revocation of 5 years**, monetary **penalties in excess of $90,000 (disproportionate)** and **(shocking to one's sense of fairness)** where **there was no evidence that Dr. Costino** was a fundamentally "corrupt licensee", had engaged in a "panoply of dishonest" acts over several years and under verifying different circumstances, and was unwilling to abide by any terms and conditions as part of his reinstatement.

# B. Relevant Procedural History and Disposition Below

On **December 5th 2007**, the Board filed the verified complaint against Dr. Costino.

On **December 10, 2007**, Dr. Costino filed an answer to the verified complaint. The Board conducted a hearing two days later over the objection of Dr. Costino's counsel who requested more time to prepare for same.

On **December 20, 2007**, the Board issued an order temporarily suspending Dr. Costino's license effective as of Dec 17, 2007.

On **July 29, 2008** the OAL issued an order requiring the Board to disclose the relevant adult medical records of the two undercover law enforcement officers who posed as patients and who were the only witnesses the Board intended to (and did) call at the plenary hearing which commenced on December 4, 2008.

On **September 10, 2008**, the Board heard oral argument on the attorney general's request for interlocutory review of the OAL's order of July 29, 2008. The Board

## Chapter 15 - Preliminary Statement of the Case

then went into executive session and issued an order requiring the undercover agents to disclose any medical problems they had with the spine, neck, or back from April 12, 2006 –through August 23, 2007 (hereinafter referred to as the "relevant time" period).

On **September 19, 2008** undercover agent Tonya Anderson (Anderson) certified in the OAL that she did not have any medical problems related to her spine, neck, or back during the relevant time period.

On **December 4, 2008 and January 27, 2009**, Anderson was placed under oath before the OAL and testified at the plenary hearing that she did not have any problems with her spine, neck or back during the relevant time period.

On **May 14, 2009,** the OAL issued its Initial Decision.

On **May 26, 2009,** Dr. Costino timely filed his exceptions and proposals to the Initial Decision pursuant to N.J.A.C. 1:1-18.4.

On **June 2, 2009,** the attorney general filed its reply to Dr Costino's exceptions to the Initial Decision.

On **June 10th 2009,** Dr. Costino filed a letter brief in lieu of a more formal sur-reply brief to two issues raised in the attorney general's letter brief in response to his exceptions to the Initial Decision.

On **July 8, 2009,** the Board heard oral argument on the parties' respective positions on the initial decision.

On **July 20, 2009** in related criminal case, in the Cape May County Superior Court, Anderson certified that during the relevant time period she went to Seaport Chiropractic Center on one occasion.

On **July 29, 2009,** Counsel for Dr. Costino (for the first time) together with an assistant prosecutor and a Cape May County superior court judge reviewed "in camera" Anderson's chiropractic records which were subsequently turned over in discovery via a court order in the criminal matter.

On **August 11, 2009**, Dr. Costino filed a motion with the Board requesting, inter alia, a remand to the OAL for the purpose of supplementing it's record based on the discovery of new evidence – ie; Anderson's chiropractic records which revealed problems with her spine, neck, and back during the relevant time period.

On **September 9, 2009**, the Board heard oral argument on Dr. Costino's motion for a remand based on newly discovered evidence.

On **November 30, 2009**, the Board issued its final decision which was entered on December 21, 2009. A timely appeal followed.

# II Statement of the FACTS

On **December 13, 2005**, investigator Joseph Landis (Landis) of the Wildwood Police Department acting under the direction and supervision of the Cape May County Prosecutor's Office ( CMCPO ) – Narcotics Task Force posed as a patient addicted to heroin and attempted to get a prescription for a pain medication from appellant John G. Costino, D.O. (Dr. Costino).

Dr. Costino did not prescribe Landis any type of pain medication because he did not want Landis to kick one addiction and gain another. Landis was unaware of any individuals who had illegally received controlled substance from Dr. Costino at or near the time of his undercover visit. Dr. Costino's actions during his undercover visit were legal.

On **April 12, 2007** approximately 16 months after Landis's undercover visit, Little Egg Harbor Township Class II special police officer Tonya Anderson (Anderson) went to Dr. Costino's office posing as a dancer from Atlantic City who wanted to establish herself as a patient in order to obtain a legal prescription for

Percocet which she had been taking after her night of dancing (instead of getting same from her girlfriends). Anderson was on her feet all day, worked at least 3 to 4 nights a week (later, Anderson told Dr. Costino that she danced for 7 straight hours and danced until 6 a.m. on some evenings), took Percocet on and after the nights she worked because it helped her to get the rest on the days she was working and because "it worked for her", and denied being addicted to Percocet or any other substance (Anderson never told Dr. Costino that the only reason she was taking the Percocet was because she wanted to get "high"). The reference to "dancer" means an exotic dancer who dances on bars and poles, moves up and down on a pole, and spins, twists, turns and does other kinds of movements. People who regularly dance 10 to 12 hours routinely, suffer acute and chronic injuries which are mostly musculoskeletal in nature - ie: sprains and strains – requiring daily management. Most professional dancers are typically going to have pain due to overuse because such activity is (rigorous work).

There are no objective tests to determine if a person has pain. Pain can be masked or hidden especially when the patient is already on opiate medication. Although there could be a "complaint of pain" from the patient in order to prescribe opiate medication, some patients never use (verbalize) or even understand the word or concept of "pain" and "discomfort" due to embarrassment, culture, or other reasons.

**In fact, Dr. Jermyn, Dr. Costino's expert testified to the following:**
*Many people don't consider pain as a medical problem. I see that all the time. When you don't ask them if they're healthy, they feel that they're physically very healthy. They just have pain.* ***They disassociate it.*** *In fact, it hasn't been until last year that even the American Medical Association declared* ***pain*** *as a specialty. So, it's not uncommon that I see that, that people feel they are 100 % healthy but still have* ***pain.***

*There are two types of* ***pain:*** *neuropathic and nociceptive. Nociceptive pain is usually sprains and strains…when a physician determines a patient is suffering from Nociceptive pain, particular testing is unwarranted. For example, if there is a diagnosis of back pain without any evidence of trauma, such as falling, the* *x-rays, MRIs and EMG would be useless, because sprains and strains cannot be seen with such tests. Further, it is not uncommon for a primary care physician to find no susceptive pain without first performing a musculoskeletal examination.*

*When determining whether it is appropriate to prescribe, (and continue to prescribe) opiate medication to a patient, the physician must determine whether the patient is a drug addict or diverter, and must continually evaluate their level of functioning. (Signs of functioning include whether the patient is working and is able to continue working while on the opiate medication.)*

*Signs of addiction include whether the patient's functioning declines after taking the opiate medication, whether the patient frequently calls the office complaining they've run out of the medication, and whether the patient is receiving opiate medication from other healthcare providers. Other signs of addiction include sedation, track marks, lesions, skin-popping and a healthy vs unhealthy appearance.*

*Signs of diversion include whether the patient specifically requests only brand necessary medications (none of the prescriptions written to Anderson or DEA special agent Margarita Abbattiscianni (Abbattiscianni) stated "brand necessary" do not substitute "brand medically necessary " which meant if the prescriptions had been presented to a pharmacy they would have only receive the generic brand. Since brand only medications (such as Vicodin or Oxycontin) have a higher street value. The number one diverted drug is Vicodin because as a Schedule III Narcotic it can be called into the pharmacy, and because it is more potent than most schedule II narcotics. A person who is diverting medication will never tell a physician that they had previously been getting medication off the street. Further, a person who is diverting would request more than 30 pills of medication which is a "conservative amount".*

During the **April 12, 2007** visit, Anderson testified that Dr. Costino was able to look into her eyes and determine if they were dilated. Her upper and lower extremities, and skin surface were clear and clean as she was wearing a low cut outfit at this examination. Her station and gait were stable. She was close enough to Dr. Costino for him to smell her breath and determine that there was no odor of alcohol. (Prior to her contact with Dr. Costino, the nurse took Anderson's blood

## Chapter 15 - Preliminary Statement of the Case

pressure which was 120/68, and her weight which was 133 pounds.)

Dr. Costino testified that Anderson had a good appearance and seemed alert and awake, that her demeanor, facial expressions, language, station, gait and movements seemed normal, ("Dr. Costino's physical findings of "normal" as to Anderson's station, gait and movements was based on his assumption that she was now refreshed after taking Percocet the night before which enabled her to get a good night's sleep) and that there were no needle marks, bruises, abrasions, bumps, or contusions visible on her skin. While making these visual observations, Dr. Costino inquired into Anderson's past medical history and determined that she had no prior medical problems, however, she had had two prior breast augmentations. He also conducted a physical examination which included listening to her heart, (finding no murmurs, rubs or gallops) and chest (finding rhonchi without any wheezes or rales) and simultaneously palpitating her back (finding no signs or spasm or abnormal motion). Although Dr. Costino was able to understand everything Anderson told him during the examination, he felt that she was having difficulty expressing the impact of exotic dancing had on her physiology which caused him to render the presumptive diagnosis of thoraco-lumbar sprain and strain. His diagnosis was based in part on his opinion that she was unhappy with her physiology, that the long hours of dancing would (and did) cause muscle fatigue, ligamentus, tenderness, strain/sprain mechanisms in the long muscles of the posterior thoracic and lumbar region, lower extremities, anterior tibialus and the quadriceps, and that she was presently taking Percocet which helped her get through a night of dancing. Dr. Costino ultimately concluded that Anderson was working hard as an exotic dancer, that the Percocet she was already taking was helping her function, that she was not a drug addict or diverter, and that her physiology was consistent with an over use syndrome synonymous with sprain/strain of the thoraco-lumbar spine. Based on this diagnosis Dr. Costino determined that it was appropriate to prescribe Percocet to Anderson. He prescribed 30 pills to be taken only the nights she worked. Based on his review of the audio recordings, the transcripts, the patient records and other information, Dr. Richard Jermyn was admitted by stipulation of the parties as an expert in the examination of patients, the management of patients, the indicators and behaviors justifying the prescribing and continued prescribing of opiate medication, and his familiarity with reviewing emergency room and primary care physician patient records. Dr. Jermyn did not retain any of the fees for his testimony – all of the fees went directly to his employer. Dr. Jermyn testified in part because it's his opinion that pain management is undertreated by evidence of the lack of any pain center, program or doctor in Cape May County and that everyone (ie: all primary care physicians) should share in providing such treatment. Concluded within a reasonable degree of medical certainty that Dr. Costino's diagnosis during the April 12 2007 was proper because Anderson gave every indication of having a musculosketetal, nociceptive injury which was acute in nature. **Dr. Jermyn's conclusion remained consistent throughout his testimony.**

### Dr. Jermyn, expert witness continued…

*"I believe after reviewing the charts and after reviewing everything we talked about that Dr. Costino believed he was treating a nociceptive pain situation,* **which he documented in his chart** *as thoraco-lumbar sprain/strain, and I do believe he felt that was his diagnosis. And as a result,* **I feel it's very appropriate for Percocet to be prescribed for a very common diagnosis that is prescribed as a first line. I'm going to say it again, I believe that Dr. Costino felt that he was treating a nociceptive pain issue, and as a result the prescribing of this medication was appropriate. I feel that – and I'm going to say it again, for nociceptive pain issues Percocet is clearly appropriate.** *For the diagnosis of noncicetive pain that I believe Dr. Costino felt he was prescribing Percocet, it is appropriate.* **I believe Dr. Costino felt he had the diagnosis of thoraco-lumbar sprain/strain and a nociceptive diagnosis.**

*One Percocet is appropriate for the diagnosis. If we have this diagnosis, it's absolutely appropriate.* **Then you ask me,** *do I feel confident based on the information that I have in front of me and my conversations with Dr. Costino that he developed - did he develop a diagnosis of musculoskeletal sprain and strain?* **And I feel confident he did develop this diagnosis".**

## Chapter 15 - Preliminary Statement of the Case

The mere fact that Anderson did not have any spine issues "did not change Dr. Jermyn's opinion because said issues related in his opinion to her past medical history (that is, no previous trauma to that area of her body). Further, the mere fact that Anderson did not use the words **"pain"**, "sprain" or "strain" did not change his opinion because some patients never use (verbalize) or even understand the word or concept of "pain" or discomfort". Dr. Jermyn also concluded that it is appropriate for a physician to render a "presumptive diagnosis" (Dr. Jermyn testified that he could within a reasonable degree of medical certainty predict that a particular person could have pain based on their occupation and normal physical activities. A diagnosis of exclusion is the typical method for specialists, not primary care physicians (such as Dr. Costino) of musculoskeletal injury based on the routine physical activities of the patient. Moreover, while a pain management specialist might use anti-inflammatory medication as a first line drug in a situation such as this case, Dr. Jermyn concluded that it was (and is) appropriate for a primary care physician (if Anderson presented herself to an emergency room the same way she presented to Dr. Costino, she would have walked away with a prescription for Percocet and a shot of Dilaudid). To prescribe Percocet as a first line drug and it is not uncommon to prescribe it at nighttime to help a patient sleep because interrupted sleep can make pain much worse. The physician's desk reference (the PDR) clearly states that the physiologic effect of Percocet is analgesia and sedation. Additionally, it was appropriate to prescribe Anderson a 7.5mg does of Percocet (in 2007 Percocet came in strengths of 5, 7.5, and 10mg.

Dr. Costino billed a "99204" for his visit with Anderson (a new patient) on **April 12, 2007**. A physician is permitted to bill either on history, evaluation and management (HEM) or on time. When a physician bills on HEM, the physician must satisfy the criteria set forth in the Center for Medicare and Medicaid services (CMS) guidelines in order to determine the appropriate code to bill for a visit with a new or established patient. When a physician bills on time, (it is well established that psychiatrists are the physicians who primarily bill on time whereas almost all other physicians bill on HEM). There are guidelines which recommend the number of minutes the physician should spend with a new or established patient in order to determine the appropriate code to bill for the visit. The level of the code – which can be either a "1", "2", "3", "4" or "5" – determines the amount of reimbursement a physician will expect to receive from a third party payer.

In order to bill for a level 3 visit on a new patient when using HEM, the physician must establish four or more of the eight elements of the history of present illness, conduct a review between two to nine of the 14 organ systems (most physicians tend to forget to conduct and separately document a review of organ systems since they have already examined same). And inquire into one of the three past medical, family, social history areas the physician must conduct an examination of at least seven of the 14 organ systems. (For example, "the constitutional organ system is a patient's appearance and /or vitals (height, weight, blood pressure and pulse), the "cardiovascular" organ system is a patient's heart (regular rate and rhythm, no sounds), and the "respiratory " organ system is a patient's lungs, and the physician must make a medical decision of low complexity.

In order to bill for a level 4 visit on a new patient when using HEM, the physician must establish four or more of the eight elements of the history of present illness, conduct a review of all of the fourteen organ systems, and inquire into two of the three past medical, family, social history areas; the physician must conduct an examination of at least eight of the fourteen organ systems and the physicians must make a medical decision of moderate complexity. In short, to bill for a level four visit on such a patient the physician must have completed a comprehensive history, and conducted a comprehensive examination.

**Glenda Hamilton,** an expert in coding testified that when she shadows physicians as part of her responsibilities, she discovered that they do not always document what they observe which effects the code that should be billed. Mrs. Hamilton concluded that Dr. Costino used HEM billing on each and every visit with Anderson. According to Mrs. Hamilton, a level 3 was proper because Dr. Costino established a detailed history of present illness (Anderson had been on her feet all day which can hurt your lumbosacral spine), conducted a review of at least two the constitutional organ system" was reviewed as Anderson's blood pressure was 120/68 and her weight was 133 lbs, and the cardiovascular organ system was reviewed when he listened to her heart, and the respiratory organ system was reviewed when he listened to her chest) of the 14 organ systems, and inquired into one of he three past medical, family, social history areas (Anderson had no medical ailments or problems such as asthma, heart disease and lung disease, she had 2 prior breast surgeries, and she denied being a drinker but admitted to being a smoker). Further, he conducted a detailed examination. Physicians make a lot of findings i.e. as to the patient's extremities, their neurology and their psychology - based purely on what they observe which is within the standard of care. Further, a diagnosis and physical examination can be and are often one in the same. Because he not only examined the constitutional, cardiovascular and respiratory organ systems but also examined Anderson's "eyes" (not dilated). "Integumentary" skin – no needle marks, bruises, abrasions, bumps or contusions visible, and psychological good appearance, seemed alert and awake, and facial expressions and language seemed normal. Finally, the medical decision-making was of moderate complexity since he prescribed her a controlled substance. Prescribing a controlled substance requires moderate decision-making.

On May 2, 2008, a nurse took Anderson's blood pressure which was 120 over 70 – weight which was 130 lbs., temperature which was 98.6 and pulse which was 68. Anderson advised Dr. Costino that the Percocet was "helping her". During this visit Dr. Costino testified that Anderson's affect, demeanor, language and movements seemed normal, that her posture and functioning were good, there were no lumps or bruises visible on her skin, and that there were no antecubital issues edema or erythema. The physical finding he made of Anderson during the first and second visits were the same findings he made of her during the third fourth, fifth sixth and seventh visits. He also conducted the same physical examinations on this visit and subsequent visits as he did on the initial visits and his findings remain the same for each visit. Because the Percocet helped Anderson continue working as an exotic dancer and because there was no evidence that she was a drug addict or diverter, Dr. Costino concluded that it was appropriate to continue prescribing her the medication. Dr. Costino's medical rationale for the prescribing and continued prescribing of Percocet to Anderson during the first and second visits remained the same for all of he subsequent visits. Dr. Jermyn concluded that it was appropriate to continue prescribing the medication to Anderson. She was working more hours which confirmed that her functioning improved and the treatment plan was working.

Dr. Costino billed a 99214 for the visit of **May 2, 2007.**

On **June 7, 2007**, the patient arrived in Dr. Costino's office, and she was presented with the "Pain Management Agreement" which in summary prohibited her from sharing medications with others, or using other practitioners for pain management, and which provided information regarding the use of pain medication. Dr. Costino has all of his pain management patients sign this "Pain Management Agreement" when he determines that the patient will remain under his regular care. After reading and signing this agreement, Anderson never told Dr. Costino that she wanted to revoke, rescind, or withdraw from his pain management agreement", leaving him to believe that she was abiding by all of the terms and conditions in this agreement. Anderson was then escorted to the examination room where she advised Dr. Costino that she had been much more active as a dancer and that "things are picking up now". Dr. Costino billed a "99213' for this visit with Anderson on June 7, 2007.

Anderson presented again to Dr. Costino on **June 26, 2007** and billed a "99214" for this visit which Mrs. Hamilton, the coding expert, concluded that the documentation by Dr. Costino for this visit was proper. He conducted a detailed examination and his decision-making was of moderate complexity.

Anderson re-presented to Dr. Costino's office on **July 13, 2007**, and advised Dr. Costino that she was very, very busy as her dancing requirement was 7 nights per week during these summer months. Dr. Costino billed a "99213" for this visit as he conducted a detailed examination when he examined her constitutional, and cardiovascular organ systems, and the medical decision-making was of moderate complexity.

On **July 26, 2007**, Anderson sought medical treatment from Dr. Joseph

# Chapter 15 - Preliminary Statement of the Case

O'Rourke, her chiropractor at Seaport Chiropractic Center. At this visit, with Dr. O'Rourke, Anderson described her "major complaint" as being upper back, neck, right shoulder, and extremities. She further stated to Dr. O'Rourke that sleep worsens her condition, and that her discomfort and pain "comes and goes", and interferes with her daily routine. Regarding her symptoms explained by Anderson to Dr. O'Rourke and clearly explained in his notes, she described neck pain and stiffness, pain between her shoulders, and sciatica. She further explained that her discomfort at times is constant.

**Dr. O'Rourke made a diagnosis which are clear in his notes of the following:**

> **Subluxation of the cervical region (739.1),**
> **Cervicalgia (723.1),**
> **Subluxation of the thoracic region (739.2),**
> **Thoracic spine pain (721.1),**
> **Subluxation lumbar region (739.3),**
> **Lumbar muscle spasm (728.285).**

His subjective findings reveal clearly in his notes the following:
> **Paravertible muscle spasms,**
> **decreased range of motion,**
> **inflammation, with normal gait, and normal ambulation**.

Dr. O'Rourke's specific findings on **July 26, 2007** revealed **cervical sharp pain, local and radiating, constant. Thoracic sharp pain local and radiating, constant. lumbar dull pain intermittent.**

**These findings of Dr. O'Rourke ultimately mirrored those of Dr. Costino, and would have completely supported Dr. Costino's diagnosis of Anderson.**

On **August 3, 2007**, Anderson was again examined in Dr. Costino's office. In addition to Anderson, her roommate, whose proper name was Margarita Abbattiscianni (A.K.A. Maggie Ortiz) also presented to Dr. Costino. When Dr. Costino said to Abbattiscianni, "what's wrong, Maggie?" her answer was, "it's just the **pain** and I'm up all night until 6 a.m.". Neither Anderson nor Abbattiscianni had a problem with Dr. Costino examining them both in the same room, and in fact, they requested to be in the same examining room during the visit. Abbattiscianni acknowledged that she did use the word **"pain"** even though the goal was for her not to mention it. The reference to "striper" means a person who dances on poles, takes her clothes off, moves up and down, hangs upside down on a pole, moves her neck, back, arms, and legs, and assumes all different positions, works long evening hours. According to the DEA, the profession of "stripper" was chosen because such a profession would be easier to obtain a prescription for pain medication. At the visit of Aug 3, 2007, Anderson's history evaluation and treatment was similar to her prior visits. Abbattiscianni testified that Dr. Costino was able to look into her eyes, to determine if they were dilated, her skin surfaces and body parts were clearly visible and there was no evidence of any edema, erythema, bumps, bruises or needle marks. Dr. Costino was close enough to smell her breath to determine any evidence of alcohol. Dr. Costino testified that Abbattiscianni's language was stable, her demeanor and facial expressions were normal, and her pupils were equal, and her movements, gait and station were stable. Examination of her heart and lungs revealed no evidence of murmurs, rubs, or gallops, and her chest sounds were clear. Abbattiscianni's past medical history was unremarkable, and she was a stable, healthy female. Based upon Abbattiscianni's complain of **"pain"** together with the fact she was working long hours as a stripper and that she had no evidence of drug addiction or diversion, Dr. Costino determined that it was appropriate to prescribe Percocet, 1 tablet, following her night of dancing. Dr. Jermyn, the Pain Management expert, concluded that it **was appropriate** to prescribe Percocet to Abbattiscianni at this visit, as there was no evidence of aberrant behavior.

During the **August 3, 2007** visit with Dr. Costino, he received a telephone call from K-Mart pharmacy which was picked up by the audio recordings of both

## Chapter 15 - Preliminary Statement of the Case

females and wherein the following exchange occurred:
K-mart pharmacy called Dr. Costino's office and wanted to make him aware that a prescription that he had written looked suspicious.

Dr. Costino's response to the pharmacist at Kmart was the following:

*Dr. Costino:* *"I'm certain that I did not order that. When did he have it filed last? He's a clever little creature isn't he? I don't want you to fill that prescription. I don't want you to give it back to the patient. I want you the pharmacist to tell the patient that you called me and these are my instructions. Furthermore, tell the patient I don't want to see him any longer as a patient. Thank you very much, incidentally, what is your name?"*

**Response:** *"Diane".*

*Dr. Costino:* *"Well you know it is very important to keep track of these things, to keep good records, because every now and then, you know, someone tried to slip something through." You know what I'm saying, Diane." You have your computer in front of you and that's excellent. Well, see. That's important. He does have ADHD, but that's no excuse. Thank you very much. Bye-bye."*

Dr. Costino testified that this is one of many telephone calls that he receives from pharmacies where there is an issue with a medication, or a prescription that he has written, and that he relies on such calls to ensure that patients are receiving the proper medication and doing the right thing.

Dr. Jermyn concluded that the aforesaid telephone conversation is and excellent example of the TEAM APPROACH that is necessary to identify diversionary and or drug addicted behaviors, and of Dr. Costino's ability to properly manage any situation of aberrant behavior.

On **August 23, 2007**, both Anderson and Abbattiscianni presented to Dr. Costino's office. Both advised Dr. Costino that they were still very, very busy, but would be taking "the show" on the road to Florida. "The Show" referred to their exotic dancing. During this visit, Anderson and Abbattiscianni attempted to solicit Oxycontin from Dr. Costino, however, he resisted their efforts admonished both of them regarding the use of Oxycontin, and did not prescribe it to them. Dr. Jermyn concluded that Dr. Costino's decision not to prescribe Oxycontin to Anderson and Abbattiscianni demonstrated very good judgment on his part.

On **December 5, 2007**, approximately 3 months after the final undercover visit, the NJ State Board of Medical Examiners filed a 2 count verified complaint against Dr. Costino. On December 10, 2007 Dr. Costino filed an answer to the verified complaint.

On **December 20, 2007,** after conducting a hearing 8 days earlier, the Board issued an order **temporarily suspending Dr. Costino's license effective as of December 17, 2007.**

On **July 29, 2008** the Office of Administrative Law (OAL) issued an order requiring the Board to disclose relevant adult medical records of Anderson and Abbattiscianni.

On **September 10, 2008** the Board heard oral argument on the attorney general's request for interlockatory review of the OAL's order of July 29, 2008. During the aforesaid hearing, counsel for Dr. Costino argued INNER ALIA that:

"And if I can use a little analogy. When you have a drug case and the FBI or the State Police in New Jersey have an informant, they're going to send that information in to go meet with the target, they may check them, make sure they have nothing on them. Then they go in, then they go out, if they have drugs on them, they take the drugs and they know that the drugs had to come from whoever it was in that room. In this particular case, I haven't seen anything in the investigative files of any kind that somebody went out, examined these people

## Chapter 15 - Preliminary Statement of the Case

and determined to 100% that they were 100% healthy people. That there was absolutely nothing wrong with them of any kind whatsoever, nothing. So, in this case, for whatever reason, they are masquerading as exotic dancers, up long hours, on their feet, obviously if you're an exotic dancer you're not just standing there. You're twisting, you're turning and doing whatever we all know what they would be doing, obviously. And then they come in with these types of subjective complaints."

When the issue turned on the efficacy of simply cross-examining the undercover agents about their medical condition during their depositions, counsel for Dr. Costino argued inter allia that:

"In terms of the deposition, you can ask questions at a deposition. What was suggested to me was that I ask the questions going back the last 6 months with regard to this. But there is no substitution for the actual records themselves, especially when you are dealing with law enforcement personnel. I don't want to say anything beyond that. But what happens is when you end up in a case and it becomes adversarial, I've had instances where, particularly in criminal cases, where there's criminal charges that are pending, where you find out later that there's documents that weren't turned over, even though in a criminal case the government has an affirmative obligation to do that. "

**Based on the aforesaid argument, a member of the board asked:**

**Question:** "Are you indicating that you have a concern that if one of these two undercover agents asks a question at a deposition, that they will not give you an honest response?"

**Answer by Mr. Zeitz:** "I'm saying the following: that I've had cases where I've had instances where people's memory is selective. I'm not making any aspirations about these two people. I'm just saying over 36 years of practice, I've had cases, without getting into them, some of which are reported federally and state, in this state, where law enforcement personnel have not turned over documents under "Brady" which they were required to. Cases I've got overturned on appeal because people didn't do what they were supposed to do in law enforcement. And sometimes, if I had the opportunity, I could give you chapter and verse. And particularly, in this state, had some of the biggest cases that were ever tried here. They were overturned because of the failure of law enforcement to turn over documents that they were mandated to turn over, let alone a situation where we're tallying about a situation, where there is going, where we're hoping for an order." When the issue is turned on the state for the honest representation of the undercover witness, the following exchange confirms the seriousness of the withheld medical records."

**Dr. Criscito states**, "I can represent to the Board that I asked both of the undercover witnesses whether they have had any back or neck injuries. They have indicated to me that they have not and they will testify in accordance with that under oath. At the depositions, if that is allowed within the scope of the deposition."

**Mr. Zeitz:** "Well let me say, I would never, I mean, a lawyer makes a representation, that's fine. You know one thing I've learned over 36 years, and I'm sure David has to acknowledge and any of the lawyers that are here, is that we don't know what the facts are. You know, we are told things by people and then we can make a representation based on what we are told. Is it always correct? I don't' think any lawyer who's ever practiced long enough could say that every time they talked to somebody and they made a representation that it turned out that what they were told was one hundred percent correct. So I don't question Mr. Puteska's integrity. But from my standpoint, he's not going to be on the stand, it's going to be them. And they're law enforcement personnel and they're adversaries. And the way that, in an adversarial system you get to the truth is by testing, and getting documents, and that's what we're asking for. The mere fact that somebody can make a statement to the lawyer and say, "Well, I've never had this problem or that problem." I can I'm sure. What he is saying right now is based on what he was told. I don't question him (meaning Puteska), but I have a right and absolute duty as a lawyer to question the people who were involved in this investigation. And those records, if there are records, should be produced."

## Chapter 15 - Preliminary Statement of the Case

**In re-emphasizing the need for actual records (over a mere representation from the witness or counsel) counsel for Dr. Costino argued inter allia that:**

**Mr. Zeitz:** "There is a legitimate basis for the production of these records and for a judge to conduct an "in-camera inspection". And you know what? You know, later on in life if it turns out that you find out, how many times have you read in the newspaper, for example, about a case where something surfaces later, and it turned out that something was withheld? It would require the attorney general, which is not that difficult, to obtain through witnesses, records. Turn them over to the judge, how do I know right now, that what's being represented to the attorney general is correct? Would you like to at least let your freedom, or your license, rest on a law enforcement officer believing one hundred percent that in no way shape or form, she would mislead anybody? I've seen it happen enough times. I'm not, as a lawyer, going to be in a situation where at least on behalf of my client being in a position where I'd rely purely on their word alone."

**The Board of Medical Examiners then went into their executive session, and issued an order requiring the undercover agents to disclose any medical problems that they had with the spine, neck or back from April 12, 2006 – August 23, 2007.**

### On September 19, 2008

Anderson **certified** in the (OAL) that "*from the time period of **April 12, 2006** through and including August 23, 2007, I did not have any medical problems related to the cervical spine, thoracic spine or lumbar spine, and that the foregoing statements* **made by me are true and that I am aware that if any of the forgoing statement s made by me are willfully false I am subject to punishment.*

### On December 4, 2008

Anderson was placed under oath before the (OAL) judge and testified at the trial in this matter. When describing her physical condition during her visit, Anderson testified that:

> Q: When you were sent to see Dr. Costino on April 12, 2007, did you have any back or neck injuries?
> A: No.
>
> Q: Did you have any neck or back *pain* or discomfort?
> A: No.
>
> Q: During the visit were you asked about any back or neck *pain?*
> A: Yes.
>
> Q: What was your response?
> A: That I had none.
>
> Q: Did you at any time during your physical with Dr. Costino on April 12, mention any problems with your neck or back?
> A: No.
>
> Q: Did you have any *pain* in your neck or back at that time?
> A: No.

When Anderson was asked if she understood the medical terms verses the layman terms concerning her neck and back she answered in the affirmative. The witness touched her neck, from the base of her skull down to her shoulder region.

When asked relative to her thoracic and lumbar region, Anderson answered affirmatively the thoracic spine is actually from where the cervical spine ends down to the lumbar region. And the lumbar spine is from the end of the thoracic spine down to the region of the hips.

# Chapter 15 - Preliminary Statement of the Case

On **May 14, 2009,** the OAL judge issued his initial decision.

On **May 26, 2009,** Dr. Costino timely filed his exceptions and proposals to the initial decision pursuant to N.J.A.C. 1:1-18.4.

On **June 2, 2009,** the attorney general, Puteska, filed his reply to Dr. Costino's exceptions to the initial decision.

On **June 10, 2009,** Dr. Costino filed a letter brief in lieu of a more formal sur – reply brief to two issues raised in the attorney general's letter brief response to this exception to the initial decision.

On **July 8, 2009** the B.M.E. heard oral argument on the parties respective positions on the initial decision.

On **July 20, 2009**, in a related criminal case in Cape May county superior court, Anderson further certified "from April 12, 2005 through and including August 23, 2007, I went to **Seaport Chiropractic Center** on one occasion, and also during the aforementioned time. I saw Dr. William Glenn for an annual physical."

On **July 29, 2009**, counsel for Dr. Costino (for the first time) together with Assistant Prosecutor and Cape May County superior court Judge Batten, reviewed "in-camera" Anderson's chiropractic records which were subsequently turned over in discovery via a court order by Judge Batten in the criminal matter.

On **July 30, 2009,** counsel for Dr. Costino sent correspondence to DAG David Puteska that "I am now in receipt of newly discovered evidence which I believe is relevant material that has the potential to effect the outcome of the case against Dr. Costino. "This evidence should have been turned over to me prior to the administrative hearing (OAL) pursuant to the order of the BME, and that this evidence is critical to this matter and involves false swearing and perjury by your star witness, Anderson.

DAG Puteska responded:

Last week assistant Cape May County prosecutor Megan Hoerner informed me that officer Anderson had informed her that in the summer of 2007, officer Anderson had a shoulder problem related to her childcare and visited a chiropractor. "This was the first time I learned of this issue." As you may recall, the Board required officer Anderson to certify that she had no back or neck injuries from one year prior to and during the undercover visits. Officer provided such a certification. This certification remains accurate as a shoulder injury is not the neck or back. Moreover, in reviewing the transcript of officer Anderson's testimony before AOL Judge Miller, I could find no reference to you asking her about a shoulder injury, or any other medical issue beyond her neck or back."

**In response to DAG Puteska's letter, counsel for Dr. Costino sent correspondence to the deputy attorney representing The Board during it's executive sessions advising that:**

Mr. Puteska is sadly misinformed. The medical records relate to complaints over and above supposed shoulder problem. They are directly related to the diagnosis of Dr. Costino, and occur during the time period of the undercover visits. Their content is contrary to both the sworn certification of Tonya Anderson and her testimony under oath before Judge Miller which was false.

Mr. Puteska confirmed that he is willing to defer to you on how this matter should be handled procedurally. I am writing to request that the final order of The Board not be entered. I intend to file a motion to reopen the record and have further proceedings before a second administrative law judge to present these medical records, and additional testimony and witnesses regarding same.

**A failure by the Board** to at least review and consider medical evidence wrongly withheld (after a Board order) that goes to the heart of the case against Dr. Costino **clearly an abuse of discretion.**

## Chapter 15 - Preliminary Statement of the Case

Consequently, I request an extension to file a motion to delay the filing of a final order until the Board reviewed and ruled upon my motion to reopen this matter for a limited evidentiary hearing so that I may present the newly discovered evidence and relevant testimony thereto.

As an officer of the court, you have an **obligation to correct false testimony,** to investigate **false swearing,** and to ensure that proceedings before the Board adhere to substantive and procedural process.

On **August 11, 2009,** Dr. Costino filed a motion with the Board requiring a remand to the OAL for the purpose of supplementing the record based upon the discovery of new evidence.

On **September 9, 2009,** the Board of Medical Examiners heard oral argument on Dr. Costino's motion for a remand based upon newly discovery evidence.

On **November 30. 2009,** the Board issued its final decision which was entered on December 21, 2009.

This timely appeal followed.

## Legal Argument:

The New Jersey State Board of Medical Examiners (The Board) **abused their discretion by denying** appellate Dr. John G. Costino's request for a **remand** to the Office of Administrative Law (OAL) for the limited purpose of confronting the key prosecution witness against Dr. Costino and calling said witness's chiropractor, Dr. O'Rourke as a defense witness based upon the post trial discovery i.e. after the OAL had issued it's initial decision, but before the Board had issued it's final decision, of evidence previously subject to a Board order that **the prosecution witness had committed false swearing and perjury**, when she certified, and later testified, that she had no problems whatsoever with her neck, back, or spine, while under Dr. Costino's care which the witness knew to be false and which would have materially supported Dr. Costino's defense that the witness was suffering neck and back **pain** warranting the prescribing of Percocet.

To qualify as newly discovered evidence entitling a party to a new trial, (or remand), the new evidence must be one (1) material to the issue and not merely cumulative or impeaching or contradictory; (2) discovered since the trial and not discoverable by reasonable diligence beforehand; (3) of the sort that would probably change the outcome. A motion for a new trial or remand in a civil case should be granted "when that evidence would probably alter judgment and by due diligence could not have been discovered before the court announced it's decision. " Material evidence is any evidence that would have some bearing on the claims being advanced. Evidence that supports a defense is clearly material. Further, when evidence relates "directly to the focal issues of the trial" it will be deemed material. Moreover, newly discovered evidence that would impeach and powerfully undermine the credibility of the prosecutor's principal witness will warrant a new trial or remand. Because there was no dispute that the second Carter Factor (the new evidence was discovered since the trial and not discoverable by reasonable diligence beforehand) has been satisfied, only first and third Carter Factors need to be addressed.

In this case, Anderson's chiropractic records are clearly material because they support Dr Costino's defense that she was suffering neck and back pain since his subjective findings were corroborated by Anderson's actual doctor (Dr. O'Rourke) during the relevant time period. Further, Anderson's chiropractic records relate "directly to the focal issue of the trial", which is Anderson's medical condition during each of her seven visits with Dr. Costino. Additionally, Anderson's chiropractic records would impeach and powerfully undermine her credibility which both the Office of Administrative Law (OAL) and the Board have in essence found to be without reproach. It is well recognized that a false certification can subject the affiant to the criminal offenses of perjury and false swearing.

With respect to altering the outcome, it is clear by virtue of the Board's order requiring the production of "any medical history, injury, or medical condition involving the cervical thoracic or lumbar spine for visits occurring within one year prior to the first undercover visit of each officer, and for the period of each undercover officer's visits that the existence of any such history, injuries, or condition of either undercover officer had the capacity to alter the finding on whether Dr. Costino's medical decision making was appropriate. It is extremely disingenuous for the Board to now summarily find that Anderson's chiropractic records would not change the result reached in this matter. That whether Anderson actually had any condition is not significant in the circumstances of this matter, and that Anderson's actual condition "is of little relevance to her initial presentation to Dr. Costino". The **quantum leap the Board has taken from initially finding that the actual medical condition of the undercover agents during the relevant time period was material to Dr. Costino's defense whereby warranting the pretrial disclosure of same, to now finding the exact opposite only underscores it's bias and prejudice toward Dr. Costino as the Board had intended all along to find him guilty of the charges in the verified complaint regardless of the evidence present, and revoke his license to practice medicine.**

With respect to altering the outcome, it is clear by virtue of the Board's order requiring the production of "any medical history, injury, or medical condition involving the cervical, thoracic or lumbar spine, for visits occurring within one year prior to the first undercover visit of each officer and for the period of each undercover officer's visits".

That the existence of any such history, injury, or condition of either undercover officer had the capacity to alter the finding on whether Dr. Costino's medical decision-making was appropriate, i**t is extremely disingenuous for The Board to now summarily find that Anderson's chiropractic records "would not change the result reached in this matter"; that "whether Anderson actually had any conditions is not significant in the circumstances of this matter"; and that Anderson's actual condition "is of little relevance to her initial presentation to Dr. Costino".**

# "Due Process" Denied

**The quantum leap the Board has taken from initially finding that the actual medical condition of the undercover agents during the relevant time period was material to Dr. Costino's defense thereby warranting the pretrial disclosure of same, to now finding the exact opposite only underscores it's bias and prejudice towards Dr. Costino as the Board had intended all along to find him guilty of the egregious charges in the verified complaint regardless of the evidence present, and revoke his license to practice medicine.**

**The Board abused it's discretion by finding that Dr. Costino had committed the allegations contained in the verified complaint since such a finding was not based on competent, credible and substantial evidence.**

On appeal from administrative determination, the standard of review is whether there is sufficient, credible evidence in the record supporting the determination.

**1. Both the initial decision and the final decision are seemingly based on the flawed premise that both Anderson and Abbattiscianni clearly presented themselves as drug addicts or diverters which made Dr. Costino's discretion to prescribe them pain medication grossly inappropriate.**

Both the initial decision and the final decision are seemingly based on the **flawed premise** that both Anderson and Abbattiscianni clearly presented themselves as drug addicts or diverters which made Dr. Costino's decision to prescribe them pain medication grossly inappropriate. **The aforesaid premise is flawed because it is not based upon competent, credible, or substantial evidence. Instead, the record supports just the opposite.**

**Neither Anderson nor Abbattiscianni presented as a drug addict.** Anderson never told Dr. Costino that the only reason she was taking Percocet was because she wanted to get "high". In fact, Anderson denied being addicted to Percocet or any other substances. Anderson and Abbattiscianni did not have any other prescription filled at a pharmacy which would have alerted Dr. Costino

## Chapter 15 - Preliminary Statement of the Case

to any aberrant behavior on their part, so that he could take proper action as he demonstrated with the Kmart pharmacy soliloquy during the visit of August 3, 2007. Additionally, neither Anderson nor Abbattiscianni had decreased functioning after taking the Percocet. They never called Dr. Costino's office claiming to have run out of medicine, there was no evidence that they were receiving opiate medication from other healthcare providers, and they did not present as sedated or with any track marks, lesions, skin popping, or other signs of an unhealthy appearance. Further, their station, gait, and movements were "normal" which was based on Dr. Costino's assumption that they were refreshed after taking Percocet the night before which enabled them to get a good night's sleep.

**Moreover, neither Anderson nor Abbattiscianni presented as a diverter**. Neither of them ever asked for brand necessary medications which have a higher street value and none of the prescriptions written to them stated brand necessary, or do not substitute. Anderson actually signed Dr. Costino's **"Pain Management Agreement"** which among it's many provisions prohibited her from sharing medications with others or using other practitioners for pain management and which provided information relative to the use of pain medication. Anderson never told Dr. Costino that she wanted to revoke, rescind, or withdraw from this pain management agreement leaving him to believe that she was abiding by all of his terms and conditions. A person who is diverting medication will never relate to a physician that they had previously been receiving the medication "off the street", namely **Percocet**, as both Anderson and Abbattiscianni had told Dr. Costino. Further, a person who is diverting would certainly request more than 30 pills, the equivalent of one month of medication.

Additionally, the functioning of Anderson and Abbattiscianni ostensively improved while under the care of Dr. Costino. Signs of functioning include whether the patient is working, and is able to continue working while on the opiate medication. Anderson advised Dr. Costino more than once that the Percocet was "helping" her, that things are "picking up now" and that she was "very, very busy." On their last visit, both Anderson and Abbattiscianni advised Dr. Costino that they were still very busy and would be taking "the show on the road" to Florida. This confirms at least in Dr. Costino's mind, that the treatment plan was working well. In sum, there was, and is, simply no evidence supporting even a mere inference, (let alone a factual finding) that Dr. Costino knew or should have known Anderson or Abbattiscianni were drug addicts or diverters which would form the basis to them, find that prescribing them (as addicts or diverters) pain medication to be grossly inappropriate.

**2. The initial decision understates and the final decision completely omits the context in which Anderson and Abbattiscianni presented themselves to Dr. Costino which clearly effects a fair determination on the appropriateness of his conduct.**

**The initial decision understates the final decision (nowhere in the final decision does the Board mention, even once, that Anderson and Abbattiscianni were posing as dancers (or strippers) who had told Dr. Costino that they were taking Percocet only after the nights they worked because it helped them get up and do it ( ie: dance another long night "all over again".), completely omits the context in which Anderson and Abbattiscianni present themselves to Dr. Costino which clearly effects a fair determination on the appropriateness of his conduct.**

**Dr. Jermyn** testified that a physician could within a reasonable degree of certainty that a particular person could have pain based upon their occupation and normal physical activities, and that it is not uncommon to find *nociceptive pain* without first performing a musculoskeletal examination. The decision to use undercover agents posing as exotic dancers (strippers) from Atlantic City who previously used medication to cope with the side effects of working long hours while on their feet all night instead of posing them as clerical workers (or some other profession that does not involve they type of strenuous physical activity one would naturally and reasonable attribute to an exotic dancer (who never used medication before and worked normal hours while sitting behind a desk all day was clearly designed **to make it virtually impossible for Dr. Costino (or any other physician) to uncover the state's deceitful and fraudulent conduct.** The Board's decision to omit (and therefore disregard) this relevant and material information from the final decision further underscores **it's biases and prejudices** towards Dr. Costino *as the Board had intended all along to find him* **guilty** *of the charges in the verified complaint regardless of the evidence presented, and* **revoke** *his medical license for five years.*

### 3. The initial decision understates and the final decision completely omits the context in which Anderson and Abbattiscianni presented themselves to Dr. Costino which clearly effects a fair determination on the appropriateness of his conduct.

The initial decision and the final decision conclude that Dr. Costino's conduct was reckless and cumulatively amounts to gross negligence is belied by the substantial evidence. First, it is not uncommon to prescribe Percocet at nighttime to help the patient sleep because interrupted sleep can make pain much worse. The Physician's Desk Reference clearly states that the physiologic effect of Percocet is analgesia and sedation. Further, Abbattiscianni clearly used the word "**pain**" during her initial visit, and Anderson was (despite falsely certifying and testifying to the contrary) actually was suffering from similar ailments that Dr. Costino had diagnosed during the relevant time period.

Second, Dr. Costino did not misrepresent the truth or conceal any material fact to induce anyone to act to their detriment. Because Anderson and Abbattiscianni were acting under the direction and supervision of the Cape May County Prosecutor's Office (CMCPO), it is factually impossible for any of Dr. Costino's conduct to be construed as causing them to act to their detriment. He did not give false impression to anyone nor did he make any false or misleading statements, and none of the statements he did make were intended to deceive anyone. With respect to the insurance company, it is clear from **Mrs. Hamilton's** testimony, the billing expert, that Dr. Costino was at all times billing on history evaluation and management (HEM), and not "time " making the issue of face to face minutes spent with Anderson during each visit completely irrelevant. It is also clear from **Mrs. Hamilton's** testimony that physicians with a vintage predating 1995 (such as Dr. Costino) commonly make innocent mistakes when selecting the billing coding level on new and established patients. Further, the difference in payments between a level 3 and a level 4 is less than $20 per visit. The net gain or loss in this entire case is ZERO. **Mrs. Hamilton** testified that two of the visits were upcoded and two of the visits were downcoded. **The total amount of reimbursement that Dr. Costino received for all of Anderson's office visits was $483.45 representing five and one half months of treatment.**

Third, there was no evidence that any of Dr. Costino's actions either individually or cumulatively could be construed as gross negligence. Anderson's diagnosis was based in part on Dr. Costino's good faith opinion that she was unhappy with her physiology, and that the long hours of dancing would (and did) cause her muscle and ligamentus fatigue, muscle tenderness, and strain and sprain mechanism in the muscular structures of the thoracic and lumbar region. Abbattiscianni's diagnosis was based in part on her complaint of **"pain"** together with the fact that she worked long hours till 6 a.m. as a stripper. Dr. Costino was ultimately convinced that both Anderson and Abbattiscianni were working hard as exotic dancers, and that the Percocet assisted them in this function, and that they certainly were not drug addicts or diverters. Their physiology was consistent with an overuse syndrome synonymous with typical strain and sprain mechanism of the thoraco-lumbar spine. Because Dr. Costino ultimately determined that they were suffering from nociceptive pain (strains and sprains) which was not caused by any trauma, particular testing such as X-rays, MRIs and EMGs were not only *unwarranted* but were also *useless* since this diagnosis cannot be seen with such testing.

Fourth, it was (and is, reasonably foreseeable that a physician would at a minimum, would presume that a person who routinely dances, moves up and down and hangs upside down on a pole, takes her clothes off, moves her neck back arms, and legs, spins, twists, turns and does other kinds of movements, assumes all different positions, and works long hours would at least have some pain and discomfort due to overuse, wear and tear, from such long and rigorous physical activity and that an opiate medication such as Percocet should be prescribed to relieve her symptoms. The aforesaid presumption is only reinforced when a physician raised certain inferences about the patient's medical condition during

## Chapter 15 - Preliminary Statement of the Case

the visit, and the patient does not tell the physician that each and every inference was incorrect or otherwise baseless. In this case there were several such instances including but not limited to the following:

These words are taken directly from the **medical office transcripts** of **Anderson and Abbattiscianni as UC1 & UC2**:

**JC:** I guess when you're done with a night of dancing you're kind of sore?

**UCI:** I am. Uh-uh.

**JC:** Just take it when you're done your work, you know, It will just relax you and it takes the pain away.

**UC2:** Uh-hm. Uh-hm.

**JC:** You know I'm sure you get these acute strains and sprains and this and that.

**UC2:** You know I'm pretty flexible so not so much "pain". I do a lot of exercise.

**JC:** Well the commercial would say oxycontin is longer acting. The fact of the matter it's not that much longer acting if you want to know the truth and that's why we reserve it for people who have significant problems, which you do not.

**UC1:** Um- hum.

**JC:** You know, not just some "pain."

**UC1:** Right.

**UC2:** Um-hum.

**JC:** (relating to Percocet) This is a nice product, you know for individuals like yourself, you do what you do for so many hours, six, seven hours.

**UC2:** Yeah.

**UC1:** About that. About seven hours.

**JC:** And you know it's just fatigue it wears on your legs, your back, your neck etc, etc. So something like this (Percocet) will soothe that pain you see, which is very nice. You get into those longer acting products, and you're just working on a trail of addiction which you don't want to get involved with. Now believe me when I tell you, you really don't want to do that. So you know, just take one a day (Percocet) take it when you're done your night of dancing.

**UC2:** Ok.

**UC1:** Isn't it…it is…it's like, not that same drug?

**UC2:** I've taken a few pills, in fact.

**JC:** I'm sure.

**UC2:** And it did work much quicker than the Percocet.

**JC:** Well, this one works quicker and that one works longer.

**UC1:** Longer?

**UC2:** Yeah, right, I guess so, so it's not much better.

**UC1:** Where do you get up in four hours and have to take another one to get back to sleep?

**JC:** You really don't want to get involved in that.

Anderson's and Abbattiscianni's tacit acknowledgement that some of Dr. Costino's inferences about their medical condition namely **pain, fatigue and interrupted sleep**, were **correct** only **reinforced** his presumptive diagnosis of sprain and strain mechanism. Further, it is clear from Abbattiscianni's testimony that she and Anderson intentionally posed as strippers because of the belief that a physician would be more likely to prescribe a medication to someone who's typical activities were rigorous in nature rather than someone who's typical activities were sedentary. **It is also clear from Landis's "testimony" that Dr. Costino was not predisposed to illegally prescribing controlled substances to patients simply because they came into his office and requested same**. Based upon the forgoing, there is **no proof whatsoever** that Dr. Costino's conduct constituted gross negligence.

**4. The initial decision and the final decision conclusion that Dr. Costino's conduct constitutes repeated acts of negligence is belied by the substantial evidence.**

The Seventh Edition of Black's Law Dictionary defines the term "negligence" as the failure to exercise the standard of care that a reasonably prudent person would have exercised in a similar situation (ie: any conduct that fails below the standard established to protect others against unreasonable risk of harm.) For the reasons stated above, Dr. Costino did not deviate from the standard of care despite being confronted with two highly deceptive patients.

**5. The initial decision and final decision conclusion that Dr. Costino's conduct constitutes professional misconduct in violation of N.J.S.A. 45:1-21 is belied by the substantial evidence.**

The seventh edition of Black's Law Dictionary defines the term misconduct "a dereliction of duty or unlawful and improper behavior". With respect to the billing there is no evidence that Dr. Costino was derelict in his duty when he coded each bill, or that he unlawfully or improperly billed a certain level. Further, as the OAL judge noted, there is no pattern of fraudulent billing in this case. Accordingly, Dr. Costino acted professionally at all times despite being confronted with two highly deceptive patients.

**6. The initial decision and the final decision conclusion that Dr. Costino's conduct constitutes the engagement of acts constituting moral turpitude or conduct relating adversely to activity regulated by the Board in violation of N.J.S.A. 45:1-21(f) is belied by the substantial evidence.**

The seventh edition of Black's Law Dictionary defines the phrase moral turpitude as "conduct that is contrary to justice, honesty or morality, or conduct that is shameful, wicked, or shocking to the moral sense of the community". In this case Dr. Costino **did not engage** in any acts that could be characterized as shameful, wicked, or shocking, as both Anderson and Abbattiscianni each acknowledge that he did not inappropriately touch them during any of the office visits, and that he otherwise acted in a professional manner towards each of them. Furthermore, with respect to the billing, there is no evidence that could be construed to effect justice, honesty, or mortality, or that it is otherwise shameful, wicked, or shocking to the moral sense of the community.

**7. The initial decision and the final decision conclusion that Dr. Costino's conduct constitutes a failure to comply with the provisions of any act or regulation administered by the Board in violation of NJSA 45-121(h) is belied by the substantial evidence.**

**NJSA 45-121(h), and NJAC 13:35-6.5(b)1 provides that to the extent applicable, professional treatment records shall reflect:**

1. **The dates of all treatments**
2. **The History**
3. **Findings on appropriate examination**
4. **Diagnosis or medical impression**
5. **Treatment ordered including specific dosages, quantities and strengths or medications including refills if prescribed, administered or dispensed and recommended follow-up.**

NJAC 13:35-7 1A(a) provides in relative part that the practitioner shall not dispense a prescription to an individual without first conducted and examination which shall be appropriately documented in the patient record. As part of the patient examination the practitioner shall:

1. **Perform a history and physical examination**
2. **Make a diagnosis based upon the examination consistent with good medical care.**

3. Formulate a therapeutic plan and discuss the plan long with the basis for the plan and the risks and benefits of various treatment options with the patient.
4. Insure the availability of the physician for appropriate follow-up care.

NJAC 13.35-7.1A(a) 1-4 NJAC 13:35-7.1A(b)4 provides in relevant part that an examination of the patient's condition shall not be required under the following circumstances or for an established patient who, based on sound medical practice, the physician believes does not require a new examination before issuing a new prescription.

NJAC 13:35-7.6(a) provides in relevant part that when prescribing controlled substances, a practitioner shall ensure that patient's medical history has been taken and physical examination accomplished, including an assessment of physical and psychological function, underlying or coexisting diseases or conditions, any history of substance abuse and the nature, frequency, and severity of any pain the medical record shall reflect.

1. A recognized medical indication for the use of the controlled substance
2. The complete name of the controlled substance
3. The dosage, strength and quantity of the controlled substance
4. The instruction as to frequency of use

With respect to Schedule II Controlled Substances, a practitioner shall not authorize a quantity calculated to exceed 120 dosage units or a 30-day supply whichever is less. The practitioner shall keep accurate and complete records including that information required by NJAC 13.35-7.6(d)1-3 as well as any agreements with the patient.

In this case Dr. Costino **complied with all of the above.** There was a separate medical record created for Anderson and Abbattiscianni of every date they received treatment; the records contained their past medical history and Dr. Costino's examination findings. The records contain Dr. Costino's diagnosis and the treatment ordered for each patient. An appropriate history and physical examination was performed by Dr. Costino on both Anderson and Abbattiscianni at each office visit as set forth above. Dr. Costino made a presumptive diagnosis of nociceptive pain based upon his overall examination together with his 38 years of experience as a physician. After explaining the risks and benefits of opiate medication, Dr. Costino determined that the appropriate therapeutic plan was to prescribe them Percocet 1 tablet following their night or dancing. Neither Anderson or Abbattiscianni presented as a drug addict or drug diverter, and they continually stated that the medication helped them to function that is, continue to do their work as exotic dancers, and their functionality improved progressively as they worked more and more nights and more hours throughout the 24 hour a day period. Dr. Costino made himself available to them as necessary for follow-up care. Furthermore, Anderson signed Dr. Costino's **"Pain Management Agreement"** and a copy of Anderson's prescription of 30 Percocet tablets to be taken one following each night of dancing was placed in both Anderson's and Abbattiscianni's chart.

**A license revocation of 5 years and monetary penalties exceeding $90,000 is "disproportionate and shocking to one's sense of fairness"**, where there is **no evidence that Dr. Costino was a fundamentally corrupt licensee**, has **engaged in a panoply of dishonest acts** over several years and under varying different circumstances and was unwilling to abide by any terms and conditions as part of his reinstatement. NJSA45:1-25(d) provides that in any action brought pursuant to this act a board or the court may order the payment of costs for the use of the state including but not limited to the cost of investigation expert witness fees and costs attorney's fees and costs and transcript costs.

**Administrative penalties shall not be disproportionate to the offense as to be shocking to one's sense of fairness. Because of occupational license is a proprietary right, the disciplinary authority must consider mitigating factors.**

## Chapter 15 - Preliminary Statement of the Case

The legal **fees "and costs' approved by the Board in this case were grossly unfair and excessive.** With respect to legal fees, if this court were to affirm the findings of the Board, **it would in effect transform DAG David Puteska into the state's highest paid employee as he would be earning nearly 8 times ($175 per hour x's 40 hours = $7,000 per week. $7,000 per week x's 52 weeks = $364,000 per year) More than his own boss** (Attorney General Anne Milgram). A fairer calculation would be to divide DAG Puteska's current salary by 52 and then divide that number by 40 to determine his actual hourly rate. Furthermore, Dr. Costino has already paid substantial legal fees to both his prior counsel, and current counsel defending this matter as well as the pending criminal matter despite being unemployed since December of 2007. Which fact, the Board should have considered when determining whether legal fees should be included in the final decision. Moreover, to require Dr. Costino to pay the cost of transcripts, a second time, would be double counting.

The Board's **egregious nature** of the underlying conduct is overstated for the reasons stated in argument B above. Neither Anderson nor Abbattiscianni as drug addicts or drug diverters. Both ostensibly improved while under Dr. Costino's care. Further, **the Board completely ignored the significance of Dr. Costino's interaction with *Landis* which established that he is not predisposed to illegally prescribing medication which is clearly relevant to his fitness to practice medicine.** Landis posed as a patient addicted to heroin, and attempted to get a prescription for pain medication from Dr. Costino. Dr. Costino **did not prescribe Landis any type of pain medication** because he did not want Landis to kick one addiction and gain another. Furthermore, Landis was completely unaware and testified as such of any individuals who had illegally received controlled substances from Dr. Costino at or near the time of his undercover visit. **Dr. Costino's actions during his undercover visit were completely legal.** This evidence is particularly relevant on the issue of whether Dr. Costino is a fundamentally corrupt licensee and had engaged in a panoply of dishonest acts over several years and under varying different circumstances. **Dr. Costino is not a fundamentally corrupt licensee and did not engage in a panoply of dishonest**

**acts.** This matter only involved 2 undercover agents under a five-month period. It did not involve the treatment of any bona fide patients of Dr. Costino nor any acts of malpractice involving bona fide patients of Dr. Costino.

Twenty-two witnesses, five physicians, **Dr. Richard Renza,** testified that he and Dr. Costino attended medical school together and that he has refereed various patients to Dr. Costino since they've been in private practice. **Dr. Robert Speer** testified that he was a classmate with Dr. Costino in medical school and that Dr. Costino takes many patients with Medicaid and welfare which other physicians do not want to treat. **Dr. Robert Maurer,** testified that he personally has been a patient of Dr. Costino and he has referred his own family and friends to Dr. Costino. **Dr. Robert Beitman** testified that he always received positive feedback from the patients referred to Dr. Costino. One retired **New Jersey state senator, the Honorable James Cafiero** testified that he and his three sons were patients of Dr. Costino and that the community misses his services tremendously. One retired **N.J. Superior Court Judge, the Honorable John Callihan** testified that he, his wife and his daughter are patients of Dr. Costino and that Dr. Costino has been essential in treating patients with drug problems as, Cape May County has the highest addiction rate per capita in New Jersey. One disabled veteran, **Dennis McDonaough**, four active retired police officers, **Wiliam Henfey, Mayor of North Wildwood, John Bartleson, Under Chief Middle Township, Charles LaRosa, Charles McNeely,** all current patients. Two school teachers, **Ruth Roach** and **Susan Hinchey** and eight other patients, who are long time friends, **Dominic Natale, Edward Fox, Roman Osadchuk, Anthony Trivelis, Barry Gehring, Kurt Kelly**, and **Donald Stafferi** and **Anthony DeSimone**. These individuals testified and or certified that Dr. Costino enjoys an excellent reputation in the community for being a truthful, honest, and law abiding citizen which confirms that he is not a "fundamentally corrupt licensee".
Furthermore, **their testimony confirms that over the past 35 years, and under varying circumstances Dr. Costino has engaged in a variety of good and altruistic activity.**

## Chapter 15 - Preliminary Statement of the Case

The Board's initial suspension followed by its revocation of Dr. Costino's medical license has been **devastating on the local community.** There is an overall shortage of primary care physicians in Cape May County, and there are no primary care physicians that will attempt to practice pain management. Furthermore, drug addiction is a serious consequence of society's flaws, and woefully underserved in Cape May County. An immediate restoration of Dr. Costino's medical license is appropriate and fair under all of these circumstances outlined above.

Wherefore, John G. Costino, D.O. respectfully requests that the court reverse the Board's final decision of November 30, 2009 and **remand** this matter for further proceeding to a second Administrative Law (OAL) court. Respectfully Submitted;

Dated: January 22, 2010
Law Office of Glenn A. Zeitz
By: Jordan Zeitz, Esq.
38 Haddon Avenue
Haddonfield, NJ 08033
(856) 795-6660

Attorneys for Respondent – Appellant, John G. Costino

# "Emotional Intelligence is the Essence of Mental Toughness"

"State vs Worthy" involves the criminal law regarding
intercepted communications between law enforcement and the accused.

It came to the attention of my attorney, Mr. Zeitz, in the summer of 2009, that Tonya Anderson was a Class II police officer from Little Egg Harbor Twp. Police Department when she became involved in my case for the Cape May County prosecutor. The intercepted communications between her and I began on **April 12, 2007**, and continued through **August 23, 2007**. At the time of these intercepted communications, Anderson was employed by Little Egg Harbor Police Department. "The New Jersey law states that a Class II officer status is limited to performing police duties only in their local unit or municipality and can only perform such duties while under direct supervision of the chief of the police of her local unit." Anderson had been appointed as a Class II officer in Little Egg Harbor Twp. for more than one year, and there were more than two such officers employed in Little Egg Harbor Twp. during that time period. When the intercepted communications occurred, Anderson was acting under the direction and control of the Cape May County Prosecutor's Office (CMCPO) which made most of the decisions in the investigation. She was **never** an employee of (CMCPO).

**On April 17th, 2007, five days after the first intercepted communication** between Anderson and myself, which occurred on **April 12, 2007**, Detective George Hallett of the prosecutor's office was assigned to handle my investigation. Hallett made an initial request to the prosecutor's office for a 30-day consensual authorization to intercept the communications between Anderson and myself, on

## Chapter 16 - Emotional Intelligence is the Essence of Mental Toughness

April 17th, 2007. The next day, **April 18, 2007,** Hallett received **approval** from Cape May County Prosecutor Robert Taylor for this **consensual authorization.**

The New Jersey law states that there must be a showing of **"special need"** before a doctor's communication can be intercepted, However, Hallett did not demonstrate to anyone, any showing of such **"special need"**. Hallett was required to demonstrate this **"special need"** to Robert Taylor, the Cape May County Prosecutor. **"He did not do this"**. When Hallett made his request for the 30-day consensual authorization, it was **5 days after the first office visit**, April 12, 2007, between Anderson and myself. Hallett was simply **unaware, and totally ignorant of the "special need" requirement.** As a result of these **gross mistakes, of both Hallett and Taylor**, *both of which should have known the law*, **Mr. Zeitz came to certain conclusions of law**.

### Mr. Zeitz wrote the following to Judge Batten:
**The court should find that:**

1. Tonya Anderson was not acting as an investigative or law enforcement officer when the intercepted communications commenced on April 12, 2007 and continued thereafter.

2. All of the intercepted communications were **unlawfully obtained** by violation of N.J.S.A. 2A:156A-1

3. The audio recordings of the intercepted communications, the transcripts of same, and all derivative evidence should be stricken from the record pursuant to NJSA2A:156A-2j.

4. That absent such evidence there is insufficient proof establishing any of the allegations set forth in the verified complaint.

**Tonya Anderson was not "investigator or law enforcement officer"** in accordance with N/J.S.A.2A:156A-4b 2f when the intercepted communications commenced on April 12, 2007 and continued thereafter. A "special Class II law enforcement officer" **is limited to performing duties only in her local unit** except when in fresh pursuit of any person, or when authorized to perform duties in another unit pursuant to a mutual aid agreement.

In this case, Tonya Anderson cannot be considered an investigative or law enforcement officer when she intercepted the communications between her and myself for several reasons.

## First:
Anderson had been a Class II officer for a term exceeding one year which is in violation of N.J.S.A40A:14-146.14A.

## Second:
There were more than two Class II officers employed in Little Egg Harbor Twp. during the same period in violation of N.J.S.A. 40A:14-146.17.

## Third:
Anderson's authority to conduct an investigation and make an arrest was **strictly limited to the territory within Little Egg Harbor Twp, Ocean County**. As a "special law enforcement officer" a Class II officer, Anderson was only on duty when under the supervision and direction of Little Egg Harbor Twp. PD, when she performed functions on behalf of, and in this township only. Because Anderson was under the supervision and direction of the (CMCPO) when she participated in the interception of the communications, and because the interceptions occurred not only outside her municipality, but also in a different county, Anderson was **devoid** of any law enforcement authority to conduct any investigation or make an arrest, and therefore**, cannot** be considered an investigative or law enforcement officer with regard to wire communications. It is also well recognized that New Jersey gives its citizens **greater protection** under its wiretap statue when compared to the federal wiretap statute.

## Chapter 16 - Emotional Intelligence is the Essence of Mental Toughness

In my case, the intercepted communications were **unlawfully obtained** because the first interception occurred before there was any approval from the Cape May county prosecutor, and because there was never any showing of a "**special need**" as required by law.

### First:

Detective Hallett **did not request approval** from Cape May County Prosecutor Taylor as required by law until five days after the first intercepted communication between Anderson and myself had occurred. Hallett ultimately received approval on **April 18th 2007**. Furthermore, Hallett **never requested** and **therefore did not receive any approval to intercept communications beyond the initial 30-day period, which meant that the authorization expired May 18, 2007.**

### Second:

"Although there must be a showing of **"special need"** as required by law before a doctor's communication can be intercepted, Det. Hallett did not demonstrate any showing of such "special need" to the prosecutor when his request was made, as he was **unaware** and **totally ignorant** of this **statutory requirement**. Because the requirements were not followed, **the court must find pursuant to the wire communication decisions of law that the intercepted communications between Anderson and Dr. Costino were UNLAWFULLY OBTAINED.** Furthermore, the audio recordings of the intercepted communications, the transcripts of same, and all derivative evidence **should be stricken from the record pursuant to N.J. S. A. 2A:156A-21.**

*"This statue provides, in relevant part, that any aggrieved person in any trial hearing, or proceeding in or before court or other authority of this state may move to **suppress** the contents of any and all communications or evidence derived on the grounds that all intercepted oral communications obtained during or after any interception is determined to be in violation of this statute under subsections A, B, or C, of this section."*

This motion by my attorney Mr. Zeitz was **granted** by Judge Batten at the time of this hearing in mid-summer of 2009.

Approximately one month later, a taint hearing was scheduled to be conducted in front of Judge Batten, however, prior to the taint hearing, Assistant Prosecutor Hoerner argued that Anderson was indeed capable and authorized as a Class II undercover police officer.

Following a lengthy discussion in court, Judge Batten said the following:
**"My sense is that I made a mistake."**

At the termination of this hearing Mr. Zeitz petitioned Judge Batten to conduct an **evidentiary hearing** on this matter.

On Aug 10th 2009, Mr. Zeitz sent a letter to Assistant Prosecutor Megan Hoerner stating, "as you know, I advised Judge Batten that it was my intention to subpoena the following witnesses for the evidentiary hearing."

1) Prosecutor Robert Taylor
2) Det. George Hallett
3) Chief of County Detectives, Rybicki
4) Lt. Lynne Frame

As you might imagine, all four individuals named above were involved in procuring this Class II police officer Tonya Anderson for the job of undercover cop. As you further might imagine, Judge Batten **refused to grant the evidentiary hearing of the above four individuals to** *elucidate the truth*.

**All four individuals had given false statements** regarding the ability for Anderson to function legally as an undercover individual prior to any approval by the Cape May County Prosecutor, Robert Taylor. *The evidentiary hearing was to establish the truth. This hearing was DENIED by Judge Batten.*

## Chapter 16 - Emotional Intelligence is the Essence of Mental Toughness

**Question:**
Why did Judge Batten deny this hearing?

**Answer:**
In my opinion, **because Judge Batten knew that all four were lying!!!!**

Furthermore, in my candid opinion Judge Batten did not want a formal record of their **lies and misrepresentations because he was afraid that one or all four would PURJURE** themselves.

"The truth is incontrovertible, malice may attack it, and ignorance my deride it, but in the end, there it is."

– Winston Churchill

**Again,** in my opinion, this episode represents the subversive and fundamentally dishonest abuse of power by Judge Batten, and underscores his cognitive bias and prejudice against me. Furthermore, and in my opinion, Judge Batten simply protected his buddy Robert Taylor in my entire five-year case, and also protected the other three individuals in this egregious violation of law.

# "OBJECTIVE DUE PROCESS ENTRAPMENT"

"All things are subject to interpretation, whichever interpretations prevail at a given time is a function of power not truth."

By way of history and further explanation, on or about January of 1977, I signed a contract with Horizon Blue Cross and Blue Shield, a PPO program, which mandated that I provide treatment to all patients insured by this company.

During the month of September 2005, the state received information from the DEA – Drug Enforcement Agency, that pursuant to a check of an uncertified and remarkably flawed and inaccurate prescription data record, it suggested an excessive amount of prescribed pain medication.

This record included patient's names, and prescriptions written for them for treatment rendered. **This document was so extensively flawed and inaccurate, that it was never brought into evidence either at one of the multiple hearings at court, or at my trial in October of 2012.**

I knew for a fact, that the morons at the prosecutor's office **NEVER** reviewed this record either for accuracy or content. Had they done an accurate review of this data prescription record, essentially, their homework, they would have discovered the gross inaccuracy of this uncertified record. The lack of due diligence on the part of the Cape May County prosecutors office is just another example of their inadequacy.

## Chapter 17 - Objective Due Process Entrapment

In all my years as a physician, I have never written anything illegal with respect to classified prescription products. Every classified prescription product that I write is in the patient's medical record, and all Class II, III and IV products are copied for accuracy and placed in the patient's medical record.

There has never been any proof that I have ever written any extraneous opioid prescriptions. **The three undercover individuals were utilized here not to detect crime, but to manufacture it, by fraudulent, misrepresentation and coercive behavior.**

**On December 13, 2005**, officer Jason Landis of the Cape May County Prosecutor's Office, Narcotics Task Force, posed as a patient addicted to heroin, and attempted to obtain a fraudulent prescription for pain pills from Dr. Costino. This entire episode of Officer Landis in Dr. Costino's office **was not provided in discovery** until 3 years later and was done so probably by mistake by the prosecutor's office. Landis was wearing a transmitting device when he met Dr. Costino in his office, **but the state claimed that they had no recording of this office visit.**

**On January 24th 2007**, a meeting was held with the following governmental agencies: Drug Enforcement Agency (DEA), United States Postal Inspector, Cape May County Prosecutor's Office, Little Egg Harbor Township Police Department. The purpose of this meeting was to commence a second proactive undercover investigation of Dr. Costino. During this meeting the decision was made that a Class II police office Tonya Anderson would pose as a patient and serendipitously record the office visits between her and myself. **At the time of their meeting in January of 2007, it was clear by virtue of the undercover visit of Detective Landis in December of 2005 that Dr. Costino had been a physician in good standing in the state of New Jersey since 1971. He was gainfully employed as a physician in his office, and was "entrapped" by law enforcement. There was no history of any lawsuits by any patients either for malpractice, or for any type of medication issue. So in reality, there was no legitimate reason, or indication, for this entrapment procedure to have ever been started.**

The complete transcripts of all of the office visits with me by the undercover agents are lengthy. In view of this, I would like to give you a small sample of my conversations with the undercover agents at the various office visits. Certain excepts are as follows:

**On April 12, 2007**, Officer Anderson reported to the Cape May County Prosecutor's office where she received the following items: a digital recorder, a fictitious health insurance card, a prepaid cellular telephone, she was given a fictitious home address, a fictitious date of birth, a fictitious Social Security number, a fictitious telephone number & fictitious employment information. Following the completion of patient forms in the office, a medical chart was established for Anderson based upon all the fictitious information that she provided. Anderson was then escorted to an examination room and the entire conversation between her and I was serendipitously recorded:

**JC:** You're from Atlantic City?

**UC:** Yeah, right. I'm kind of in transition now. I'm working up there. And you know, staying with friends. You see I'm a dancer.

**JC:** When you say a physical, what are you looking for, what do you need?

**UC:** I guess I work nights, you know, long hours I'm on my feet all day, you know, it's a little hard for me to unwind, I guess. At the end of the day one of the girls that I work with told me…and she, I think she had given me Percocets and I had taken them after work to sleep and you know, to get up and do it all over again. I don't know what is your suggestion?

**JC:** Percocet is a **pain** pill.

**UC:** OK.

## Chapter 17 - Objective Due Process Entrapment

**JC:** Do you understand what I mean?

**UC:** Right?

**JC:** You don't really want something for **pain** which is addictive unless you really got a real problem. You know, if you wanted something to just relax...

**UC:** ...Well I've got to say they did work for me...

**JC:** Well usually they do.

**UC:** Regardless of what theyre for...

**JC:** Usually that kind of pain medication is not for relaxation

**UC:** Right...

**JC:** It really kind of peps you up and enables you to function if you've got a bad back, or a bad leg, or a bad, knee, of a bad neck, or something like that. That **pain** medication enables you to..to function because it takes your **pain** away.

**UC:** Um-hmm.

**JC:** It doesn't really relax, you know, now, something like valium... that is something at the end of the day if you're kind of strung out you know what I mean, from dancing and running around the stage all night, you know, that's something you could take to just kind of relax you take some of the anxiety, that sort of thing.

**UC:** Right.

**JC:** Just kind of relax you know, that makes sense.

**UC:** Um-hmm.

**JC:** But I mean, you don't really want Percocet or Vicodin, or any of that stuff cause first of all, it's addictive and you don't really want an addictive medication unless you really need it.

**UC:** Right. Well as I've said I've taken it, and it does seem to work for me. I mean, I gotta say it does, it works for me.

**JC:** Well, are you addicted to Percocet?

**UC:** No, cuz I'm only taking it on nights I work. I'm only working 3 to 4 nights a week now. It's not something I take when I'm not working or anything like that. The fluctuation of the schedule between the days I'm off and being up during normal hours so it helps me to get that rest on the days, you know, that I'm working.

**JC:** I mean do you have **pain**?

**UC:** No, I wouldn't say **pain.**

**JC:** So if you really don't have **pain** you don't want Percocet. It's really a **pain** pill. It's not a sedative.

**UC:** Right. Well I don't want to be sedated either, like I said it works for me. I don't know... yeah like I said 3 to 4 nights a week...

**JC:** You would take one? Is that it?

**UC:** Yeah, it doesn't take much with me. I have no problem coming in and getting rechecks or whatever is necessary.

**JC:** Well, I really have no problem giving you that as long as you understand, A, it IS a narcotic and B, it can be addictive so you don't want to start taking Percocet like M&M's.

**UC:** Right.

## Chapter 17 - Objective Due Process Entrapment

"In sum, the aforesaid exchange confirms that officer Anderson falsely presented herself as a dancer from Atlantic City who was on her feet all day and night, and takes pain medication only on the nights that she has worked because it helps her to get the rest on the days that she is working, and because it works for her. "

It also confirms that officer Anderson never stated that the inferences raised by Dr. Costino concerning her medical condition were either incorrect or otherwise baseless. Officer Anderson's unnecessarily false statements about her employment together with her tacit acknowledgement that Dr. Costino's inferences about her medical condition were correct, was clearly intended to **unfairly,** and **unconstitutionally,** induce him into prescribing her this medicine.

**On May 2, 2007,** Anderson again reported to the county prosecutor's office, where she received the digital recorder, and was instructed to get another prescription for pain medication from Dr. Costino. The following relevant exchange took place between her and I in the examination room:

**JC:** Slide down there. Are you doing alright with this medication?

**UC:** Yeah, doing fine, doing fine. It's helping me, yeah.

**JC:** I guess when you're done with the night of dancing you're kind of sore?

**UC:** I am, um-hmm.

The aforesaid exchange confirms that when officer Anderson states that the medication is helping her, and acknowledged when she is done with a night of dancing she is "kind of sore" was again clearly intended to ***unfairly and unconstitutionally*** induce Dr. Costino into prescribing medication.

**On June 7, 2007** Anderson again reported to the Cape May prosecutor's office where she received the digital recorder and similar instructions. When she arrived at my office she was presented with **my "Pain Management Agreement"**, which clearly states that the patient takes medication for her **pain**, which prohibited her from sharing medications, or using other practitioners for pain management, and provided voluminous information about the use of pain medication. After signing this agreement, Anderson was escorted to the examination room and the following relevant exchange took place:

**UC:** I did…well I did want to mention or ask if it'd be possible to get something a little stronger that lasts a little longer or I don't know go up to a higher milligram.

**JC:** Well, I can give you 10 milligrams since you are now on 7.5 mg.

**UC:** Yeah, cuz they just seem to like wear off in 4 hours.

**JC:** See what happens is that you've become tolerant to medication. You take it at night when you're done your dancing?

**UC:** Yeah, yeah

**JC:** You're active, and this as you know, does help.

**UC:** Right, right. Things are picking up now, working six to seven nights per week.

The aforesaid exchange confirms that when Anderson stated that the medicine wears off in 4 hours and acknowledged that she was more active as "things are picking up now" was again clearly intended to **unfairly** and **unconstitutionally** induce me into prescribing her more medication. I explained to her that tolerance occurs with every patient, however, 10 milligrams will only last 3 to 4 hours, similar to the 7.5 milligram dose.

## Chapter 17 - Objective Due Process Entrapment

**On June 26, 2007** Anderson reported to the prosecutors office, received the digital recorder, with similar instructions to my office. The following relevant exchange took place at this office visit:

**JC:** Really busy…what's new, anything?

**UC:** Nothing really. I didn't really notice any difference with the 10 milligrams. It's the summer now working seven nights a week.

**JC:** No?

**UC:** No, it's pretty much the same. I mean they still lasted the same amount of time. I was hoping they would last longer like as far as how long they're effective.

**JC:** You think they really would. It's peculiar isn't it?

**UC:** It's almost like you could set a clock to it. It's 4 hours.

**JC:** well the thing is, you become a little tolerant.

**UC:** Right.

**JC:** That's still an issue, however they still, I'm sure have the effect.

**UC:** Yeah, oh, yeah, they just seem to wear off too soon.

**JC:** You think they would really? It is peculiar, isn't it? That's still an issue. I mean, they still, I'm sure have a good effect.

**UC:** Yeah, oh, yeah, they just seem to wear off too soon.

The aforesaid confirms that when Anderson states that she was "hoping the medication would last longer as how long they're effective" was again, clearly intended to unfairly and unconstitutionally induce me into prescribing her more medication however, **I would not,** ***and did not.***

**On July 13, 2007** Anderson reported to the Cape May County prosecutor's office and similarly reported to my office where the following exchange took place:

> JC: What's happening?
>
> UC: What?
>
> JC: Have you been busy?
>
> UC: Very, very busy.
>
> JC: I guess you're really busy there.
>
> UC: Yeah. Working seven nights a week, ten hours per night.

The aforesaid exchange confirms that when Officer Anderson stated that she had been very, very busy was again clearly intended to **unfairly** and **unconstitutionally** induce him into prescribing her additional medication. **I would not *and did not.***

**On August 3, 2007**, DEA Special Agent Margarita Abbattiscianni reported to the CMCPO along with Tonya Anderson where they received a digital recorder, and presented to Dr. Costino's office. An additional medical chart was established for Abbattiscianni with all the fictitious information given to her by the prosecutor. Both were in the examination room when I entered the room and the following relevant exchange took place:

> UC1: Maggie wanted to see you. She...
>
> JC: Maggie, what's wrong?
>
> UC2: **It's just the "pain". Up all night...long hours**
>
> JC: Well they are...when you dance...

**JC:** Just take it when you're done work. You know, it will relax you and take the <u>pain</u> away.

**UC2:** Um-hm...um-hm....

**JC:** You know, I'm sure you get these acute strains and sprains with your work...

**UC2:** You know, I'm pretty flexible. Not much "<u>pain</u>". I do a lot of exercise...

**UC1:** Oh my god, I got to get up and I've been sitting for too long.

**UC2:** I know, I know and then we need to sit in a car for another couple of hours or so.

The aforesaid exchange confirms that Margarita Abbattiscianni also presented herself as a dancer which caused her **"pain"** and to "be up all night". It also confirms that agent Abbattiscianni never stated that the inferences raised by Dr. Costino concerning her medical condition were either incorrect or otherwise baseless. Abbattiscianni gave unnecessarily false statements about her employment together with her tacit acknowledgement that my inferences regarding her medical condition were correct, was clearly intended to **unfairly and unconstitutionally** induce me into prescribing her medication for her alleged condition.

**On August 23, 2007**, both Anderson and Abbattiscianni again reported to the prosecutor's office, received digital recorders and presented to my office with instructions to obtain a prescription for pain medication. The following relevant exchange took place:

**JC:** You're still busy up there?

**UC2:** Summers coming to an end.

**JC:** Yes it is. And you're doing fine with the medication?

**UC2:** I'm doing good, yep.

**JC:** No problems?

**UC2:** No problems at all.

**UC1:** Let me ask you now, how many of them can I take safely?

**JC:** Now what do you mean by that?

**UC1:** Well, I mean, it doesn't come any higher than 10 mg, right?

**JC:** Nope. Nope, this is the highest dose. You understand what I mean?

**UC2:** As far as getting adverse, you know, effects and stuff; I mean how many? Two or 3 at a time or…

**JC:** No, just one at night following your work…

**UC1:** Now what's the difference between Percocet and Oxycontin?

**JC:** Well, you see, Oxycontin is a longer acting product. It's much more addicting.

**UC1:** Um-hm.

**JC:** And it's a problem drug.

**UC1:** Oh, Ok.

**JC:** It's a problem…you don't want to start that. You don't want to take those. (meaning Oxycontin) unless you have a real serious problem, which you don't.

**UC1** Right, right.

## Chapter 17 - Objective Due Process Entrapment

**UC2:** Right.

**UC1:** No, I just…if it were longer acting meaning it doesn't, meaning it doesn't wear off as fast.

**JC:** Well, the commercial would say it's longer acting…the fact of the matter is it's not that much longer acting if you want to know the truth and that's why we reserve it for people that have significant problems.

**UC1:** Hm-um.

**JC:** You know, not just "some pain"…

**UC1:** Right.

**UC2:** Mm-hmm.

**JC:** This is a nice product (meaning Percocet) you know, for individuals like yourself. I mean…you do what you do for how many hours, five, six, seven hours each night.

**UC2:** Yeah.

**UC1:** About that. About seven hours…

**JC:** **And you know it's just fatigue, it wears (meaning their work) on your legs, your back, your neck, et cetera, et cetera. So, something like this (meaning Percocet) will soothe that pain, you see, which is very nice. You get into those longer acting products and you're just working on a trail of addiction, which you don't want to get involved in. Now believe me when I tell you, I mean you really don't want to do that. So you know, let's continue to take one per day following your night of dancing.**

**UC2:** Ok.

**UC2:** Isn't it, is it, it's like not the same drug?

**JC:** No.

**UC1:** I was under the impression that it's the same thing. Just a lower thing and it has, like, somebody said, like Tylenol or something in it.

**JC:** It does. Its like Oxycodone and Tylenol.

**UC1:** Ok.

**JC:** Oxycontin is a different synthetic. It's more potent, a little longer lasting, it's stronger, and you, I'm telling you, you don't want to get involved in that, period.

**UC2:** I've taken a few pills in fact...

**JC:** I'm sure.

**UC2:** And it did work much quicker than Percocet.

**JC:** Well this works quicker, that one works longer.

**UC1:** Longer?...

**UC2:** Yeah, right. I guess so. So it's not much better...

**UC1:** Where you get up in 4 hours and have to take another to get back to sleep.

**JC:** **You really don't want to get involved in that...**

The aforesaid exchange confirms that when Abbattiscianni acknowledged that she had been busy, "still very busy" was again clearly intended to **unfairly, and unconstitutionally** induce me into prescribing her additional medication further, it confirms that neither agent Abbattiscianni nor officer Anderson ever stated that the inferences raised by me concerning their medical condition were either incorrect or otherwise baseless.

During each office visit for each patient, I conducted a physical examination conforming to the various billing codes for payment. Furthermore, I determined at each visit, in their medical chart, the improved functionality of both undercover females, as well as making the determination of the **absence of addiction, diversion or aberrant behavior.**

## ARGUMENT:

*The indictment should be dismissed based upon the objective "due process" theory of entrapment because:*

1. The state was solely responsible for creating and planning the alleged crimes;

2. The state primarily controlled and directed the commission of the alleged crimes;

3. The methods used by the state were unreasonable and unfairly deceptive;

4. The legitimate law enforcement for creating and planning the alleged crimes is dubious.

"**Objective due process entrapment**" is like traditional entrapment in that it concentrates on the extent of the government's involvement on the crime. **State vs Johnson "127N.J.458,470 (1992).** "The essence of due process entrapment inheres in the egregious or blatant wrongfulness of the government's conduct". "The defense arises when the conduct of government is patently wrongful in that it constitutes an *abuse of lawful power, perverts* the proper role of government, and offends principles of fairness". Justice Stewart defined the standard to be used under the objective test as follows:

"When the agent's involvement in criminal activities go beyond the mere offering of such an opportunity, and when their conduct is of a kind that could induce or instigate the commission of a crime by one not ready or willing to commit it, then regardless of the character or propensity of the particular induced – entrapment has occurred."

<u>United States Russell 411 U.S. 423 445 (1973)</u> (Stewart J. Dissenting) When determining what conduct of the police will society tolerate, Justice Frankfurter said:

> "Certain police conduct that ensnares a person into further crime is not to be tolerated by an advanced society…in holding out inducements the police should act in a manner as likely to induce the commission of the crime only persons ready and willing to commit further crimes should the occasion arise, and not others who would avoid crime…"

<u>Sherman v United States 356 US 369-382-84 (1958)</u> (Frankfurter J. Concurring) Justice Roberts found that the objective test protects society and the administration of justice concerns, reasoning that:

> "The protection of it's own functions, and the preservation of it's own temple belongs only to the court. It is the province of the court and of the court alone to protect itself, and the government, from such prostitution of the criminal law. The violation of the principals of justice by the entrapment of the unwary into crime

**should be dealt with by the court, no matter by whom, or at what stage of the proceedings the facts are brought to it's attention."**

**Sorrells v United States 287 US 435, 457(1932)** "When the police conduct revealed in a particular case falls below standards, which common feelings respond, for the proper use of governmental power", "**the charges should be dismissed.**" A prosecution will be barred when the nature and extent of the police involvement in the crime is so overreaching even where there is evidence that the defendant might be predisposed to commit the crime. Once a defendant presents some "evidence of due process entrapment" the state then bears the burden of proving by "clear and convincing evidence" that it did not entrap the defendant. Clear and convincing evidence must be " so **clear, direct, weighty and convincing** as to enable either a judge, or jury to come to a clear conviction, without hesitance, of the truth of the precise facts in issue."

When determining "**objective due process entrapment**" the court must consider:

1. Whether the government or the defendant was primarily responsible for creating and planning the crime,

2. Whether the government or the defendant primarily controlled and directed the commission of the crime,

3. Whether objectively viewed the methods used by the government to involve the defendant in the commission of the crime were unreasonable,

4. Whether the government had legitimate law enforcement purpose in bringing about the crime, Johnson, supra, 127 n.j. at 474.

The court must also consider "the circumstances surrounding the creating of the crime, the methods undertaken by the government to induce the defendant to commit the crime, and the actions entailed in the commission of the crime itself."

Furthermore, the court must specifically consider **"the nature of the efforts directed to encourage defendants to commit the crime"**. Including such "tactics" like **heavy-handed pressure; repetitive and persistent solicitation, or threats, or other forms of coercion.**

The use of **false** and **deceitful appeals** to such humanitarian instincts such as **sympathy, friendship, personal need, and the promise of exorbitant gain** which are disallowed because they can overwhelm the resistance of ordinary people".

*"Vaccaro"* states in part under Drugs and Narcotics pg. 168 of the record, that "a physician's license and registration authorizes him to dispense controlled substances, but under this statute, he is "immune" from criminal liability when he dispenses same in good faith, in the course of his professional practice only. "

Remember, I am a licensed physician, registered in the state of New Jersey, with full authority as a licensed physician to prescribe Class II, III, IV and V controlled pharmaceutical products according to the laws of the state of New Jersey.

**In my case, all of the Johnson factors favor a finding of "objective due process entrapment."**

1. The state was solely responsible for creating and planning the alleged crimes since the undercover agents initiated all of the visits with me, and advised me after the first visit that it would be "no problem coming in and getting re-checks". The only contact between the undercover females, and myself occurred in my office, which again was always initiated by the undercover agents under the direction of the Cape May County Prosecutors Office. The undercover females related to me that they had been taking the prescribed medication, **"only on the nights as exotic dancers as it would enable them to dance all night and do it all over again the next day and**

**night."** Besides writing the prescription, I never took any action to help or otherwise assist these undercover agents to obtain their medication or to refill their medication by any pharmacy. In fact, none of the prescriptions written by me to the undercover agents were ever filled by any pharmacy.

2. The state primarily controlled and directed the commission of the alleged crime, as set forth above. The state through the undercover agents, initiated all seven office visits with me and persistently related to me of their progress with the prescribed medication with **fictitious reasoning,** while posing as legitimate patients.

3. The methods used by the state were *unreasonable and unfairly deceptive.* The state's decision to use undercover agents posing as exotic dancers from Atlantic city who **were already taking Percocet** to cope with their effects of pain while working long hours on the their feet, days and nights, instead of posing them as clerical workers, *(or some other profession that does not involve the type of strenuous physical activity one would naturally and reasonably attribute to an exotic dancers)*, who worked normal hours while sitting behind a desk all day, was clearly designed to make it virtuously impossible for myself, or any physician, to uncover the states **deceitful** and **fraudulent conduct**. Furthermore, because I was a participating physician on the Horizon Blue Cross, Blue Shield PPO network, **I was mandated** to provide treatment to Anderson which formed the basis for their **"health insurance fraud counts"**.

4. The legitimate law enforcement purpose for creating and planning the alleged crimes was **dubious** simply because I have never been named as a party in any civil law suit involving any patient who received a prescription for medication from me. Any other information relied upon by the state came from sources who were **convicted criminals, known drug abusers, and were otherwise unreliable and not credible.**

Each "Johnson" factor standing alone is a basis for the court to **dismiss the indictment with prejudice** in my case. The basis to dismiss the indictment is even stronger when the "Johnson" factors are considered collectively. **It is essential to have objective morality and ethics in law.** It is repugnant to that concept, to justify the apprehension of **"honest citizens"** on the basis that "the end justifies the means". It is improper to utilize the tools of **lies and deceit** to affect criminal justice. When the means of obtaining a desired end is **distasteful and objectionable**, it eventually undermines rather than enhances the high standards of conduct in the administration of justice required of law enforcement agencies and the courts of the state. In sum, to permit the prosecution to go forward based upon the state's **egregious** and **unconstitutional conduct** during the investigative phase, and continuing through it's presentation to the grand jury, would severely undermine the confidence and fairness in the outcome in these proceedings, and violate my right to "**due process**".

**An evidentiary hearing is necessary so that each of the four Johnson factors and other relevant facts can be properly considered by the court when making it's determination on whether the state has met it's burden of providing by "clear and convincing evidence" that it did not entrap Dr. Costino.**

Judge Batten eventually conducted an evidentiary hearing, and Assistant Prosecutor Megan Hoerner defended the state. After all the evidence, and all of the facts of this case were presented to Judge Batten in open court, he continued to support his buddy Robert Taylor and **refused to dismiss my case** on the "objective theory of due process entrapment". **Please be aware that at this time in my criminal case, Judge Batten and every prosecutor present were totally ignorant of the law in the state of New Jersey namely "Vaccaro".**

The state of course **did not meet** its burden by providing clear and convincing evidence that it did not entrap me. **It was obvious that the state did entrap me.** Again, "**due process**" was ignored by Judge Batten. I repeat again, an evidentiary hearing **was necessary** so that each of the four Johnson factors were properly considered by the court when making the determination as to whether or not the state had met it's burden, that the state did not entrap me. **The facts in this case were perfectly clear to enable the judge to come to a clear conviction, without hesitancy of the truth of these precise facts at issue.**

"The methodology employed by the state was not only **unreasonable, and unfairly deceptive,** but when the entire issue is examined, it clearly defines **"objective due process entrapment". "The protection of it's own functions, and the preservation of the purity of it's own temple belongs only to the court."** "It is the province of the court and the court alone to protect itself and the government from such **prostitution** of the criminal law." "The violation of the principles of justice by the entrapment of the unwary into crime should be dealt with by the court, no matter by whom, or at what stage of the proceedings are brought to it's attention."

"When the police conduct revealed in a particular case falls below standards to which common feelings respond, for the proper use of governmental power, the charges **should be dismissed.**" Prosecution will be barred when the nature and extent of the police involvement in a crime is **overreaching, unreasonable, and unfairly deceptive.**

## "Once a defendant presents evidence of "due process entrapment" the state bears the burden by proving by clear and convincing evidence that it did not entrap the defendant."

**Furthermore, I am a physician with medical licensure and registration in the state of New Jersey, to prescribe Class II, III, IV, and V controlled pharmaceutical products in accordance with the laws of the state of New Jersey and specifically, "Vaccaro", which the cast of characters in the Cape May County prosecutor's office were completely ignorant.**

Furthermore, the law in the state of New Jersey is "**State v Vaccaro**" which states in part:

> **"A physician's license and registration authorizes him to dispense controlled substances, but under this statute, he is "immune" from criminal liability when he dispenses same in good faith, in the course of his professional practice only."**

Judge Batten **refused to dismiss my case** after clear and convincing evidence was presented by Mr. Zeitz in court that the state was **absolutely guilty** of **"objective due process entrapment"**. Judge Batten was **ignorant** of the law, "State v Vaccaro," and was duped by Assistant Prosecutor Megan Hoerner, who was also ignorant of **"Vaccaro"**. Furthermore, this refusal to dismiss represents another glaring example of the **cognitive bias and prejudice** against me, **an innocent pain management physician**, to protect and support the soiled reputation of his colleague and good friend, Robert Taylor.

# Driver Hearing

"A casual stroll through the lunatic asylum of the justice system demonstrates that faith alone does not prove anything. The war must be won on logic, principle, and evidence."

"There is a universal truth, a universal principal of life, of morality, which must prevail in the milieu of the intellectual pygmies that one must deal with."

"The primacy of the intellect must reign supreme"

By way of history, our county sanctions the use of sound recordings where the matter contained therein is competent and relevant. We adopt that view as a condition to admissibility however the speakers should be identified and it should be demonstrated that the device is capable of taping the conversation or statement, and it's operator competent. The recording must be **authentic and correct, without alterations, additions, or deletions,** and in instances of alleged confessions, that the statements were solicited **voluntarily** and without any **inducement.**

This statement is the introduction to **"State vs Driver"**, a case which occurred in 1962, in New Jersey regarding **"transcriptions" from sound recordings.**

This controversy in my criminal case is the following:
The two undercover females, Anderson and Abbattiscianni came into my office, as individual patients. The transcripts of their recordings were UC1 for Anderson, and UC2 for Abbattiscianni. Serendipitous recordings of all office visits with

both females were made at each individual visit. At the completion of each visit, the recordings were taken from them by the DEA character, **Thomas Prevoznik,** and given to the postal inspector, **Alex Sylvester.** Sylvester then gave the CD recordings to a second individual, **Michelle Stankiewicz,** also a postal employee, for transcription. The transcripts were then sent to the prosecutor's office and to my attorney. The controversy is concerning the fact that somewhere along these lines of custody between the DEA character Prevoznik, the postal inspector, Sylvester, and the typist, Stankiewicz, there were at least **"three" alterations in the transcription record.**

This **"driver hearing"** was conducted two years following the production of transcripts, by my attorney Glenn Zeitz. The "driver hearing" was conducted specifically because of the alterations that were produced either in the recordings themselves or in the transcriptions or both. **Clearly and unequivocally, these alterations were produced by someone in the justice department. On August 3, 2007,** Undercover II entered my office, and I said to her, **"Maggie, what's wrong?"** She responded, **"it's just the "pain" and up all night long hours 'til four am".** Early in my case Edwin Jacobs was my attorney, and we reviewed the transcripts of all of the visits, and the original transcript of August 3rd clearly stated Maggie's response, **"It's just the "pain" and up all night long hours 'til four a.m.".** We received this transcript in October of 2007 and relied upon its accuracy.

Some time in mid February of 2008, an email was sent to Detective **George Hallett** at the CMCPO from **Thomas Prevoznik** who stated in the email that there was an "error" regarding the transcript of August 3, 2007. Instead of *"it's the pain and up all night 'til four in the morning,* Maggie really said: *"Well, I mean, it's basically the same as Tonya again here, just up all night and I just need something to bring me down during the day, long hours"*. **In other words, the transcript was altered.** Furthermore, in addition to the email to Hallett, a second August 3rd, 2007 transcript **with the altered statement** was sent to Hallett. He then delivered this altered transcript to my attorney, and immediately **I knew something nefarious was going on in Cape May County**, at the Drug Enforcement Agency, and with

## Chapter 18 - Driver Hearing

the U.S. Postal Service agency.

# TREACHERY!!!

During this period of time, there were a number of issues regarding not only the criminal case in chief, in Cape May County but also other issues as well with the State Board of Medical Examiners. My attorney and I scheduled a meeting with Assistant Prosecutor Megan Hoerner regarding this alteration. At this meeting in the prosecutor's office, Detective Paul Worrell, a former patient of mine, was also present. Paul Worrell was a patient, his wife was a patient, and his mother was a patient of mine prior to my arrest in September of 2007. I knew all three very well, and I did know that he was employed at the prosecutor's office as a detective. At this meeting, and without Horner present, I asked Worrell a confidential question: "Tell me Paul, are you able to alter the recording device and change the words?" His answer was, **" Yes. "**

My attorney and I then again listened to the CD recordings representing each office visit with the two undercover females, and there were additional discrepancies that were clear to me that had been **eliminated** from the CD recordings and from the transcriptions as well.

### Eliminated from the CD recordings and transcript:

Tonya Smith (UC I) asked me the following question at her second office visit.

**Question UC1:** "Can I bring several other of my girlfriends to your office for treatment?"

**My Answer:** "I would prefer not to have any additional young females from Atlantic City who are dancers at any one time in my office because they would disturb my elderly patients."

### Eliminated from the CD recording and transcript at her third visit:

Tonya Smith asked the following:

**Question UC1:** "Do you date?"

**My Answer:** "No, I'm married."

# "Due Process" Denied

**These two factual recorded statements by UC I and answered by me, were also eliminated from the serendipitous recordings and transcripts that were produced at her office visits.**

After realizing that there were a total of **three major alterations** in my conversations with the undercover females, in my office, I was certain, that I was dealing with **corrupt law enforcement,** who were *not just corrupt* but extremely **subversive**, and wanted nothing more than *to convict me of something*.

After the meeting with Assistant Prosecutor Megan Hoerner and Paul Worrell, I had some difficulty with Edwin Jacobs, and hired another attorney, **Glenn Zeitz** from Haddonfield, NJ to continue my defense.

In the summer of 2008, Glenn Zeitz and I began preparing for the administrative law hearing (OAL) and in an effort to ensure accuracy regarding the office visit of August 3, 2007 with Abbattiscianni (UC II), and the fact that she clearly said to me that she had **"pain"** while "working long hours and up all night". My attorney scheduled a video deposition of Abbattiscianni prior to the Office of Administrative Law civil trial - hearing, to absolutely identify what was said on August 3, 2007.

**The video deposition, under oath of Abbattiscianni was performed by my attorney Glen Zeitz, and DAG David Puteska, was also present.**

*The statements posed to Abbattiscianni (UCII) by Glen Zeitz were as follows:*

1. This is the original transcript of the conversation between you and Dr. Costino. This is the official transcript that we were given. Based upon your recollection, does it accurately reflect what was said by the parties on August 3, 2007?
   Her answer was: **Yes**

2. As you follow along with the transcript, the recording is being played, does that transcript fairly and accurately portray what you just heard?
   Her answer: **Yes**

3. Early in the visit we heard in the recording that you mention to Dr. Costino **"pain"**. Is that correct?
Her answer: **Yes**

4. Just for the record again, you have looked at the transcript, is it accurate?
Her answer: **Yes**

5. Does it accurately depict what took place?
Her answer: **Yes**

6. It says, "just the **pain** and up all night long hours". Now you're leading him to believe what happens after a night of dancing and doing all of this exotic stuff you've got **pain,** correct?
Her answer: **Yes**

7. You went there with the following goal. Posed as a striper, up long hours, who has **"pain"**, and going to a doctor, and the very first thing when he asked you "what's wrong Maggie?" you clearly tell him, **"pain"**?
Answer: **Yes**

The video deposition of Abbattiscianni was clear and concise. She agreed that she did say **"pain"** at her video deposition and she also agreed to all of the other statements posed by Mr. Zeitz.

In late December of 2008, the administrative court hearing, trial, (OAL) began. When asked these same questions under oath, Abbattiscianni gave the same **honest answers.**

Fast forward to the actual "driver hearing" which is now two years later in **2010.** It's called the "driver hearing" because the New Jersey case was "State vs Driver". This hearing is an attempt to clear some or all of the discrepancies with the undercover recordings. It is an effort to obtain the facts, regarding the idiosyncrasies in the transcripts and recordings themselves, the methods of handling them,

# "Due Process" Denied

and whether or not, and how much, they were **tainted by law enforcement.**

The principle individuals in the "driver hearing" were DEA Investigator Prevoznik, Postal Inspector Alex Sylvester, and postal employee and transcriber, Michelle Stankiewicz. Additionally there were two or three other individuals who according to their testimony, handled the recorders, as well as the CD discs. The "driver hearing" was conducted at superior court in Cape May County under the control of Judge Raymond Batten.

Mr. Zeitz sent a letter to Assistant Prosecutor Hoerner several months prior to this hearing which stated: "It was our understanding that the undercover officers utilized digital recording devices to record their visits with Dr. Costino, and that after each visit these digital audio files were transferred from the portable device to a law enforcement computer."

Please provide the following:

1. A log as to who the audio file was transferred to and accessed on the law enforcement computers.

2. The identity of the person who transferred and accessed the audio files.

3. The reasons why the audio files were accessed for information.

4. The documentation of any viruses, malfunctioning, or other problems with the digital recording devices, audio files, or law enforcement computers used in this matter prior to, during, or after the relevant period.

5. Information and or documentation of the digital recording devices used.

6. The identity of the persons who transcribed the audio files.

7. The date each transcript was prepared.

8. The location and identity of the recording devices used for each office visit.

# Chapter 18 - Driver Hearing

Shortly thereafter, we received an order from Judge Batten that the recording devices actually used in this matter be **preserved** should same still exist. Should the recording device or devices no longer exist then the state should advise the court defense counsel that they have been destroyed together with a **date of destruction.**

As a result of this order, there were several letters back and fourth regarding the existence, or non-existence of these recorders. The devices used were Eagle-8 digital recorders bearing specific serial numbers.

## You guessed it!

They never found the recorders, therefore, we could never examine them or determine exactly how the information had been altered. **Another very clever and corrupt characteristic of both the DEA, and the Cape May County Prosecutor's office.**

## In spite of all the efforts by Mr. Zeitz, the recorders were *NEVER* recovered.

**Under oath in superior court, in Cape May County and under cross-examination by Glenn Zeitz, Thomas Prevoznik was asked the following questions:**
*The following is taken word for word from the superior court hearing*

1. "Did you ever tell Agent Abbattiscianni before she gave her video taped deposition that there was a transcript error somewhere?"
   **Answer:** "Yeah. I probably would have."

2. "When you say you probably would have, what made you do it?"
   **Answer:** "I didn't know she was having a video deposition."

The fact of the matter is that Prevoznik **never** told Abbattiscianni that there was a transcript error anywhere. Prevoznik **simply lied under oath at this hearing.** Prevoznik is the group supervisor for the Drug Enforcement Agency (DEA) and the diversion investigator in the Atlantic City office. Mr. Zeitz asked the question again:

3. "Did you ever tell Abbattiscianni prior to her video deposition about the fact that there was an error like this?"
   **Answer:** "Yes, we had that discussion."

4. "When was that discussion?"
   **Answer:** "A few weeks ago"

5. "I'm not talking about a few weeks ago, her deposition was in November of 2008. Are you telling the judge that you had a conversation with her before that or not?"
   **Answer:** "I can't tell you if I did or I didn't."

6. "Glen Zeitz then questioned Prevoznik relative to the video deposition of Abbattiscianni when she clearly states that she said, "It's just the "<u>pain</u>" and up all night long hours. " Is that true?"
   **Answer:** "Yes."

7. "So, notwithstanding the email, or anything that you listened to, this, ...or someone else, listened to, that this was **her testimony** under oath at her video deposition which you just reviewed, correct?"
   **Answer:** "Yeah, after the fact, yeah."

**Attorney Zeitz:** "I have nothing else for Your Honor."

Chapter 18 - Driver Hearing

## Michelle Stankiewicz testified at the "Driver Hearing":
*The following is taken word for word from the superior court hearing*

Zeitz: Who do you work for?

Stankiewicz: I work for the Postal Inspection Service. I did then and I do now. I am a general analyst for the Inspection Service. I support a team of postal inspectors in 3 main areas. Investigative research, asset forfeiture, and victim witness issues."

Zeitz: Did you do the typing of the transcripts between Dr. Costino and the two undercover females?

Stankiewicz: Yes.

Zeitz: On page 3 *(of the Aug 3rd transcript)* did you type, **"it's just the "pain" and up all night long hours?**

Stankiewicz: Yes.

Zeitz: **You prepared this transcript based upon instructions that you were given by someone, correct?**

Stankiewicz: **Correct.**

Zeitz: And **who was the person who instructed you to prepare this transcript?**

Stankiewicz: **The case agent, Alex Sylvester.**

Zeitz: And I assume his instructions to you were to prepare the transcript of what you heard as accurately as possible?

Stankiewicz: Yes.

Zeitz: Following the transcription and at some point in time, did you give him, meaning Sylvester, the transcript that you identified as the **August 3rd visit?**

| | |
|---|---|
| Stankiewicz: | Yes. |
| Zeitz: | Did there come a time when **Mr. Sylvester stated to you that there was an error in this transcription?** |
| Stankiewicz: | **Yes.** |
| Zeitz: | What did you supposedly type incorrectly? |
| Stankiewicz: | **The word "pain"** |
| Zeitz: | Did Mr. Sylvester ask you to review again the disc and **retype page 3?** |
| Stankiewicz: | Yes. |
| Zeitz: | **Was it the August 3rd, 2007 transcript?** |
| Stankiewicz: | Yes. |
| Zeitz: | Now were you told to change anything else other than the word **"pain"?** |
| Stankiewicz: | Not that I recall. |

*On further questioning, Michelle Stankowictz states the following:*

| | |
|---|---|
| Stankiewicz: | After listening to the recording on the CD again in the presence of Alex Sylvester, the question to Abbattiscianni, was "Maggie, what's the matter?" |

In reality, my question posed to Abbattiscianni in my office that day was **"Maggie, what's wrong?"**

# Chapter 18 - Driver Hearing

Furthermore, **instead of accurately typing "it's just the pain and up all night till 4 in the morning"** she typed the following:

```
"I mean it's just the same as Tonya here,
it's just I'm up all night, and I just
need something to bring me down a little
bit during the day."
```

**This CD recording, this transcript, this EVIDENCE, WAS ALTERED.** Michelle Stankowicz typed, with Sylvester right next to her, instead of seven words, she typed **29 fictitious words.** Mr. Zeitz then asked Ms. Stankowicz the following:

**Zeitz:** Did you have custody of those tapes?

**Stankiewicz:** **I did not.** I only had custody while they were in my possession to transcribe, and other than that, **custody of these CDs were with other agents.**

**The next witness questioned by Mr. Zeitz was Alexander Sylvester, the Postal Inspector:** *The following is taken word for word from the superior court hearing.*

Zeitz: By whom are you employed?

Sylvester: The United States Postal Inspection Service.

Zeitz: Were you part of the investigation involving Dr. Costino?

Sylvester: Yes, I was.

Zeitz: The lady who just testified, do you know her?

Sylvester: Yes.

Zeitz: Did you give her any assignment with regard to this matter?

Sylvester: Yes, she had an assignment to transcribe *some* of the recordings that were made.

Zeitz: Have you ever done that with her before?

Sylvester: Yes, (and then Sylvester says,) "I don't recall."

Zeitz: What were your instructions to Ms. Stankowicz?

Sylvester: Just to listen to the tape and transcribe.

Zeitz: Did she do that?

Sylvester: Yes.

Zeitz: On the original transcript of August 3, 2007, what was the original answer to Dr. Costino's question?

Sylvester: "It's just the "**pain**" and up all night long hours."

## Chapter 18 - Driver Hearing

**Zeitz:** Did there come a time when that was changed to a different transcript, a change in that language?

**Sylvester:** Yes.

**Zeitz:** When was that?

**Sylvester:** February, the following year.

**Zeitz:** And did you listen to the tape?

**Sylvester:** No, I did not do that.

**Zeitz:** Would that be your standard procedure normally?

**Sylvester:** It depends, it was really time consuming, I had to go back and go word by word. **That's not what we did.**

**Zeitz:** Isn't it important that you get an accurate transcript as soon as possible?

**Sylvester:** Of course.

**Zeitz:** **The only way you can get an accurate transcript is to compare the transcript, and listen to the tape, correct?**

**Sylvester:** **Correct.**

**Zeitz:** **In this particular case, are you saying that you never sat down with the tape, and the transcript, and compared the tape and the transcript?**

**Sylvester:** I'm saying I didn't go line by line and compare the transcripts to the tape. "After she was done, meaning Stankowicz, we reviewed not the whole tape, we sat down and went over the wording."

**Zeitz:** **Did you go over the entirety?**

**Sylvester:** **No,** it was just given over to the DEA after we were done transcribing.

**Zeitz:** Did you have any conversations with David Puteska?

**Sylvester:** Yes, I believe so.

**Zeitz:** And the CD was provided to the postal Inspector by the DEA, correct?

**Sylvester:** Correct.

**Zeitz:** Then it was a copy that they had provided to you, correct?

**Sylvester:** Correct.

**Zeitz:** Was that copy between the first time Abbattiscianni was transcribed and the second time it was transcribed, was it ever altered by yourself or was it ever altered by anyone to your knowledge?

**Sylvester:** Not to my knowledge.

**Zeitz:** Was there any alteration done between the first transcription and the second transcription?

**Sylvester:** No

**Zeitz:** What did you do following the transcription?

**Sylvester:** I turned it over immediately to Tom Provosnik.

**Zeitz:** How would you know that it was the same one, that it wasn't changed in some fashion by somebody in the interim? How would you know that?

**Sylvester:** I'm sorry, are you asking me, the CD that was given to me by the DEA initially was transcribed on August 3, was that the same CD, where did the second CD come from? Is that the question?

**Zeitz:** I'm saying, how would you know during that interim if somebody didn't do anything to it?

## Chapter 18 - Driver Hearing

**Sylvester:** Because the CDs are locked up, they're stored in my office.

**Zeitz:** In your office?

**Sylvester:** Yes.

**Zeitz:** And you're saying that was for the entire time?

**Sylvester:** Yes, it was.

Interestingly enough, Mr. Sylvester stated that the CD recordings are stored in his office, however Prevoznic, the DEA supervisor, and the other characters in the DEA, stated that the CDs were stored in the New Jersey State Police files, not the DEA files, and not the postal service files.

As strange as this sounds, these are the **facts** stated at the "driver hearing " by law enforcement. Abbattiscianni stated clearly to me at the office visit of August 3, 2007, " It's just the "**pain**" and up all night long hours." The August 3, 2007, transcript **was altered**, and the alteration, instead of seven words, consisted of 29 words. **They are the facts, as I have both transcripts from the prosecutor's office as proof of this CRIMINAL ACTIVITY AND DECEPTION.** However there has been no admission of guilt assigned to any party.

The "Driver hearing " was certainly interesting, as it placed several characters involved with the actual recorders used by the undercover females, which in my opinion, were **destroyed** by law enforcement. The Driver hearing underscores a number of **inaccuracies, and perjury** under oath by both Thomas Prevoznik, and Alex Sylvester. Mr. Zeitz and I were **never able to identify the original recorders, or where the original CDs were stored.** We do, however, have both transcripts which begs the question, **who really altered the CD recordings and the transcripts?**

## "Due Process" Denied

*FAST FORWARD to MY CRIMINAL TRIAL for a moment…*

Both Prevosnik and Sylvester testified for the prosecutor at my **criminal trial** in **November of 2012.** At this trial the jury members listened very carefully throughout, and understood the s̲**ubversive and fundamentally dishonest testimony** of Prevosnik and Sylvester, and realized the level of **legal tyranny** that law enforcement was able to accomplish for five years. **None of these liars, and perjurers in my criminal case either in Cape May County or at the Board of Medical Examiners in Trenton** *EVER RECEIVED* **any punishment from the so-called, "justice system", for their dishonesty, perjury, and** *ABUSE OF POWER.*

**The "Driver hearing" is another example of the subversive, and corrupt conspiracy between law enforcement agencies to create their narrative…by** *altering the office recordings.* Fortunately my attorney, Mr. Glenn Zeitz, was both **intuitive** and **perceptive** in his ability to disassemble their fundamental errors and bring them to the surface.

# Healthcare Claims Fraud

"The natural aristocracy of talent should dictate the culture, not democracy or politics."

"The truth is incontrovertible, malice may attack it, and ignorance my deride it, but in the end, there it is."
- Winston Churchill

## The Drama is in the Details

*Between the criminal case in chief orchestrated by Robert Taylor and assisted by certain detectives, and assistant prosecutors in Cape May County, and in collusion with Sandra Dick at the Board of Medical Examiners, assisted by David Puteska, Mr. Taylor decided, in an attempt to persuade me to plead to his egregious charges, Taylor indicted both my wife, Barbara and myself for Healthcare Claims Fraud. The following represents the two healthcare claims fraud indictments that this moronic prosecutor created out of thin air, through his delusional thought process, and caused further grief to both myself and my wife, and had to be defended completely.*

In the early part of 2009, Assistant Prosecutor Megan Hoerner notified my attorney Glenn Zeitz that the Cape May County Prosecutor Taylor accused both myself and my wife of 62 separate criminal counts of healthcare claims fraud, and 62 criminal counts of conspiracy. As absurd as this may seem to my reading audience, this actually happened. According to the moronic Prosecutor Robert Taylor, this indictment was produced as a result of an investigation by none other than Detective George Hallett, in the prosecutor's office regarding my office billing concerning "physical therapy". First of all, the morons should know that I do not practice physical therapy, I am a licensed physician. As a physician, I practice "rehabilitative medicine", and have been doing rehabilitative medicine in my office in North Wildwood for thirty-five years.

The genesis of this escapade was commenced by a dishonest lawyer by the name of Alan Lands of Pleasantville, New Jersey. By way of history, a patient of mine was injured as a result of an accident that occurred in the North Cape May Acme market in November 2001. As a result of this accident, the patient sustained multiple trauma to her trunk and extremities, with multiple contusions, strain and sprain of her cervical thoracic and lumbar areas, and right upper extremity, along with a tear in the posterior horn of the medial meniscus of her right knee.

The patient came under my care initially in the acute phase, and several weeks later, she began a rehabilitative program in my office in an attempt to relieve her symptoms, improve her ambulation, and general welfare. The patient was a 64-year-old female, treated in my office for several months. During the pendency of her treatment program, she sustained another injury in the form of a slip and fall with fracture of her right wrist in her home. As a result of the fracture in her right wrist she was referred to an orthopedic specialist for both the right wrist fracture and the torn meniscus in her right knee.

The patient eventually retained a lawyer by the name of Theodore Smith of Pleasantville, NJ. Mr. Smith did send to my office the required letters of protection to ensure payment to my office for treatment received. For one reason or another, the patient's legal representation was transferred to a second lawyer, his friend, Alan Lands.

The patient's past medical history included a cerebral vascular accident in 1996 with residual left sided weakness, a myocardial infarction in 1997, a left carotid endarterectomy in 1992, a history of diabetes mellitus, and pancreatitis. The patient was treated in my office for her injuries, from December 2001 to September 2002. During this period of time the patient eventually received a program of "rehabilitative medicine" on and off directed primarily to her lumbar region, right knee, and right wrist. I examined this patient at each office visit to assess her progress. Her medical treatment continued under her family physician, and she was also treated by a local orthopedic surgeon. As a result of her significant past medical history, and her current injuries, I personally spent a great deal of time with her and obviously treated her on a conservative basis. The referral orthopedic surgeon declined to perform any surgical procedures for her as a result of her past medical history, and underlying vascular disease. The patient was discharged from my care in mid-September of 2002 with reasonable improvement in her clinical status with certain residuals relating to both her significant past medical history, and current injuries.

Her legal case eventually went before a judge, and Mr. Lands was able to obtain a reasonable monetary settlement. Lands received my total bill for treatment, which was conservative, and following his settlement, decided to release only a partial payment of this bill for service. After multiple discussions with Lands, and also with the patient's prior attorney Theodore Smith, Lands made a decision **not** to fulfill the signed written agreement for payment. The letter of protection signed by Mr. Smith and assigned to Mr. Lands is a **legal document.** This refusal by Lands became an ethical violation of the attorney's obligation, and following my attempts to collect a reasonable fee, I reported Lands to the **ethics board** of the state of New Jersey. This "ethics violation" eventually came under the Disciplinary Review Board of the Supreme Court of New Jersey at the Richard Hugh's Justice complex in Trenton. The issue however was heard at the local Atlantic County Review Board completely controlled by two of his lawyer buddies in Atlantic County.

**My formal complaint charged Lands with "allegations of unethical conduct, a violation of truthfulness with regard to statements to others which provides in pertinent part, representing a client."**

1. "A lawyer shall not knowingly make false statements of a material fact of law to a third person."

**2.** "A violation of misconduct which provides that it is professional misconduct for a lawyer to engage in conduct that is prejudicial to the administration of justice."

**3.** "A violation in safekeeping of property, which provides upon receiving funds or other property in which a client or third person has interest, the lawyer shall promptly notify the client and deliver to the client any funds or other property that the client or third person is entitled to receive."

The state of New Jersey provided me with an excellent lawyer, **Willis Flowers, Esq.**, to defend my position in this **ethics violation** case. A hearing was conducted in May 2006, and Lands retained an attorney to defend his position. The major problem that existed is the following:

There were three lawyers from Atlantic County, at this hearing, all colleagues of Lands, who essentially defended his actions in spite of the fact that there was a signed contract for payment for services rendered. This panel of his buddies stated, "that we find that Mr. Lands failure to fulfill the contract made with Dr. Costino regarding payment for services rendered to his client, **does not rise to the level of unethical conduct.**" Furthermore, The District 1 ethics committee formed by his three buddies found that "Mr. Lands failure to call back Dr. Costino and appraise him of the windfall settlement that was reached one hour after he cleverly had Dr. Costino's bill conditionally compromised did not rise to the level of <u>unethical conduct</u>." As a result, and as you might imagine, I was never paid the proper conservative fee regarding the treatment of this patient and the matter was then concluded.

Now fast forward to early 2007, at the Cape May County Prosecutor's department, while planning to send two undercover females into my office in an attempt to entrap me. Lands, the dishonest lawyer that I had dealt with several years prior, called a meeting and invited Assistant Prosecutor Megan Hoerner, DEA Investigator Thomas Prevoznik, and postal inspector, Alex Sylvester. He

## Chapter 19 - Healthcare Claims Fraud

also serendipitously notified the Board of Medical Examiners that I had billed his former client, the client in question, for office visits without seeing her as a patient. **This of course is a blatant lie, from a very clever liar.** At the meeting of the above characters, Lands stated that my office billed his client for several "physical therapy modalities" that were never performed. Again representing another **blatant lie** from this **fundamentally dishonest lawyer.** Lands cleverly portrayed to the above individuals his false statements and misrepresentations in an effort to criminalize my practice of medicine. Alan Lands, however, never testified to his blatant lies, under oath, in superior court.

In September 2008 two detectives from the prosecutor's office were sent to interview several members of my office staff who assisted on a part-time basis with medical patients and with my rehabilitation patients. The two detectives were Paul Worrell, and Trish Kalita.

As a licensed physician, registered in the state of New Jersey, to practice both medicine and surgery, I have been in the practice of **rehabilitation medicine** for approximately thirty-five years. I am not a physical therapist, therefore, I do not perform physical therapy. In my thirty-five years of practice I have treated all types of injuries and accidents, motor vehicle accidents, worker's compensation accidents, and sports injuries. I have in my office a full rehabilitative array of treatment modalities ranging from mechanical massage table for soft tissue injuries, whirlpool therapy for upper and lower extremity issues, muscle stimulation, and ultrasound equipment, both stationary and recumbent bicycle modalities for upper and lower extremity issues, and the full "Cybex Isokinetics dynamometry" equipment for the "rehabilitation" of **surgical knees, hips, and shoulders.** I've been doing this work for more than thirty-five years, beginning as a medical student in the 1960s when I assisted in an industrial medical clinic performing multiple types of rehabilitation.

Both Paul Worrell and Trish Kalita, **interviewed and intimidated** my innocent staff employees who assisted my wife Barbara Haas R.N.P.A., and myself in the administration of rehabilitative medicine. These modalities were performed two or three times per week relative to the type of injury, and severity of injury sustained by each individual patient. **According to my employees, both Worrell and Kalita questioned and intimidated them in an attempt to criticize, and criminalize my rehabilitative practice without any critical knowledge of the subject.** My employees told both detectives that their job was to bring patients into the room for rehabilitation, do the paperwork, set up additional appointments, and assist with the injured and older patients on and off the various apparatus, set up and assist in the rehabilitation program administered primarily by my wife Barbara, *R.N., P.A.*

Their job was to assist patients in the office, and to avoid further injuries to the patient while under rehabilitative treatment. Furthermore, these part-time staff members accompanied the patients throughout the treatment program to prevent any additional injury, and to schedule the patient with the appropriate paperwork for the next appointment. My employees were responsible individuals who took great care, and great concern regarding the welfare of the patients treated in my office.

98% of these patients treated in my office improved, and we're happy with their treatment program. A few, of course, are always unhappy regardless of the outcome. Both Worrell and Kalita attempted to twist the words of my staff members, and the contents of these interviews in a methodology, that would cloud the issues of treatment. I have examined all of these interviews carefully, and my impressions are as follows:

Both Worrell and Kalita represent another example of **dishonesty, and abuse of power,** in an attempt to coerce my employees into a dialogue that would favor them in an attempt to implicate my office personnel and myself in some nefarious activity. This represents an additional attempt to **criminalize** my practice of medicine. Please be aware that neither Hoerner, Kalita, nor Worrell, or any of my employees, ever testified against me at my criminal trial in October of 2012.

**On July 28, 2009** a Cape May County Grand Jury orchestrated by Assistant Prosecutor Megan Hoerner, and Detective Trish Kalita, through PROSECUTORIAL MISCONDUCT, DECEPTION AND MISREPRESENTATION OF THE FACTS, **returned a 124 count indictment charging both myself and**

## Chapter 19 - Healthcare Claims Fraud

my wife with **62 counts** of **healthcare claims fraud, and 62 separate counts of conspiracy,** *WITHOUT EVER EXAMINING ANY REHABILITATION PATIENT MEDICAL RECORDS.*

**Stop and think about that for a moment and consider the fact that I have been in practice for thirty-five years in North Wildwood following five years full-time as an emergency room physician, and these morons in Cape May County feel very comfortable with their** *ridiculous accusations* **with absolutely no knowledge whatsoever of what I do in my office. Furthermore,** *neither the Cape May County detectives, or prosecutors, ever examined any of my 62 rehabilitation patient medical records.*

**Please understand the following:**

There are certain rules and regulations that a physician must follow in order to perform "rehabilitation medicine" in a professional office. In addition to office personnel, the regulations require at least one licensed medical personnel in the office at all times for the administration of "rehabilitation medicine". Both myself, a licensed physician, and my wife Barbara a licensed registered nurse and a certified physicians assistant, were present 100% of the time in the office performing these rehabilitative medical treatments. My female employee / assistants, were hired to assist both myself and Barbara collectively in the care of these patients. **My assistants did not "treat anyone". I am the treating physician.**

**Healthcare claims fraud** is defined as:

> "making or causing to be made a false, fictitious, fraudulent, or misleading statement of a material fact in or omitting a material fact from or causing a material fact to be omitted from any record, bill, claim, or other document in writing, electronically or in any other form, that a person attempts to submit, submits, causes to be submitted, or attempts to cause to be submitted for payment, or reimbursement, for health care services"

# "Due Process" Denied

"An indictment must be dismissed if the prosecutor's misconduct is **EXTREME**, and clearly infringes upon the grand jury's decision-making function. An indictment must be dismissed if upon a palpable showing of fundamental unfairness, or when there is conduct of the prosecutor, or his witness, that amounts to an interference with the grand jury's decision-making function. "The court should not hesitate to dismiss an indictment if the evidence establishes that the conduct of the prosecutor in obtaining an indictment amounted to an intentional subversion of the grand jury process. If the record in the case demonstrates such conduct of that quality, dismissal of the indictment is the only appropriate remedy."

It was clear to Judge Batten, that neither detective Kalita or Assistant Prosecutor Hoerner understood the CPT coding system, and the associated modalities that patients received in my office. Kalita **erroneously** stated that the investigation focused on five physical modalities which all required a licensed healthcare provider. Early in the grand jury testimony Kalita was asked by Hoerner certain questions regarding the types of physical modalities utilized. Kalita stated to the grand jury that the defendant administered five different physical modalities that were required to be provided by a licensed healthcare provider. **Kalita, however, never identified these specific modalities to the grand jury. The billing and CPT codes, demonstrate that her statements were false.** Later in her testimony Kalita repeated this information relative to the CPT coding system, and she again stated to the grand jury that there were five types of therapeutic procedures and activities that were given to patients which required a licensed healthcare provider.

Notably, Kalita testified that these modalities were identified, however she failed miserably to specifically identify any of them. **Kalita, Hoerner, and the state completely misunderstood, and misrepresented the relevant CPT codes, and furnished inaccurate and false information to the grand jury.** Kalita **erroneously** stated multiple times, that my office administered five specific modalities, that all required a licensed healthcare provider. **The CPT codes however demonstrate that her testimony was totally incorrect.**

## Chapter 19 - Healthcare Claims Fraud

**Furthermore, the state did not submit any relevant billing to the grand jury.** The state did not go through the individual billing with the grand jury, and did not identify any false or fictitious billing information to the grand jury. The billing accurately identified my "rehabilitative treatment", and "exercise program", that each and every patient received in my office. **The evidence demonstrates that the state presented erroneous and misleading testimony to the grand jury.** **This presentation by Horner, and Kalita, represented "prima fascia" evidence** of <u>**prosecutorial misconduct**</u>, which <u>**required dismissal of the entire indictment**</u>.

In open court, and in his wisdom, after listening to this erroneous and misleading testimony given by Detective Kalita, and directed assistant prosecutor Megan Hoerner, Judge Batten **dismissed this entire indictment**. The presentation by Hoerner, and Kalita, **was erroneous, incongruent, and false**. Our attorneys Glenn Zeitz, and John Tumelty, defended these false and erroneous statements made by the state concisely, and completely. The final result was that Judge Batten **dismissed the entire 124 criminal count indictment**.

This entire episode regarding my rehabilitative medical practice began as a result of the **pernicious, venomous,** and **malicious lies** rendered by Alan Lands in an attempt to criminalize my medical practice. Judge Batten dismissed the entire indictment because both the **optics, and kinetics** of my rehabilitation medicine we're completely **misunderstood and misrepresented** by both **ignorant,** and frankly, **stupid** detectives and prosecutors in Cape May County.

If this dismissal was not clear enough for Taylor, approximately one year later, in August of 2010, this moronic prosecutor, Robert Taylor, decided to re-indict my wife and I, **for a second time, for health care claims fraud.**

Taylor assigned a second assistant prosecutor, Matthew Weintraub, and Trish Kalita *again,* for this task. When I express that certain members of the Cape May County prosecutor's office, and certain detectives, are both **stupid and ignorant**. **I have a firm basis for my opinions.**

The second indictment for healthcare claims fraud is the textbook example of the **Dunning-Kruger effect:**

**INCOMPETENT PEOPLE think they are amazing, and they rate themselves as near expert, while they lack the critical thinking and knowledge of the discipline that they attack.** *The drama is in the details.*

This represents a **perceptual blindness, a cognitive bias,** and the **anchoring effect** that they simply cannot discharge from their "medieval brains". The **molecular labyrinth** in which these prosecutor creatures and detectives existed, created nothing more than an advanced level of **confusion, and lunacy** in which they all *spun around,* for another ten months.

The **second indictment** for healthcare claims fraud was produced on August 24, 2010. Instead of 126 criminal counts, this indictment was based upon three counts. Detective Kalita was again the lead investigator and Matthew Weintraub the assistant prosecutor in Cape May County. Kalita and some of her fellow detectives arrived in my home with a subpoena demanding 25 additional rehabilitative medical charts. After finally reviewing these rehabilitative medical records, the morons whittled the 25 down to 3 medical records. All three criminal counts were concerned with the treatment, and billing of the office visits of 3 patients. Eventually, a hearing to dismiss was again held by Judge Batten on October 21, 2010. Briefs and motions were filed to dismiss this indictment on the following grounds:

1. **The state engaged in prosecutorial misconduct by providing false and misleading testimony to the grand jury on critical facts and relevant administrative code sections.**

2. **The state failed to present exculpatory evidence.**

3. **The state improperly introduced inflammatory, and erroneous evidence that tainted the grand jury presentation.**

## Chapter 19 - Healthcare Claims Fraud

Matthew Weintraub presented the testimony of Detective Kalita to the grand jury. Kalita stated to the grand jury that she **examined and collated** the **billing records, medical records, and the insurance records** of these three patients. Kalita stated to the grand jury that she interviewed my employees who assisted in my rehabilitative process. Kalita **erroneously testified** to the grand jury that defendants committed **billing fraud** by allowing an unlicensed employee to perform **"electrical stimulation T.E.N.S. therapy"**. *Please let that statement by Kalita sink in!!!*

Kalita stated to the grand jury in more than **25 individual statements** that my office submitted fraudulent bills for a "physical therapy" modality that she **erroneously titled, "electrical stimulation T.E.N.S. therapy."**
There *IS NO SUCH MODALITY*
in the CPT coding system!!

**There *is no such modality* in the CPT coding system, yet Kalita stated to the grand jury, more than 25 separate times, this erroneous statement.**

Kalita's testimony to the grand jury represented a **flagrant misrepresentation** regarding the modalities contained in my **billing records, my medical records, and the insurance documents.** It is imperative that the reader understands that "T.E.N.S. therapy" treatment and mechanism is completely separate from a second modality called electrical stimulation given to the patient in a different setting altogether. Therefore, THE **GRAND JURY WAS DELIBERATELY MISINFORMED AND MISLEAD.**

Kalita *conflated* legitimate, and separate physical modalities into one **fictitious treatment modality that she "invented in her head".** There is simply no CPT code for her fictitious statement. The grand jury transcript was replete with **false statements, and misinformation,** regarding the critical aspects of my rehabilitative practice. **This grand jury presentation was false, unfair, and substantially tainted by the erroneous and fictitious information which required a dismissal of the indictment.**

**This indictment should also be dismissed based upon prosecutorial misconduct, by presenting FALSE AND MISLEADING EVIDENCE to the grand jury.** Detective Kalita presented **false testimony** regarding my rehabilitative therapy services clearly identified in the *billing records, my medical records, and the insurance records.* **Kalita never introduced to the grand jury any of these records, or any other relevant documents.** Kalita, however, *unequivocally* stated to the grand jury that she both **"examined"** and **"collated"** my treatment *records, billing records, and insurance statements,* **over and over again in more than 25 separate statements to the grand jury!!!**

**Kalita erroneously stated more than 25 times that I submitted fraudulent bills for "electrical stimulation T.E.N.S. therapy".** Furthermore, Kalita **misrepresented the actual comments of all three patients that she interviewed in preparation for her grand jury testimony.** Additionally, Weintraub and Kalita FAILED to present exculpatory evidence to the grand jury.

Assistant prosecutor Matthew Weintraub received our defense briefs, outlining the **false factual statements,** made by Kalita at the grand jury presentation for healthcare claims fraud. It became clear to assistant prosecutor Weintraub, that Kalita **completely misrepresented the facts** when stating to the grand jury that she **"examined" and "collated"** my *treatment records, billing records, and insurance records*. After digesting our briefs, it was clear to Mr. Weintraub that Detective Kalita gave **completely false testimony under oath to the grand jury with gross misconduct, knowingly, willfully and maliciously.**

In open court, and at the beginning of the **"hearing to dismiss"** in superior court with Judge Raymond Batten, the judge asked Assistant Prosecutor Weintraub if he was ready to begin the hearing. Following the judge's question to Weintraub, this is what occurred, *word for word, and it's a classic:*

*Mr. Weintraub abruptly rose from his chair, and stated to the judge:*
> **"I am at this time leaving the county of Cape May, thank you very much."**

## Chapter 19 - Healthcare Claims Fraud

*In all seriousness, following his statement to the judge, Weintraub abruptly left the courtroom...never to return.*

The rest of the courtroom sat there in amazement and the judge was then forced to terminate this "hearing to dismiss" at that time for 30 days, as it was necessary for the county of Cape May to replace Assistant Prosecutor Weintraub with yet another prosecutor. This, of course, presented a problem for the county of Cape May. So, approximately one month later, they recruited a third assistant prosecutor to carry on with this hearing.

The next prosecutor assigned to this task was Tina Kell. On March 22, 2011 we again assembled in the courtroom for the "hearing to dismiss." Assistant Prosecutor Kell appeared to be a "deer in the headlights", who knew nothing regarding my rehabilitative office practice, and next to nothing regarding this case. At this point in time, Mr. Tumelty represented my wife, Barbara, and I represented myself, *"pro se"*. Assistant Prosecutor Kell wrote a brief in which she attempted to explain, and to rectify, the flawed grand jury presentment done by Weintraub and Kalita. Her brief was replete with **errors, and misrepresentations,** regarding my rehabilitative practice, in her attempt to correct the **false and incongruent statements** given to the grand jury by Weintraub and Kalita.

I wrote a brief *"pro se"*, to counter Kell's numerous **mistakes and false testimony** defined in the presentation by Kalita from both a legal and professional perspective. In short, Kell attempted to counter the **errors, false narratives, and misrepresentations,** made by Kalita, however, Kell's brief was **miserably defective on factual representation.** Furthermore, **all exculpatory evidence** was withheld from the grand jury by Weintraub, Kalita and Kell, regarding **CPT coding, medical billing, and the relevant modalities** incorporated in my "rehabilitative medicine practice".

To reiterate, detective Kalita falsely stated to the grand jury that **"electrical stimulation T.E.N.S. therapy,"** was identified on the super bills, and that patients were billed for this modality but did not receive this treatment. **There is no such CPT code for "electrical stimulation T.E.N.S. therapy."** There *has never* been submitted to any insurance company, *bills* for this modality since **it does not exist. It *has never* been found in any of my treatment records, insurance statements, or the patient's medical chart because IT DOESN'T EXIST.** Both Weintraub, and Kalita, made reference to a CPT code that *"was never in my treatment records or billing records"*. **"Electrical stimulation T.E.N.S. therapy" does not exist as a CPT code or anywhere else**. Kalita provided this false and misleading information to the grand jury **more than 25 separate times during her grand jury presentation**. These *false and misleading statements* represent **GROSS PROSECUTORIAL MISCONDUCT AND PERJURY on the part of Detective Kalita.**

Assistant Prosecutor Tina Kell attempted to rectify the **errors and misrepresentations** outlined above by Weintraub and Kalita. Unfortunately, Tina Kell was completely **ignorant** of the practice of "rehabilitative medicine" and represents another example of the "Dunning-Kruger" effect.

This second healthcare claims fraud indictment **was dismissed** by Judge Batten as a result of the **gross prosecutorial misconduct,** by both the prosecutors and detectives. Collectively, they presented **false, misleading, and incongruent statements** to the grand jury throughout the entire presentment. Furthermore, at the conclusion of the "hearing to dismiss," **Judge Batten said the following**:

> "**How in America can an indictment return substantially predicated upon facts not accurate be permitted to stand, and this indictment was an indictment based upon factual inaccuracy, and no one in this court's view at least, should be required to stand trial based upon inaccurate tracks, however developed before the grand jury, but this, to this court is not, not a close call. And that's my decision."**

Robert Taylor, George Hallett, Paul Worrell, Trish Kalita, Matthew Weintraub, Megan Hoerner, and Tina Kell are just a few representatives of the **pernicious, dangerous**, and **destructive operatives** of the Cape May County Prosecutor's Office. Their leader, Robert Taylor, exemplified **gross misconduct** in a public official. These creatures are **not elected**, but are **simply appointed**,

## Chapter 19 - Healthcare Claims Fraud

and represent the **paradox of perception, and hypocrisy** of many public officials not only in Cape May County, but throughout the state of New Jersey**, especially at the Board of Medical Examiners.**

My medical practice was under siege by these **corrupt** individuals principally, because they **have no understanding of medicine, the practice of medicine, or medical law.** They have no understanding with regard to the caring concern that doctors render to their patients. With both rehabilitative medicine indictments, it was clear to Judge Batten that these prosecutorial creatures and their detectives were **completely ignorant**, regarding their interpretation of my practice, representing gross misconduct, and perjury which was given knowingly, willfully and maliciously, to the grand jury.

**I am a physician, licensed to practice medicine and surgery, registered in the state of New Jersey, and additionally licensed and certified, for the treatment of opioid addiction by the Drug Enforcement Agency, and devoted to my patients.**

**The above characters, and especially Taylor, the chief lunatic, couldn't give a damn regarding my practice of medicine, my office staff, my wife and family, or my patients. His goal was simply to destroy me**. The above characters, in my opinion, are *devoid of a moral compass, fundamentally dishonest* **and have an innate ability to** *weaponize law-enforcement,* **and continue the criminalization of medicine.** With their **abuse of power**, these detectives and prosecutors were able to **threaten and intimidate** my office staff, who are all law-abiding citizens. **In my opinion, they are** *narcissistic,* **suffer from** *personality deficits,* **along with their** *egomania, and delusional manifestations.*

Notwithstanding the indictments against me, **these two indictments against my wife, Barbara Haas,** *RNPA,* **represents the perfect example of the corrupt, deplorable, and fundamentally dishonest action by the CMC Prosecutor, his assistants and detectives associated with this case.**

**These creatures are the bottom feeders representing the so-called "justice system".**

**"Unfortunately, the justice system today consists of mostly inadequate personalities with evil intent".**

In my absolute opinion, the real criminals in my case are the justice system personalities identified throughout this text, who are **fundamentally dishonest, subversive, and devoid of a moral compass,** with their only goal, to criminalize my practice of medicine with their abuse of power, and legal tyranny.

"Reliance on authority becomes a paradox,
those with authority my be criminal with poor judgment, or narcissistic,
and incompetent, and plainly ignorant, with no common sense."
- John G. Costino

Crime is a defective exercise of free will,
a betrayal of one's character.

"Distrust all in whom the impulse to punish is powerful"
- Frederick William Nietzsche

*My impression* since September 2007 is simply:

# Distrust all authority.

# The Criminal Trial and Outcome

"What happens, happens to everyone sooner or later.
It's not what happens that determines your life's future,
it's what you do about what happens."

It's one thing to spar with an opposing attorney who is challenging my testimony as an expert witness in a workers compensation case. It's a different thing altogether however, to be that other physician, whose judgment is on trial. My defense attorney tells me that the outcome of the trial will ultimately come down to me, whether the jury believes I am a good physician, who does my best for my patients, and did what a reasonable and prudent physician would do.

The issue now lies in the hands of the twelve jurors of my peers. They may be as unhappy to be here as I am, twelve individuals whose only real criterion for involvement is that they live in the same county where I practice medicine. They will be asked to understand a complex set of often conflicting medical facts, and reconcile competing portrayals **of my medical decision making**. They will be asked to decide if my practice conformed to that of a board certified family physician of ordinary learning, judgment, and skill, the definition of the standard of care that seems impossibly vague.

In the courtroom, the prosecuting attorney makes statements that cannot be challenged, makes scientific claims that are **fundamentally false**, and accuses me of failures to which I cannot respond. The courtroom is arranged with a jury box very close to where the witness sits. To look at the jury would require me to actively turn in my chair, bringing me within a few feet of the nearest juror, **which**

# "Due Process" Denied

**is exactly what I did**. As a former high school teacher, I must convince the jurors that I am a fundamentally good and prudent physician, attempting to do so in a way that is simple, but not condescending. I must be confident but not arrogant, concerned but not disingenuous, in front of family members, the press, and random members of the public who may wander into the court room to observe.

My position is clear as I attempt to look both confident and professional with my ongoing testimony. Physicians are used to being in control however being a defendant in the courtroom means giving up this control. The night before the final day of the trial, my attorney spends several hours preparing his closing argument, and this is the moment for trial attorneys when they are most on stage, when they need to be most **persuasive, eloquent, and honest**. It is powerful experiences to watch my attorney John Tumelty, a master professional perform on my behalf in front of a full courtroom, the judge, the prosecutor, and the public. As the jury is given final instructions, my fundamental belief is that I did the right thing, and that I would make the same decisions again, and then whatever the jury decides my life as a physician should go on. **We waited less than two hours, for the verdict.**

The jury returned to the quart room, and Judge Batten then said to them ladies and gentlemen of the jury have you reached a decision. The jury foreman responded "yes we have your honor…**not guilty**".

We spend our lives as physicians attempting to predict the future however, the answer is rarely never, and never always, as physicians we work in shades of gray. The law attempts to work only in black and white. I am either right or wrong. There are no other choices. Finally twelve jurors said I was all right. It must be the truth.

My criminal trial began in late October 2012, and lasted for approximately 10 days. Dara Paley assistant prosecutor of Cape May County controlled by Robert Taylor, attempted to frame her prosecution in such a way as to **eliminate my judgment** as the physician in the practice of medicine. The law in the state of New Jersey as stated previously is "State V Vaccaro". It is the superior court appellate published decision which outlines the issues regarding the prescribing

## Chapter 20 - The Criminal Trial and Outcome

of class two, three, four, and five pharmaceutical products by the physician.

**"Vaccaro"** states in part under drugs and narcotics page 168 of the record, that "a physician's license and registration authorizes him to dispense controlled substances, but under this statute he is **"immune"** from criminal liability when he dispenses same in good faith in the course of his professional practice only". A physician who is honest and ethical and who dispenses these drugs in a good faith effort to treat and cure patients, has no fear of the criminal sanctions of the statute". "A physician's license and registration authorizes him to dispense controlled dangerous products. " "This statue makes it clear that he is **immune** from criminal liability when he dispenses these products in good faith in the course of his professional practice only." "Furthermore, and when the statute circumscribes the limits of this exemption from its criminal consequences, by the utilization of the term "good faith" he knows, that is the physician knows full well what is meant and how he must comport himself." "There is nothing vague or ambiguous about the requirement that the legal dispensing of drugs by the physician must be carried out in "good faith" in the course of his professional practice only**". "It is a standard which is clear and understandable to the mind of any reasonable physician**, and is therefore beyond constitutional attack."

**"Vaccaro" is the law in the state of New Jersey,
and it has been the law with regard to
controlled pharmaceutical products since 1976.**

Early in my criminal trial, assistant prosecutor Dara Paley played the CD recordings of all of the conversations of the seven visits between myself and the two undercover females. Along with the CD recordings, all seven written transcripts were provided in order for the jury members to understand each and every word of each office visit as to what was said by myself, as well as the response from the individual females. The jury was permitted at any time during this exercise to ask questions regarding the words spoken, and or the words written. **I thank God that we were able to provide the written transcripts to the jury, to enable them to understand the entire dialogue at each office visit.**

Following the office visit renditions, which took a considerable amount of time, Dara Paley then called her witnesses one at a time for questioning. Following her questions, my attorney, John Tumelty, very **capably and concisely** conducted cross-examination.

Tonya Anderson, Thomas Prevoznik, and Alex Sylvester were **untruthful** under oath on the witness stand, **similarly to their untruthfulness** during the pendency of the criminal case, and especially at the "driver hearing", and office of administrative law hearing. Margarita Abbattiscianni, was truthful under oath on the witness stand, as she was truthful with her certifications, and truthful at the OAL civil trial and with her video deposition.

The prosecution's expert physician witness, Dr. Kaufman, was examined by the prosecuting attorney, Paley, and she was **unable** to create even a suspicion of guilt on my part, because Dr. Kaufman, the state's expert, knew that my judgment with regard to both undercover females was *legal, responsible, and conformed to the law*. He was *truthful* with regard to his responses.

John Tumelty cross-examined **Tonya Anderson**, [who would have been a perfect actress in the movie *Police Academy*], brilliantly precipitated, and brought to the surface Anderson's perjury with her first certification in 2008 and her perjury under oath at the administrative law civil trial before Judge Miller in December of 2008. By the time Mr. Tumelty finished his cross-examination of Tonya Anderson, it was clear to the jury members that Anderson had **zero credibility**. **She was disgraced under oath on the witness stand as the state's star witness.**

John Tumelty cross-examined the DEA supervisor **Thomas Prevoznik** and again he perjured himself stating to the jury that "Dr. Costino, *sold* prescriptions of controlled substances to both undercover females, and they *bought* these substances from him. **Prevoznik's attempt to convince the jury that my treatment was unlawful, (with regard to prescribing one pill at night after their dancing activity was unlawful), fell flat.** Prevoznik lost his credibility with the jury early on with his perjurious statements. Additionally the issue of Prevoznik attempting to convince Undercover II (Abbattiscianni) to alter her story with regard to whether or not she said **"pain"** at the August 3, 2007 office visit

## Chapter 20 - The Criminal Trial and Outcome

was also brought to the surface by Mr. Tumelty. These two issues were salient to the jury members, and clearly convinced all members of the jury that this DEA supervisor **was a first class confabulator of the truth**.

John Tumelty cross-examined postal service supervisor **Alex Sylvester,** and his testimony was also confusing to the jury. Sylvester you may remember was responsible for the completion of the transcripts of the office visits from the CDs to the printed format. Sylvester played a role in altering the transcripts of Undercover II along with other statements extracted from the transcripts mentioned earlier in this text. Recall if you will Prevoznik, and Sylvester, along with Hallett played a significant role in eliminating the word "pain" from the August 3, 2007 office visit transcript along with providing an additional 29 words in it's place. Additionally, there were two other main topics, removed from the CD recordings, and transcripts.

Recall the "driver hearing" which was held in an attempt to discover who indeed altered the transcripts. Who actually tampered with the undercover female recorders in this escapade? Recall, in addition to removing the word **"pain"** from the August 3 transcript, the words, " Do you date? ", with my answer " No, I'm married " was also removed. Additionally, Anderson asked me if she could bring additional girlfriends to my office for examination and treatment. "My answer was simply that I really did not want any more of these young women scantily dressed in my office simply because they would disturb my elderly patients."

The "driver hearing" was riddled with **lies and perjury under oath** on the part of both Prevoznik and Sylvester, along with confusing testimony by Michelle Stankiewicz, the postal employee, and typist of the office transcripts. The explanations at the "driver hearing" given by all witnesses, were unclear and arguably vague, as they never really revealed the truth regarding who altered the CD recordings and the transcripts. Furthermore, we never really found out the facts regarding the custody of the CD recordings or who actually stored these recordings for the many months during the pendency of the criminal case. Additionally, neither witness revealed the fate of the two recorders that the undercover females used that were probably destroyed by certain actors in the justice system. The recorders obviously were never examined by my experts.

**John Tumelty through cross-examination, was able to reveal all of the *lies, discrepancies, and inaccuracies* regarding Sylvester's testimony as it became clear to the jury members that this postal inspector was simply untruthful**.

Dara Paley made a very smart decision not to present George Hallett under oath on the witness stand, at my trial. I say it was a very smart decision simply because both Taylor and Paley realized that Hallett had previously given **perjured testimony** at the initial grand jury presentment in February 2008. Mr. Tumelty would have precipitated Hallett's **stupidity, and ignorance,** as well as his **perjury** with regard to his handling of a number of issues if placed on the witness stand.

John Tumelty cross-examined **Margarita Abbattiscianni.** Her testimony was brief, as this DEA employee was reasonable with her responses in the past, and she did not perjure herself at my trial.

The final prosecution witness was **Dr. Kaufman,** the state's expert, under questioning by Mr. Tumelty, was **unable** to create even a suspicion of criminal guilt with regard to my treatment of the two undercover females. Parenthetically, **Dr. Kaufman, through the brilliant cross-examination by Mr. Tumelty, essentially became a witness for my defense**.

**Upon completion of the prosecution witnesses, Mr. Tumelty then called our defense witnesses to the stand:**
**Detective Joseph Landis** testified in my behalf. Detective Landis as you may recall was sent to my office as the first undercover in December 2005 posing as a heroin addict. He was treated perfectly in my office, and placed on **Suboxone** for his addiction. Detective Landis was an excellent witness, and was able to reiterate to the jury members the entire narrative of his office visit with me. Following his office visit, he wrote an excellent report regarding this visit,

## Chapter 20 - The Criminal Trial and Outcome

and stated unequivocally there was no evidence, of any past issues with my work in pain management, or addiction therapy in the county of Cape May. Please recall that this entire episode of Detective Landis and the glowing report that he wrote in the prosecutor's office which is part of discovery, **was withheld from my attorney for 3 years.**

**Michelle Stankiewicz,** the postal service employee, and typist, next testified in my defense. She clearly stated to the jury that she originally typed the seven transcripts from the CDs provided by the DEA supervisor Thomas Prevoznik. She further stated several months later, she was given a second CD by her supervisor Alex Sylvester, also titled August 3, 2007. She was then asked to retype a certain portion of this CD by Sylvester. She was asked to do this retyping with Alex Sylvester sitting right next to her during this exercise. This second CD titled August 3, 2007 subtracted the word **"Pain"** from the original transcript, and added an additional 29 words. The first transcript stated **"it's just a pain and up all night till four in the morning".** The second transcript subtracted **pain**, but added an additional 29 words. When asked to explain this to the jury, Mrs. Stankiewicz became upset, and was simply unable to explain the differential between the original CD recording, and the second one both titled August 3, 2007.

Michelle Stankiewicz was visibly upset on the witness stand regarding this issue, and the jury members understood her anxiety with respect to the differential in the two transcripts. This witness was very clear on the fact that she was asked to do this second typing by Sylvester as he sat right next to her while she performed this task. Mr. Tumelty did not press her any further, as the jury members certainly understood her dilemma. The Jury members understood her testimony, and coupled with the previous cross-examination of both Alex Sylvester, and Thomas Prevoznik, it became clear to the jury members that flagrant violations of **evidence tampering** had taken place. It was clear to the jury members that the CDs and transcripts **were altered**. As a result of this alteration, it was further clear to the jury members that this alteration represented **criminal activity by law-enforcement**.

**Glenda Hamilton,** my expert in medical records and medical coding also testified in my behalf. She stated clearly to the jury under direct questioning that the medical records of both undercover females were better than average, and the medical coding for reimbursement with regard to Undercover I was better than acceptable. There were two sessions that were under coded, and two sessions that were overcoded. This represents a differential of **"zero dollars"** as far as payment from Blue Cross and Blue Shield is concerned. Coding of office visits is done by the billing company directly relating to the patient's office visit record. These codes represent an average reimbursement in dollars and cents rendered by the insurance industry. The physician is generally unclear as to what this reimbursement may be. Mrs. Hamilton as you may recall, also testified as my expert in the administrative civil law hearing in December 2008. Judge Miller, did not understand the concepts delineated regarding medical coding for reimbursement. Miller did not understand the utilization of templates for medical record keeping, or the methodology of the coding itself. As a defense witness, Mr. Tumelty guided Mrs. Hamilton through this endeavor to enable the jury members to understand as much as they could regarding these billing issues. Judge Batten also listened intensely regarding the explanations of coding, recordkeeping, and template formation by Mrs. Hamilton. She gave an excellent explanation of this material in detail, and at the end of her testimony the jury members, as well as the judge, had a reasonable level of understanding regarding this business. Taylor's prosecutors of course never understood these issues, nor did the members at the Board of Medical Examiners understand many of the facts concerning coding, billing, and template formation in the practice of medicine.

I testified in my behalf for a full day in Superior Court. **John Tumelty brilliantly covered all important aspects and statements in the transcripts of all seven office visits.** His questions to me were to the point, concise, and meaningful to the jury's understanding of the dialogue between the two undercover females and myself at all seven office visits. The physician must be able to interpret words, demeanor, and inferences during the doctor patient interaction, along with the physical appearance and deportment of each individual patient that he examines. The physician must use good common sense, as well as the science of medicine, to arrive at a true and valid judgment regarding presumptive diagnosis and treatment.

The federal government through the Medicare Law, proscribes the utilization of History, Examination, and Evaluation (H.E.M.). This is the mechanism by which the physician will, through physical, psychological, and historical perspectives, have the ability to make a reasonable diagnosis, and manage the patient with regard to treatment. H.E.M. is the hallmark of the doctor patient interaction, and provides an excellent format for the evaluation of patients, and for the provision of a reasonable treatment program. Mr. Tumelty covered all of these concepts with me under oath, on the witness stand. We went word for word through the transcripts specifically for the jury member's understanding, sentence by sentence through all seven transcripts. When this exercise was finalized the jury members understood the full scale of my experience with these two undercover females. My testimony was orchestrated by John Tumelty in a systematic approach for the jury, so they could understand everything said by me, and all of the responses of both undercover females. During my testimony, there came a point where the prosecutor Paley, decided to object to my answers given to the jury.

**"I object your honor",** said Paley:

**"Dr. Costino seems to be lecturing to the jury".**

Judge Batten retorted:

**"Dr. Costino is simply answering questions by Mr. Tumelty, and he may do this at his discretion for the jury members to understand completely, I will allow it."**

Through the diligence of my attorney, John Tumelty, my testimony to the jury was *forthright, clear and concise,* and at its completion, this record convinced the jury that my treatment of the two undercover females was both *honest and sincere.* Furthermore, **my treatment of both females was within a reasonable degree of medical certainty, responsible, legal, and represented an exercise of good judgment.**

Following my direct testimony, assistant prosecutor Dara Paley had the opportunity to cross-examine me. At this point in time, my direct testimony was extremely complete, with no "residual meat" left over for her to chew on. She did ask me a few simple questions, certainly nothing important or relevant. There was no reason for redirect testimony, or re-cross-examination.

Following the trial, the judge takes the opportunity to present what is called a "jury charge" for the jury to read and understand concerning a number of boiler-plate statements as to the deportment of the jury in their deliberations. The first three pages of the jury charge however represents the judge's interpretation of the trial. The first three pages of the jury charge are written by the judge in order to render his assessment and interpretation regarding the trial to the jury.

I might mention at this point in time, that **Hurricane Sandy** struck the east coast creating obvious well-known damage to Cape May County, and additional damage to central and north jersey as well as New York. As a result of Hurricane Sandy, jury deliberations were suspended for approximately one week. During this time Judge Batten did call the two assistant prosecutors, John Tumelty and myself to review his jury charge.

The two prosecutors along with John Tumelty and myself, presented to the courtroom on Wednesday morning after Sandy was over, when the judge presented the first three pages of his jury charge for us to examine and argue. The initial three pages of Judge Batten's jury charge were not suitable to either Mr. Tumelty or myself. The prosecution and Mr. Tumelty argued this issue for a while, and the decision was made to return on Thursday morning for another session. The judge gave Thursday morning we again appeared in the courtroom, and the second set of three pages to us. These were still not acceptable by either John Tumelty or myself. We argued the matter with the prosecutor and decided to return Friday morning for similar pursuit.

On Friday morning the two prosecutors, John Tumelty and myself again presented into the courtroom and at this point in time Mr. Tumelty presented to Judge Batten the law in the state of New Jersey. **The law, of course, is "Vaccaro".** Mr. Tumelty also gave a copy of "Vaccaro" not only to the judge, but also to the two assistant prosecutors in the courtroom. In his wisdom, Judge Batten then addressed the courtroom with the following:

"I will read **"Vaccaro"** over the weekend and finalize my jury charge on Monday morning." The judge followed through with his statement, he read the law over the weekend, and on Monday morning presented the four of us with his

## Chapter 20 - The Criminal Trial and Outcome

final jury charge which conformed to "Vaccaro", prior to the jury's entrance into the courtroom.

Judge Batten presented to the courtroom at 9am and gave his fourth three-page jury charge to the prosecutors, and to Mr. Tumelty, and myself. Following this distribution, Judge Batten said to the prosecutors:

### "Are there any questions regarding this jury charge?"

*The immediate response from the two prosecutors was:*
### "We object."

*Judge Batten then immediately stated the following to them:*
### "Please sit down, "Vaccaro" is the law in the state of New Jersey, and that's it."

**I do credit Judge Batten for his decision to produce his first three pages of the jury charge compliant with the law in the state of New Jersey, "Vaccaro"**

The completed 25-page jury charge was then given to the jury members, they were escorted to their isolated room for deliberation, and lunch was provided for them by the county of Cape May. In less than two hours, and following their lunch, their unanimous verdict was announced in open court by the jury supervisor. The jury's findings were **"not guilty"** on **all 26 criminal charges.**

I, of course, was substantially relieved by the jury's verdict, and I thanked the jury members on their way out of the courthouse, and then returned home with my family. I graciously thanked both **Mr. Tumelty** for his excellent work on my behalf, and also graciously thanked his assistant, **Marianne Bluhm**, for her tireless effort in my case.

# "Due Process" Denied

# The Case Against A Doctor

Page 1 of 1

The Case Against a Doctor

FROM: bmaurer789@...

C126

Hide Details

Friday, November 16, 2012 2:29 PM

### The Case Against a Doctor

My major concern has always been about the abuse of power of multiple regulatory agencies and the lack of due process involved, at an enormous cost of time, money, and resources.

It particularly involved the removal of a doctor's ability to earn a living in order to properly defend himself against the alleged charges. At the same time, the state and other regulatory agencies had unlimited funds and unlimited resources to
pursue a frivolous case that in the end actually proved to have NO criminal charges.

To the best of my knowledge, there was never any evidence of this doctor causing harm to any of his patients.

The action of the SBME by suspending his license, especially without proper time to obtain good coverage, thereby preventing patients from appropriate care by their personal physician, was far more harmful than anything the doctor might have done had he been allowed to continue to practice in his office in this remote community.

Actually, this doctor successfully treated hundreds of patients that no other doctor in the community would treat in the proper manner, because of the nature of their disorder.

He was a dedicated osteopathic physician, loyal to his patients, to his family, and to his profession. He was heavily involved in his local community and its politics, which might have been the underlying motivation for many of the actions taken against him.

What will the State now do to give this doctor, his family, and his patients back that which was taken away from all of them so abruptly?

11/21/2012

Exhibit C126

# CONTEMPT

"If a man cause a blemish to his neighbor, as he hath done so let it be done to him. Breach for breach, eye for eye, tooth for tooth, as he hath caused a blemish in a man, so shall it be done to him."
- Leviticus 24:19-20

"Look beneath to see things as they truly are."

Following my criminal trial in November of 2012, and my acquittal of all 26 criminal charges, the rotten, irresponsible, and moronic prosecutor Taylor indicted me for the **fifth time** for contempt, a charge by **Judge Batten**, which occurred three years earlier. This fifth indictment references a court hearing on August 10, 2009.

This indictment charges me with a fourth-degree criminal contempt. This criminal contempt charge was levied by Judge Batten **irrationally** for a perceived offense regarding a judicial order relating to my criminal case, and the State's star witness, Tonya Anderson. The indictment referenced a court hearing on August 10, 2009 before Judge Batten where his statement was made releasing Anderson's chiropractic medical records to the prosecutor, and counsel for defendant for use in the criminal case. The indictment "alleges" that Judge Batten released the records for trial preparation, expert witness review, and prohibited the use, photocopying, or dissemination of the record beyond that purpose.

On August 10, 2009 Judge Batten presided over this hearing that dealt with several significant pretrial issues, including the motion to release Anderson's medical records. Batten granted the motion to release her medical records to the parties for trial preparation, and expert witness review. Judge Batten expressly directed defense counsel to submit a written order on the court's rulings. My attorney, Glenn Zeitz, submitted an order under the five-day rule. Without delay or objection from the state, Assistant Prosecutor Megan Hoerner, or Judge Batten, regarding this written order, the judge then signed the order. The order signed by Judge Batten, was then filed with criminal case management on August 19, 2009.

This formal, signed, order addresses Anderson's medical records, and specifically provides for the immediate release of these records to the prosecutor, and defense counsel for the following purposes:

- Trial preparation
- Expert witness review
- Use at trial

Also, provides a copy to:
- The N.J. Board of Medical Examiners
- The deputy attorney that is handling the administrative law proceeding
- The administrative law judge

Notably, **the formal order** of August 19, 2009 differs substantially from Judge Batten's courtroom statement at the hearing on August 10, 2009 regarding Anderson's medical records. *First,* the formal order signed by Judge Batten **expands the scope** of the permitted use of the medical records of Anderson to include evidence at trial. *Second* the order **does not "seal" the medical records,** and does not prohibit defendant (me) from discussing the contents of the records. The formal order is devoid of any specific language prohibiting the parties from discussing the records in any venue. The executed, written, formal order signed by Judge Batten must be construed as the **controlling order** regarding the release and use of Anderson's medical records. **I could not violate a court order that did not specifically prohibit my conduct.**

**At the grand jury presentation, regarding criminal contempt, by assistant prosecutor Dara Paley, she *DELIBERATELY FAILED TO SUBMIT the formal order signed by Judge Batten to the grand jury.* Paley did not**

## Chapter 21 - CONTEMPT

otherwise inform the grand jury that Judge Batten signed a formal order nine days after the court hearing that addressed the release and use of the medical records. The state completely withheld this information from the grand jury, and instead conveyed a *false impression* to the grand jury members that Judge Batten's decision of August 10, 2009 was the final word relating to these records.

Notwithstanding the **August 19, 2009** order signed by Judge Batten, the state alleges to the grand jury that I disobeyed Judge Batten's courtroom ruling of August 9, 2009 by revealing the contents of Anderson's medical records. The state contends that sometime in 2010, I published a **"Letter to My Patients"** that discussed the medical records of Anderson. The state further alleges that I talked to a reporter from the *Herald* newspaper regarding these records, which precipitated a published article by the *Herald*, on my case where some of Anderson's records were disclosed.

Anderson was a Class II police officer employed by Egg Harbor Township, and was the primary witness involved in the undercover investigation that targeted me in my medical office. While Anderson was in a treatment program of "pain management" in my office, she attended her chiropractor's office for treatment of her "pain", and discomfort, continuing over a four-year period. This information was brought to the surface at my criminal trial in October of 2012, when I was completely acquitted of all criminal charges. **The medical records of Anderson were highly relevant as to her lack of credibility as the state's star witness**.

The August 19, 2009 the formal order signed by Judge Batten *did not* prohibit me from discussing Anderson's medical records. "The Letter to My Patients", published in the *Herald* newspaper, occurred several months after the August 19, 2009 order was executed and filed in the Cape May courthouse. **This August 19, 2009 order must be construed as the controlling order, relative to the release and use of these records.** I had a **constitutional right** to rely upon the language in the formal order signed by Judge Batten, and my actions did not constitute any violation of this formal, signed court order.

## Legal arguments by my attorney John Tumelty:

"This indictment should be dismissed based upon the state's misconduct in presenting misleading evidence to the grand jury, and failing to provide "exculpatory evidence", specifically the formal order signed by Judge Batten."

"Dismissal of an indictment is appropriate if it is established that a violation substantially influenced the grand jury's decision to indict, or if there is grave doubt that the determination ultimately reached is arrived fairly and impartially. When a person's fate is before a grand jury, he is constitutionally entitled to have his case considered by an impartial and unbiased body capable of deciding the issue of "probable cause" on the evidence fairly submitted to it."

"Indictments may be dismissed upon a palpable showing of a fundamental unfairness or when there is conduct of the prosecutor that amounts to an interference with the grand jury decision-making function. The court should not hesitate to dismiss an indictment if the evidence establishes that the conduct of the prosecutor in obtaining an indictment amounted to an intentional subversion of the grand jury process. If the record in the case demonstrates such conduct of that quality, a dismissal of the indictment is the only appropriate remedy."

"Consequently, jurisdiction rests with this court to review the facts of the case at bar and consider defendants motion to dismiss the indictment for prosecutorial misconduct. Moreover, our state constitution envisions a grand jury that protects persons who are victims of personal animus, partisanship, or inappropriate zeal on the part of the prosecutor. The grand jury cannot be denied access to evidence that is credible, material, and so clearly exculpatory as to induce a rational grand juror to conclude that the state has not made a *prima facia* case against the accused. If evidence of this character is withheld from the grand jury, the prosecutor, in essence, presents a distorted vision of the facts and interferes with the grand jury's
decision-making function. A prosecutor's interaction with a grand jury, and prosecutorial misconduct, is subject to judicial review."

## Chapter 21 - CONTEMPT

"The prosecutor's abuse of his special relationship to the grand jury posses enormous risk to defendants. For while in theory, the trial provides the defendant with a full opportunity to contest and disprove the charges against him, in practice, the handing-up of an indictment will often have a devastating personal and professional impact that later dismissal and acquittal can never undo."

"Where the potential for abuse is so great, and the consequences of a mistake and indictment so serious, the ethical responsibilities of the prosecutor, and the obligation of the judiciary to protect against even an appearance of unfairness, are correspondingly heightened."

"The New Jersey Supreme Court found that precedence make clear that this court may invoke it's supervisory power to remedy perceived injustices in grand jury presentations. Consequently jurisdiction rest with this court to review the facts of this case at bar and consider defendants motion to dismiss the indictment for prosecutorial misconduct."

I had a **first amendment right** to inform my patients of the truth regarding my criminal case orchestrated by Robert Taylor in Cape May County. The only mechanism available to me to inform my patients was through the press. **Remember, a judge's order cannot be ambiguous. His order must be unambiguous.** The signed order from a judge cannot be open to interpretation. In my case Judge Batten created a conduit for dissemination of Anderson's medical records, not only to the Board of Medical Examiners, but also to all other entities in my case. Furthermore, **there was no gag order submitted by Judge Batten, regarding Anderson's medical records.** The formal order was agreed to by assistant prosecutor Meghan Horner, and signed by Judge Batten. This order could have been revisited by Horner, and revised to her liking, however none of this was done. Furthermore, there was no HIPPA, restrictions connected to Anderson's records which were sent to superior court by Dr. O'Rourke at Seaport Chiropractic clinic.

The **"Letter to My Patients"**, was published in the *Herald* newspaper, and was done **in response to the lies, deception, and perjury of the actors of the**

Cape May County prosecutor's office, and at the Board of Medical Examiners in Trenton. Furthermore, I did not publish anything over the internet, nor did I publish anything anywhere else. **The editor of the local paper, the *Herald*, said to me that he would have to give this article that I wrote to prosecutor Taylor for his approval before he published it.** I agreed, and the editor did just that, and Taylor gave his tacit approval.

**Furthermore, if an individual is going to masquerade as an undercover creature for the state, against a law-abiding physician, this creature has waived her right to privacy.** We know that Anderson informed deputy attorney David Puteska at the BME that she sought medical treatment. This of course, was not revealed to my attorney until Anderson's second certification was completed, following a direct order from Judge Batten. Following the "in camera" inspection by Judge Batten, Glen Zeitz, and Megan Hoerner, Anderson's medical records became part of the public hearing in Trenton at the Board of Medical Examiners. There was *no infringement* of Anderson's privacy at any level.

I was *not* **guilty of contempt** as Judge Batten made a gross error, when assistant prosecutor Tina Kell rushed into the courtroom and blurted out, "look what he did", referencing the "Letter to My Patients". As assistant prosecutor Kell rushed into the courtroom disturbing Judge Batten during an active hearing on my criminal case, she shouted out loud,
"Look what he did, your honor, look what Dr. Costino did."

The **drama queen**, Tina Kell, of course, did this to entice Judge Batten to react. As a result of Kell's immature activity, referencing my "Letter to My Patients" printed in the *Herald* newspaper, **Judge Batten reflexively, and without a reasonable thought process, charged me with criminal contempt.**

The medical records of Anderson were previously discussed in open court in Cape May County, and at the Board of Medical Examiners in Trenton. **I never violated any judicial order.** Furthermore, I did not release the four pages of Anderson's medical records personally to anyone OR to any newspaper.

The hearing to dismiss was conducted in Atlantic County before Judge Donio on April 4, 2013. My attorney John Tumelty, **courageously attacked**

## Chapter 21 - CONTEMPT

this frivolous indictment executed by assistant prosecutor Dara Paley under the direction of the moronic chief prosecutor Robert Taylor. Mr. Tumelty clearly identified all of the flaws in the indictment, and enumerated **the fact that Judge Batten's written order was never presented to the grand jury which, if it had been, would have exonerated me. This of course represents absolute prosecutorial misconduct,** *knowingly, willfully, and maliciously.*

Judge Donio instead of considering this overwhelming evidence of **prosecutorial misconduct**, made one of the **dumbest statements** that I have ever heard in any courtroom.
**Donio stated, in open court:**
"Because Judge Batten held the defendant in
criminal contempt for whatever reason, I feel I must
abide by his decision".

In the face of clearly **exculpatory evidence**, Judge Batten's written, formal and signed order, was *not presented* to the grand jury. Donio, **instead of following the law and dismissing the indictment**, decided "to punt".

John Tumelty clearly identified this indictment as *false, and disgraceful behavior and misconduct* on the part of the county prosecutor, Taylor, and Assistant Prosecutor Paley. Donio *abandoned and disregarded* the facts, and the **exculpatory evidence, specifically Judge Batten's formal order**. Donio was *biased, with absolute prejudice* against me, following my vindication and acquittal in the criminal case in chief.
Another example of legal tyranny.

As a caveat, and at the end of this "hearing to dismiss", Donio suggested to Mr. Tumelty and myself, in open court, that *I plead to criminal contempt*, after **his refusal to dismiss this "despicable" contempt case**. My attorney, John Tumelty, at my request while sitting next to me in the courtroom, addressed Judge Donio and said to him, "Dr. Costino *will not plead* to criminal contempt, and we will see you at trial".

My second criminal trial for criminal contempt, was held one month later in Cape May County Superior Court by **Judge Garofalo**. Donio failed to attend this trial. Assistant prosecutor Dara Paley attempted to entice Judge Batten to be her witness. Judge Batten very wisely declined this offer by Paley since it was his signed court order that carried the case. The jury of my peers, in this contempt trial, exonerated me with a formal acquittal of this **despicable criminal contempt charge.**

This additional episode in my life, became, in my opinion, another example of the **prejudice and cognitive bias** of Judge Donio, eliminating "**due process**" in the face of **overwhelming exculpatory evidence**. Furthermore, and in my candid opinion, this failure to dismiss represents another example of a **biased political judge** utilizing his **abuse of power, and legal tyranny,** to compel me to a second criminal trial, because *I would not plead guilty* to this **disgraceful** and **prejudicial** criminal contempt charge.

LAW OFFICES OF GLENN A. ZEITZ
BY: GLENN A. ZEITZ, ESQUIRE
38 Haddon Avenue
Haddonfield, New Jersey 08033
(856) 795-6660

Attorneys for Defendant John G. Costino, D.O.

SUPERIOR COURT OF NJ
CAPE MAY COUNTY
CRIMINAL CASE MANAGEMENT
F I L E D

AUG 1 9 2009

| | |
|---|---|
| STATE OF NEW JERSEY, | SUPERIOR COURT OF NEW JERSEY |
| PLAINTIFF | LAW DIVISION<br>CAPE MAY COUNTY |
| vs. | INDICTMENT NO.: 637-08-08 |
| JOHN G. COSTINO, D.O., | CRIMINAL ACTION |
| DEFENDANT | ORDER |

AND NOW this matter having been brought before the Court by the Law Offices of Glenn A. Zeitz, by Glenn A. Zeitz, Esquire, attorney for defendant John G. Costino, D.O., in the above-captioned matter, and Assistant Prosecutor Meghan Hoerner appearing on behalf of the State of New Jersey, and for the reasons stated by the Court on the record during the motion hearing of August 10, 2009 and for good cause shown;

IT IS on this 19th day of August, 2009, ORDERED that the State's motion to reconsider the Court's Order dated August    , 2009 which found the State in violation of N.J.S.A. 2A:156A-1, et seq., is returnable on Thursday, September 24, 2009 at 1:30 p.m. Defendant shall file and serve his reply brief to the aforesaid motion no later than two weeks prior to the return date on this matter.

IT IS FURTHER ORDERED that the "taint hearing" to determine what "derivative evidence" is to be suppressed based on the State's violation of N.J.S.A. 2A:156A-1, et

Page -1-

# "Due Process" Denied

seq., is returnable on Thursday, September 24, 2009 at 1:30 p.m. and that both parties shall simultaneously file and serve their respective briefs concerning the aforesaid hearing no later than two weeks prior to the return date on this matter;

IT IS FURTHER ORDERED that defendant's motion to suppress the statement of defendant John G. Costino, D.O. given on September 14, 2007 is GRANTED;

IT IS FURTHER ORDERED that defendant's motion to dismiss the indictment on an objective (due process) theory of entrapment and request for an evidentiary hearing is DENIED;

IT IS FURTHER ORDERED that the Court will conduct a status conference on Thursday, September 24, 2009 at 1:30 p.m. under Indictment No. 584-07-09; and

IT IS FURTHER ORDERED that the State shall forthwith inquire of Tonya Anderson concerning the extent to which her annual physical performed by Dr. William Glenn during the relevant time period previously determined by this Court contains records or information appropriate for in camera inspection. Additionally, the State shall forthwith inquire of Tonya Anderson concerning the extent to which she received chiropractic care from any other medical provider during the relevant time period previously determined by this Court and submit any medical records obtained to the Court for in camera inspection.

IT IS FURTHER ORDERED that the medical records of Tonya Anderson reviewed by the Court in camera with both the prosecutor and counsel for defendant shall immediately be released in-full to both parties.

IT IS FURTHER ORDERED that counsel for defendant may utilize the released records for trial preparation, expert review, use at trial, and may further release same to the New Jersey Board of Medical Examiners, the Deputy Attorney Generals handling the administrative law proceedings against defendant, and the Administrative Law Judge.

_____
HON. RAYMOND A. BATTEN, J.S.C.

# "Stand up for what you believe in, even if it means standing alone, nothing brings you peace but yourself."

"A man can be destroyed but not defeated."

**The tort of malicious abuse of process** lies not for commencing an improper action, but for misusing, or misapplying process after it is issued. To be found liable for malicious abuse of process, a party must have performed additional acts after issuance of process, which represents the *perversion or abuse* of the legitimate purpose of that process. It is further clarified that process is not abused unless after issuance, the prosecution reveals an ulterior purpose for securing it by committing "further acts' where they demonstrably use process as a means to coerce or press the plaintiff or defendant. In order for there to be abuse of process, therefore a party must use process in some fashion, and in that use must be *coercive or illegitimate*. To prevail in a malicious use of process case you must prove four elements:

1. That the original action complained of was brought without "probable cause"
2. The action was actuated by malice
3. The action was terminated favorably to the plaintiff or defendant
4. The plaintiff suffered a special grievance

My criminal case orchestrated by Robert Taylor and Sandra Dick is a perfect example of **malicious prosecution**, and **malicious abuse of process**. There was never "probable cause" for my criminal prosecution. "Probable cause" is an element that has a well-established meaning arising in criminal law, and

## Chapter 22 - Stand Up for What You Believe In

therefore an equally plain meaning when used in the context of an action for malicious prosecution. "**Probable cause**" is a matter of law to be determined by the court, and only submitted to the jury if the facts giving rise to "probable cause" are themselves in dispute when decided by the court. The inquiry into whether there was "probable cause" is determined by means of an objective analysis. The question to be decided is whether in the prior action the facts supported the actor's honest belief in the allegations. In this context, *honest belief* means using the reasonable, prudent person standard. A reasonable belief that there was a good or sound chance of establishing the claim to the satisfaction of the court or the jury.

In my case, you see "malicious abuse of process", and "malicious use of process" without "probable cause". Taylor conducted this abusive process with malice in conjunction with Sandra Dick, against my pain management medical practice and me.

The individuals associated with this **abuse of process** includes the following:
- *County Prosecutor,* **Robert Taylor**
- *Assistant Prosecutors* **Megan Hoerner, Matthew Weintraub, Tina Kell, and Dara Paley.**
- The *detectives* associated with this abusive process include: **George Hallett, Trish Kalita, and Paul Worrell**.

Both **malicious abuse of process** and **malicious use of process** are clearly evident **at the Board of Medical Examiners** with:
- *Deputy Attorney* **David Puteska**
- *Chief Deputy Attorney,* **Sandra Dick**, the main architect at the BME

At the time of my criminal trial in November of 2012, the twelve-member jury clearly understood the **lies,** the **perjury under oath,** the **deception,** and **corrupt elements** of the Cape May County law enforcement. **Within 2 hours, the jury members found me NOT GUILTY, and I was acquitted of all 26 criminal counts with complete vindication**. The jury understood clearly the **malicious *abuse* of process** and the **malicious *use* of process** that both my wife and I endured for five long years.

> "Crime is a defective exercise of free will,
> a betrayal of one's character."

> "Nate que severious extra"
> ("Don't seek yourself outside yourself")
> -Ralph Waldo Emerson

## A Brief Overview
## – A brief synopsis of the years between 2007 and 2012

Over criminalization of medicine has become a national plague. When more behaviors are criminalized there are more and more occasions, for prosecutors, who embody the **state's monopoly for illegitimate political violence**, to fully participate in humanity's flaws, **and make grave mistakes**.

My criminal case was flawed from day one by the Cape May County prosecutor, Taylor. **Robert Taylor, in conjunction with Sandra Dick** at the Board of Medical Examiners arrested me with absolutely no knowledge of criminal law, or medical law in the state of New Jersey. Taylor represents the worst type of leadership as he disregarded the New Jersey law **"State vs Vaccaro"** in September 2007 when he had the **audacity to arrest me for practicing medicine as a licensed physician.**

In December 2007, the first hearing at the BME, my medical license was suspended by the **"Star Chamber"** Board of Medical Examiners. DAG Sandra Dick and her cohorts, aided by certain disgraceful and corrupt physicians on her Board, suspended my medical license without an indictment, and certainly without any conviction, thereby terminating my ability to earn a living.

## Chapter 22 - Stand Up for What You Believe In

The first criminal indictment, was conducted by Assistant Prosecutor Megan Hoerner, and the moronic Detective George Hallett. The grand jury presentation in February of 2008 was full of **lies, misrepresentations, and absolute perjury**, omitting all of the **exculpatory evidence** which would have certainly exonerated me. **"In this instance, I was the first to discover this lack of truth, by being the first to experience the lies, as lies, by law enforcement".**

A few months following this indictment, certain actors in law-enforcement then **altered my medical records**, and **removed at least three major statements, including the word "pain" from the CD recordings and transcripts of both undercover females.**

In December 2008, the office of administrative law, in conjunction with the Board of Medical Examiners, held my civil trial hearing with Judge Miller acting as both **judge** and **jury.** Miller of course works for the state of New Jersey, and maintains a close affiliation with DAG Sandra Dick and the BME. **Miller essentially dismissed my testimony, and dismissed the testimony of my experts Dr. Jermyn, Glenda Hamilton, and detective Landis.**

Several months later my attorney, Glenn Zeitz, discovered the **false** and **perjurious** certification of Tonya Anderson written by DAG David Puteska. Tonya Anderson committed perjury on her first certification, and also committed perjury at the Administrative Law civil trial before Judge Miller. **Miller, however, stated that her testimony was credible.**

Simultaneously, in the county of Cape May, the chief lunatic, Taylor, indicted both my wife and myself for **medical claims fraud**. This indictment was **dismissed** by Judge Batten for **prosecutorial misconduct**, and approximately one year later the psychiatrically impaired Cape May County prosecutor Taylor **re-indicted both my wife and myself for similar medical claims fraud**. In his wisdom, Judge Batten **dismissed** this second indictment for medical claims fraud again for **prosecutorial misconduct,** followed by a strong statement by the judge as a matter of record suggesting both indictments were incompatible with the truth. These two indictments were performed with **"prosecutorial misconduct," knowingly, willfully and maliciously,** committed by assistant prosecutors, Megan

Hoerner, Matthew Weintraub, Tina Kell and detective Tricia Kalita.

The **"objective due process entrapment" hearing** was conducted by my attorney Glenn Zeitz, in Superior Court in Cape May County with Judge Batten. The **"Johnson factors"** clearly favored dismissal of this flawed criminal indictment. Judge Batten failed to dismiss the criminal case in chief either because of **ignorance** of the laws regarding controlled substances, ie **"Vaccaro"**, or a **cognitive bias** against me. **In either instance, the case in chief was not dismissed and continued for a total of five years.**

The **"driver hearing"** was held several months later, and both DEA supervisor Thomas Prevoznik and postal inspector Alex Sylvester, **lied under oath** and **misrepresented** the issues regarding the altered medical transcripts and CD recordings. **The alteration of my medical records represents, in my opinion, criminal activity. Essentially, no one was ever held responsible or accountable for the lies and misrepresentations at the "driver hearing".** Furthermore, there has never been full disclosure with regard to these issues, including the destroyed recording devices used by the undercover females. No doubt, they were destroyed by law-enforcement.

## "The quest for truth is neither easy or pleasurable, but a battle requiring courage and vigor!!!"

During the pendency of my criminal case, there were several hearings at the Board of Medical Examiners. Each hearing was controlled by DAG Sandra Dick and her cohorts in Trenton. Their **lies, misrepresentations and confabulatory statements** have continued my medical license in suspension. Following all the evidence regarding the **state's star witness**, Tonya Anderson, and all of her **perjury** which has been well documented, my attorney demanded a hearing at the BME to petition the Board for a **"remand"** to a second administrative law court. A return to a second administrative law judge, and a **"remand"** hearing, to delineate the facts with regard to the Board's disgraceful activity in my case, is necessary in order to demand testimony from the **state's "star witness"**, Tonya Anderson.

## Chapter 22 - Stand Up for What You Believe In

There was a conspiracy between Robert Taylor in Cape May County, and Sandra Dick at the BME prior to my arrest in September of 2007. It was also clearly obvious that there was a conspiracy between Sandra Dick, David Puteska, and Tonya Anderson regarding all of her **perjury**. A **"remand"** to a second administrative law hearing is absolutely necessary to elucidate the **facts, and the truth**, regarding these issues which was completely denied by **Sandra Dick** and certain *disgraceful board physicians*. I was denied **"due process of law, and justice"**, under the constitution of both New Jersey and the United States of America.

As a result of the Board's egregious and disgraceful denial of "due process", my attorney Glenn Zeitz appealed this decision to the Superior Court appellate division of the state of New Jersey. Remember, these appellate characters are also state employees and they completely favor Sandra Dick and her Board of Medical Examiners.

You have read the **"statement of the case"** by my attorney Jordan Zeitz which clearly, delineates all of the issues and principles concerning the New Jersey regulations. This document by my attorney Jordan Zeitz was eventually argued at the Superior Court appellate division by Glenn Zeitz in front of the three female appellate judges, **Dorothea Wefing, Edith Payne, and Linda Baxter**.

I was present at this appellate hearing, and listened to my attorney Glenn Zeitz, and also to these three appellate judges who I will call "the "three blind mice". These three appellate judges, **made certain that their decision was to deny me a remand to a second OAL civil trial, and to deny me "due process" of law, and my constitutional rights.** In spite of the **lies, deception, perjury, and fraudulent activity** of both Sandra Dick, David Puteska, and Tonya Anderson, **these three appellate judges denied me a "remand" to a second OAL civil trial, and a second OAL judge.**

The "three blind mice", Wefing, Payne and Baxter, made certain that no one would *ever read their opinion,* as this entire hearing is "unpublished". This *"unpublished decision"* essentially ended my ability to obtain a fair trial and honest evaluation of the evidence.

"The three blind mice" terminated my ability to return to my medical practice, and essentially confiscated my medical license for a five-year period, along with my ability to earn a living. By denying a **"remand"** to a second OAL civil trial, they have denied me **"due process" of law** in the face of absolute evidence of **false swearing and perjury** of Anderson, **and illegal activity** at the BME between Sandra Dick, David Puteska and Tonya Anderson. **This decision by these three appellate judges is again, a perfect example of the "legal tyranny" exhibited by political appointees who commit injustice with impunity, and will never be held accountable for their "disgraceful behavior".**

> "Due process is inextricably rooted
> in the Constitution of the
> United States of America."

The creatures at the BME, along with Judge Miller at the office of Administrative Law, and the three appellate judges, **failed in their duty** to provide me **"due process" of law,** and thereby have **failed their oath, the public trust, and the laws of the state of New Jersey and of the United States of America.**

It is unbelievable to me that these state creatures who work for the government, are so **dishonest.** They *lie and deceive,* and get away with it scot-free, *without reprisal* and *without any oversight.* **Essentially, no one in New Jersey state government really gives a "shit". In my candid opinion, there is a significant fundamental level of dishonesty, corruption and legal tyranny in the state of New Jersey.** My criminal trial in November 2012 was decided by a jury of my peers, citizens in Cape May County. My attorney, John Tumelty, **with precision of thought and expression**, presented all of the salient issues to the jury members. **My criminal trial ended with complete acquittal of all 26 criminal charges.**

# Chapter 22 - Stand Up for What You Believe In

Following acquittal of all criminal charges in November of 2012, I then faced another criminal charge of **"contempt"** as a result of the major mistake by Judge Batten as previously discussed. I refused again to plead to the *stupidity and ignorance* of Judge Donio who **refused to dismiss** this **spurious charge of "criminal contempt".** I then had to endure a second jury trial as a result of this absurd criminal contempt charge. My attorney, John Tumelty again with *"precision of thought and expression"* presented the salient facts to the jury members resulting in a complete acquittal of this **disgraceful, biased criminal charge.**

In my candid opinion, Cape May County Prosecutor Robert Taylor, DAG Sandra Dick, and DAG David Puteska at the Board of Medical Examiners, and of course, Judge Miller at Office of Administrative Law (OAL), **FUNCTIONED IN UNITY** to destroy my medical practice, and made a full-press effort to destroy my entire life. They injured *my family, my wife, my children, my grandchildren,* and also destroyed the lives of many of *my patients* with their **legal tyranny, abuse of power, and prosecutorial misconduct,** *knowingly, willfully and maliciously*.

Fortunately, I'm still alive, still standing, with self-reliance, individualism, and in reasonably good health. I thank the Lord for the God-given strength, endurance and courage bestowed on me by both of my wonderful parents who are now deceased. Following the acquittal for the contempt charge I began filing law suits against the county of Cape May, Little Egg Harbor Twp. and the detectives and prosecutors involved in this **illegal abuse of power** which was titled "State vs Costino". Additionally I commenced an appeal to the Board of Medical Examiners for the reinstatement of my medical license.

# "The Justice System in New Jersey is Composed of Mostly Inadequate Judges and Prosecutors with Evil Intent, and are Infected by the Intoxication of Power."

"I also noticed that under the sun there is evil in the courtroom. Yes, even the courts of law are corrupt! In due season God will judge everyone, both good and bad, for all their deeds."
-Ecclesiastes 3:16-17

If the dishonest prosecutors and detectives were not enough to deal with in Cape May County, at the Board of Medical Examiners in Trenton, and at the Office of Administrative Law, I was subject to a variety of **judges,** most of which were *objectively dishonest, and politically motivated.*

**The following represents my objective and *honest opinion* of the various judges in my case over the past thirteen years.**

## Judge Batten

The first judge in my criminal case was **Raymond Batten**. Judge Batten's best buddy was Cape May County prosecutor, Robert Taylor. From the very onset of my criminal case it was clear to me that Judge Batten demonstrated both a *cognitive bias, and prejudice* against me in favor of Taylor. Batten should have dismissed the first indictment **by Megan Hoerner and George Hallett**, in February of 2008, based upon **the perjury of Hallett,** the **complete exclusion of multiple, significant exculpatory evidence by Hoerner and Hallett, and prosecutorial misconduct.** Hallett's testimony completely **omitted detective Landis's office** visit in December 2005. Hallett and Hoerner **omitted my "Pain Management Agreement"** signed by Tonya Anderson. Hallett and Hoerner **omitted the four thefts of my prescription pads** from my locked cabinet in my office, and **omitted all of the illegal prescriptions** written by these thieves. Hallett and Hoerner **omitted the issue of misspelling** Maggie **O-R-T-I-Z** to " *A-R-T-I-Z* ", and **Hallett stated to the jury that I was taking payment in cash from this patient, and not producing a medical record**. Hallett and Hoerner **omitted Maggie Ortiz's statement to me on August 3, 2007, that she had "pain, and up all night till 4 am."** In my opinion, Hallett is a **liar and a perjurer,** and Hoerner is a **grossly inadequate, and flawed prosecutor**. Furthermore, Judge Batten should have dismissed the entire criminal case based upon the "**objective due process theory of entrapment" by law enforcement.**

Judge Batten in his transient wisdom did dismiss both medical fraud indictments against my wife and I, which were conducted with **prosecutorial misconduct** by assistant prosecutors *Hoerner, Weintraub and Kell,* and detectives *Kalita and Worrell*. Both indictments were **fundamentally dishonest, corrupt**, with associated **perjury**, and **prosecutorial misconduct** performed **knowingly, willfully, and maliciously**.

Judge Batten was compliant with the request of Glenn Zeitz regarding the medical records of Tonya Anderson, and he finally realized the **dishonesty and perjury** of Anderson, when her medical records were obtained and evaluated by him "in camera". I take this opportunity to thank Judge Batten for his indulgence in this matter, finally realizing the dishonesty of the **state's star witness**, Tonya Anderson. I additionally give the judge credit for eventually understanding the medical law in the state of New Jersey, **"Vaccaro."** Fortunately, my attorney John Tumelty produced "State v Vaccaro" for Judge Batten to read and digest, and his final jury charge did conform to the medical laws of the state of New Jersey.

## Judge Gorman

The initial administrative law judge in the winter of 2008, **Judge Bruce Gorman** was very *responsible,* and very *honest.* He became acutely aware of the *dishonesty, and prejudice,* exhibited by DAG Sandra Dick and David Puteska at the Board of Medical Examiners, and demanded the medical records of the two female undercovers be disclosed. He clearly understood the necessity for this medical record evaluation. I take this opportunity to thank **Judge Gorman** for his **honesty and perseverance** against the *disgraceful and unethical behavior* of Sandra Dick, David Puteska, and other uninformed physicians on the Board of Medical Examiners who denied me **justice.** Unfortunately with the departure of Judge Gorman from my administrative law bench trial, a second judge, Todd Miller, a total disgrace, was appointed to my case.

## Judge Miller

**Todd Miller** represents another example of a **cognitive bias and prejudice** against me. He listened to the **perjured testimony** of Tonya Anderson, and called her credible. Miller completely eliminated my testimony, and the testimony of my experts in *"pain management", "billing", and "recordkeeping"*. Miller completely eliminated the testimony of **Detective Landis**, the first under cover officer who I treated as a heroin addict in December 2005.

I testified for approximately four hours, and Miller basically REJECTED **all of my testimony** and **eliminated** the testimony of my experts in his "conclusions of law". **Without *any reasonable thought process,* Miller further stated that my experts were essentially "unqualified"**. Both **Dr. Jermyn and Glenda Hamilton** are stellar **experts** in their field, specifically **"pain management", "recordkeeping" and "Medicare law".** In my opinion, **Miller is simply a disgrace to his profession.**

Miller, was both judge and jury at the administrative law hearing, **and in my candid opinion**, he was *subversive, devoid* of a *moral compass,* and a *perfect shill* for Sandra Dick and David Puteska. His "conclusions of law" report to the Board of Medical Examiners was nothing but a *false narrative,* and mimicked Puteska's insufficient "conclusions of law". Miller's "conclusions of law" were *corrupt and fundamentally dishonest.* Miller had the opportunity to come forward when Tonya Anderson's **perjury** was apparent to all parties, including superior court Judge Batten in Cape May County. My attorney Glenn Zeitz demanded a **"remand"** to a second administrative law court civil hearing, however, Miller kept silent.

## Judge Donio

My next criticism is directed to **Judge Donio.** At the hearing to dismiss the criminal contempt indictment *reflexively* rendered by Judge Batten, Donio missed the entire boat. *Similar to a deposed Napoleonic figure, Donio relates in open court:*

> **"If Judge Batten holds Costino in contempt, I cannot go against his opinion."**

**In view of the record, how stupid is this statement???**

A judge's order cannot be **inconsistent or ambiguous**. Here Judge Batten's written and signed order was clear and concise. Donio should have dismissed this criminal contempt indictment immediately based upon the law. To his shame, he failed to do so.

## Judge Garofalo

**Judge Andrew Garofalo**, assembled a jury, and heard this criminal contempt case. When all of the evidence was given to the jury, it was obvious to them that Judge Batten's **written and signed order did not** preclude me from writing my "Letter to my Patients". Furthermore, the jury certainly recognized that the prosecutor in this case, Dara Paley, **failed** to reveal to the grand jury that Judge Batten's order was a **fact matter. This failure represents another example of prosecutorial misconduct, where significant exculpatory evidence was withheld from the grand jury.** My attorney John Tumelty explained to the jury that the prosecutor **withheld** this very important exculpatory evidence, and following his *expert* and *candid explanation* to the jury, **they acquitted me of this charge**. I thank **Judge**

**Garofalo**, and **the jury** for their **honesty and fortitude**, and I thank my attorney, John Tumelty, for his expertise.


## Judge Gibson

My next criticism is directed to **Judge Christopher Gibson.** Following my dual criminal acquittals, I hired two civil attorneys to file a **1983 civil rights case in Superior Court, Cape May County.** The 1983 civil rights case was filed against the disgraceful prosecutors and detectives in Cape May County involved in my criminal case in chief. Unfortunately, I was represented by two *irresponsible and disgraceful lawyers,* who failed to prosecute this civil rights case in a proper, legal manner, and after a period of time my lawsuit was dismissed by Judge Gibson for **"lack of prosecution".** During this lapsed period of time, I never received notice of "failure to prosecute", nor did I receive any "notice of dismissal" of my case from the Cape May County court system.

Hercules Pappas and Paul Stewart, the attorneys representing me in the 1983 civil rights case, **lied to my wife and I for a period of two years regarding the status of this case.** To this day, I simply do not understand why these two attorneys were so **fundamentally dishonest**.

Judge Gibson eventually scheduled a hearing for **reinstatement of the 1983 civil rights case**. Hercules Pappas represented both my wife and I at this hearing. Pappas presented a reasonable explanation for his "failure to prosecute" the case, before Judge Gibson. Both my wife and I were present and listened attentively. I thought for sure that Judge Gibson would reinstate my 1983 civil rights case, against the *county of Cape May,* certain *prosecutors* and certain *detectives*. **Gibson instead, denied this petition and refused to reinstate my very important 1983 civil rights case.**

My question, of course, is why would Judge Gibson refuse to reinstate my civil rights case? There's only one answer!!! Why Gibson refused to reinstate this civil rights case, **in my opinion**, is rather clear. **Gibson was simply protecting Taylor, and the four assistant prosecutors and three detectives who were** accused of prosecutorial misconduct and other egregious deeds including perjury. Please understand, these creatures in Cape May County are guilty, **not only of prosecutorial misconduct, but certain persons were also guilty of perjury.** The facts are clear to any reasonable individual.

By failing to reinstate my case, Gibson **absolved** all of the above. **In my very calculated and candid opinion,** this refusal of Judge Gibson represents another example of the "**political legal tyranny**", **and the abuse of power of the justice system against two innocent citizens to protect the guilty.**

## Judge Rodriguez

The next judge that I'd like to discuss is **Joseph Rodriguez,** the federal judge in Camden County. Rodriguez clearly demonstrates, in my opinion, a **cognitive bias, and prejudiced against me,** and he should have recused himself from my case for the following reasons:

*By history,* Judge Joseph Rodriguez lived on Cornell Road in Audubon, New Jersey, when my family moved from Camden to Audubon, to Cornell Road, just up the street from the judge, in the 1960s. At this specific time, his brother, Mario Rodriguez Senior was a politician in Camden County, and assisted one of my sisters in obtaining a position with the state of New Jersey. Another sister of mine babysat Judge Rodriguez's children on multiple occasions in our neighborhood in Audubon.

Judge Rodriguez knew my family well, and eventually I established my medical practice and residence in North Wildwood, New Jersey in 1976. The judge's nephew, Mario Rodriguez Jr., and my brother, Gregory, were very good friends in their high school years. My brother Gregory, Mario Jr., and Mario's sister were guests at my house in North Wildwood on many weekends during the summer months for several years. My brother Gregory eventually enlisted in the Air Force after high school, and lost contact with Mario Jr.

Unfortunately, several years later, Mario Jr. died of drug and alcohol related circumstances. Mario Jr. was very close to his uncle Judge Joseph Rodriguez, and this is a relevant fact. **It is my opinion** based upon the relationships outlined above, that Judge Rodriguez and his brother Mario Rodriguez Senior were very familiar with myself, and my family members. Furthermore, and **again, in my opinion**, Judge Rodriguez developed a jaundiced view of *"pain management"*, and the treatment of patients with *opioid addiction*.

By the time I came to federal court with my lawsuit against certain Cape May County prosecutors and detectives, for their **misconduct and perjury**, the facts of my innocence were clear to the jury in Cape May County, as I was acquitted of all charges within two hours. I was falsely accused of drug related crimes by the Cape May County prosecutor, and this fact was clear to Judge Rodriguez following the initial briefs and oral arguments that were performed in open federal court. Judge Rodriguez was presented the **facts** of my case, and was given all of the **exculpatory evidence** which clearly identified the absence of **"probable cause"** in the Cape May County indictment presented by Megan Hoerner and George Hallett. Early in this federal case Judge Rodriguez seemed clear on these issues. However, as time went on, Rodriguez gave complete immunity to all five prosecutors, and certain detectives, even though it was clear that they had committed **prosecutorial misconduct** *knowingly, willfully and maliciously* in my criminal case. **It was also clear that there was no "probable cause" for my arrest, or for any criminal indictment. The entire grand jury presentation** *was flawed* **with misconduct of both prosecutor and detective.**

**Judge Rodriguez made the most egregious statement in his opinion brief that "because an indictment was handed down by the grand jury, this becomes prima facia evidence of "probable cause".**
*(This represents another irresponsible statement by a ninety year old judge.)*

Rodriguez completely disregarded the **lies and misrepresentations,** and **perjury** of Hallett, in addition to completely disregarding all of the **exculpatory evidence** *withheld from the grand jury* **knowingly, willfully, and maliciously**, by Megan Hoerner and George Hallett in order to obtain their indictment.

Judge Rodriguez completely disregarded all of the facts in my case, and gave summary judgment to the defendants.

The **cognitive bias**, apparent with certain prosecutors and detectives in my case along with certain judges lead me to believe that the **stigma of accusation** persists disregarding any factual evidence to the contrary. It was clear to Rodriguez initially that there was no **"probable cause"** for my arrest or prosecution. His **cognitive bias** extended to **pain management physicians** and **opioid treatment**, as he protected the two remaining defendants, Tonya Anderson and George Hallett, who both lied and committed **perjury** under oath.

**It is *further* my opinion** that Judge Rodriguez should have recused himself from my federal 1983 civil case against these Cape May County personalities. Rodriguez knew my family well, was ethically compromised, and should have recused himself because of his cognitive bias against the practice of **"pain management"**, and the treatment of patients with opioid addiction.

After three years in federal court with Rodriguez, he summarily **canceled final oral arguments, and refused to give me a jury of my peers to decide my case**. Instead, he gave "summary judgment" to the opposition. **Again in my opinion,** Judge Rodriguez, **age 90,** represents a clear example of the **abuse of power, fundamental dishonesty, and legal tyranny of this weaponized justice system.**

## Judge Wefing, Judge Payne & Judge Baxter
"The Three Blind Mice"

The next group of judges, who I call the "the three blind mice," are the three Superior Court appellate judges who refused to **"remand"** my OAL civil case to a second administrative law judge and a second OAL civil hearing - **Dorothea Wefing, Edith Payne and Linda Baxter**.

In the face of **absolute perjury** on the part of Tonya Anderson, along with many other lies and misrepresentations at the Board of Medical Examiners, with Sandra Dick and David Puteska, these three judges refused to allow me a second OAL civil trial to elucidate the **truth**. My attorney Jordan Zeitz wrote a clear and concise **"Statement of the Case"** which identified all the issues of this BME fiasco.

## "Due Process" Denied

**Any reasonable citizen off the street,** would have understood the brief by Jordan Zeitz, clearly defining all of the **false statements** made by the Board of Medical Examiners, and the **perjury** of Anderson, aided by Puteska and Dick. **The failure of the "three blind mice" to "remand" my case to a second administrative law judge for an honest determination of these issues is both completely DISGRACEFUL and UNBELIEVABLE to my attorneys and myself.**

**These three female appellate judges, in my opinion, are fundamentally dishonest, and they abandoned my 14th Amendment Constitutional right to "due process".** By neglecting "due process" the "three blind mice" have deprived a board-certified physician in good standing in the state of New Jersey, his normal existence as a practicing physician. **They have taken my liberty, my property, my medical license, and have denied me equal protection of the law. In my candid opinion, these appellate judges represent nothing more than political appointees who lack a moral compass, and chose to continue the legal tyranny, and the criminalization of medicine.**

---

*Note...*
The decision of these "three blind mice"
**remains unpublished for a reason.**
Their decision was completely unjust, and they simply did not want anyone assessing
**their deceit and their failure** to
render "due process" in my case.

---

The "three blind mice" are employed by government, and view their opinions specifically to protect the delinquents in control of the Board of Medical Examiners.

As a result, DAG Sandra Dick, and her cohorts will never answer to the attorney general for their subversion of the law, and their illegal disgraceful behavior.

Furthermore in my opinion, these appellate judges, are **fundamentally dishonest**, and have abandoned my 14th Amendment Constitutional right to "due process". By negating "due process", these appellate creatures, as well as certain BME creatures have **deprived a natural born citizen of the United States of America, my fundamental rights as a practicing physician, my liberty, and my medical license, and have denied me equal protection of the law.**

As I have outlined earlier in the text, a complete appeal was then rendered to the Supreme Court of the state of NJ in a timely fashion. **The Supreme Court simply refused to hear my case.**

In other words: **F. U. Dr. Costino.**

## Judge Hardiman, Judge Greenaway & Judge Bibas

The last group of judges represented in this book are the third circuit court of appeals: Judge Hardiman, Greenaway & Bibas.

My federal case attorney comprised excellent briefs regarding the **factual evidence** in my criminal case. **Judge Rodriguez took three years in federal court to ultimately deny final oral arguments, deny me a jury of my peers, and gave summary judgment to the opposition**. Rodriguez **disregarded the prosecutorial misconduct of all of the players, prosecutors and detectives in Cape May County.** There was *never* any "probable cause" to arrest me in September 2007, and Rodriguez was certainly well aware of this. The indictment by Megan Hoerner and George Hallett was presented with lies, deceptions, and the complete elimination of **all critical exculpatory evidence.**

Following the result in federal court, my attorney petitioned the third circuit court of appeals, thinking that **I** *may finally receive* **justice**. He produced a very accurate assessment of my federal **1983 civil rights** case to the third circuit. **To my amazement, this "third circuit court of appeals" canceled *all* oral arguments, and produced a report that appeared to be written by a fourth grader in grammar school**.

The third circuit report **mimicked** Rodriguez's report, and was simply an **abomination**. My civil rights case ended abruptly in that manner. My attorney never had the opportunity to present final arguments in federal court with Rodriguez, and was denied the ability for oral argument at the third circuit Court of Appeals. *They simply did not allow the truthful record to see the light of day, and certainly refused to allow a jury to decide this most significant matter in accordance with our Constitution of the United States of America.*

**My fourth and fourteenth amendments to the federal Constitution have been obliterated by the legal tyranny of the so-called justice system.** Both Rodriguez and the three creatures of the third circuit systematically denied me a **jury of my peers**, thereby terminating **any possibility of ever obtaining justice. These political judges prevented me from my right to a jury trial simply because they knew that once my case was presented before a reasonable jury, I would prevail.**

**It's almost impossible to obtain justice today because the system of lawyers, prosecutors, detectives, and judges** *protect* **each other. Judges condone "prosecutorial misconduct" which occurs on a routine basis.** In my candid opinion, the justice system is a *corrupt, subversive, and fundamentally dishonest system, devoid of a moral compass*, supported by *legal tyranny*, and *abuse of power* that I have experienced over the past thirteen years. It's clear to me that this **fundamentally dishonest justice system** has been orchestrated to continue the **criminalization of medicine**, essentially denying me "due process" of law.

# "The Largest Lessons are Learned from the Largest Tragedies."

"Concentration is the source of strength"

The "herd instinct" is prevalent in our society, the higher man attempts to elevate himself above the herd which upsets those with lesser qualities. The prudent physician must be true to himself, he must be courageous, and ignore the contemptible elements of society.

The Constitution of the United States was established for the protection of its citizens, not for the suppression by government. The first ten amendments specifically ensure the sovereignty of every U.S. citizen.

Since the constitution was enacted in the 1780's, the federal government has expanded it's grip on society, to such a degree that it now employs the "power to punish" with impunity through the "corrupt justice system".

**James Madison** put it this way in the "*Federalist #47*", "the accumulation of all powers, legislative, executive, and judiciary, in the same hands, whether of one, a few, or many, and whether hereditary, self appointed, or elective, may justly be pronounced the very definition of tyranny".

Following the conclusion and acquittal in my criminal cases, I sent a letter to the Board of Medical Examiners requesting a hearing in an effort to return my medical license and continue my practice of medicine. This correspondence was initially done in 2012, and it is now 2021 however, my medical license remains in Trenton at the Board of Medical Examiners along with their *$90,000 fine* levied by the BME **and an additional $100,000** fine levied by the State of NJ representing the state's egregious activity.

During the past nine years, I have filed a number of civil lawsuits against several individuals, principally lawyers, prosecutors and detectives that I've found to be, in my opinion, **dishonest, irresponsible,** and **ignorant of the law.**

A lawsuit was filed against **Alan Lands, Esq.** the *disgraceful* attorney in Pleasantville New Jersey. The attorney handling this case against Alan Lands, Hercules Pappas, failed to prosecute this civil suit properly, and the presiding judge eventually dismissed it.

A lawsuit was filed against **Edwin Jacobs, Esq.** in Philadelphia, PA, for failing me at the Board of Medical Examiners in December 2007. This lawsuit was also dismissed because of a venue issue. My attorney **Stanley Cheiken**, refused to re-file the case in New Jersey without additional money, which at that time, I simply did not have. I therefore was unable to pursue Edwin Jacobs any further.

**I filed a 1983 civil rights lawsuit** against five prosecutors, and four detectives, for **prosecutorial misconduct, in superior court in Cape May County**. As outlined earlier, this civil case was dismissed by Judge Christopher Gibson for "failure to prosecute", and following a later hearing with Judge Gibson to reinstate this case, *he, in my opinion, for political reasons, refused to do so.*

**The two attorneys responsible for this botched civil case were completely irresponsible. Furthermore, I failed to receive any notification from the Cape May County court system of this "failure to prosecute" or it's dismissal. By failing to reinstate this case, Judge Gibson, in my opinion, protected Robert Taylor, Matthew Weintraub, Megan Hoerner, Tina Kell, Trisha Kalita, Paul Worrell, and of course, George Hallett, from civil prosecution, completely protecting Cape May County and the State of New Jersey.**

## Chapter 24 - The Largest Lessons Are Learned from the Largest Tragedies

**I filed a 1983 civil rights lawsuit** in federal court in Camden New Jersey against five prosecutors, three detectives, Cape May County, and Egg Harbor Township, for their **prosecutorial misconduct, multiple lies, deceptions, and perjury in my criminal case.** After three years of back-and-forth briefs, a final hearing was scheduled, and then **abruptly canceled by Judge Rodriguez** *with no explanation*.

He then *canceled* additional arguments *with no explanation*.

Judge Rodriguez is a 90-year-old character who has been retired for many years, receiving his federal pension, but still a judge in federal court. After abruptly canceling final oral arguments, Rodriguez then gave **summary judgment** to the other side, *eliminating* **my jury trial in federal court.** Furthermore, also eliminating my ability to recover the hundreds of thousands of dollars representing the costs of defending myself and my wife in superior court and at the Board of Medical Examiners for five years, and the costs of my lawsuits thereafter.

**Rodriguez** is a federal employee, who **protects dishonest prosecutors and detectives.** Furthermore, in my opinion, this judge exemplified a **cognitive bias, and prejudice** against me with his **egregious and dishonest decision**. The third circuit court of appeals, simply mimicked Judge Rodriguez "to a T". This third circuit was another perfect example of the **legal tyranny** in this coordinated justice system.

**It's like banging your head against a brick wall for an innocent, law-abiding physician to file a lawsuit against the state or the federal government.** I endured five years of **incompetent, illegal behavior** and **prosecutorial misconduct knowingly, willfully and maliciously** by the Cape May County Prosecutor's office and the Board of Medical Examiners. **These disgraceful and incompetent creatures were able to LIE, FALSIFY FACTS, and certain personalities, to COMMIT PERJURY under oath with impunity.**

Collectively, they performed this corrupt activity throughout my five-year criminal case, and have essentially gotten away with all of their egregious activity, because, as state employees, **there is *NO OVERSIGHT*, and they are essentially**

**untouchable.**

The creatures at the Board of Medical Examiners, principally Sandra Dick and David Puteska, employed by the state of New Jersey, are also **essentially untouchable** with *"layers of immunity"*. There's nothing more that I can do regarding their **abuse of power** and **corrupt behavior**. They, unfortunately, possess significant immunity in the face their CORRUPTION, LIES, AND PERJURY that I endured. **They are completely protected by the state, with regard to their illegal activity without sanction. Furthermore, and in my opinion, they're** *all ethically compromised with complete protection through fabricated immunity.*

The Cape May County prosecutor **Robert Taylor**, along with the Board of Medical Examiners chief deputy **Sandra Dick, colluded to arrest me, and destroy my medical practice**. They made a full court attempt to **destroy my life, my wife's life, my children's life, and my entire family in general.** They destroyed the lives of many of my patients, with their **legal tyranny,** but fortunately I am still standing with *self-reliance and in reasonably good health.*

**Sandra Dick** (alias Sandra Y. Ben-Asher)**,** is now retired from the Board of Medical Examiners, and Robert Taylor is now retired as county prosecutor. There are currently newly assigned deputy attorneys at the Board of Medical Examiners, and a different county prosecutor has been appointed. **My criticism and anger is confined** *to ONLY the characters* **outlined in this text. William Roeder**, however, continues as executive director of the BME.

Roeder has been the executive director at the BME for more that 25 years. I have written numerous letters to him, his response has been uncooperative. Several months ago I spoke to one of his assistants**, Jacqueline Johnson,** an employee, at the Board. She was very cordial to me, and almost to the point of encouragement. She directed me to the current physician in charge at the board, **Dr. Leseig**. After several phone calls to the Board, I was able to speak with Dr. Leseig and implored him to schedule a hearing for me regarding my license reinstatement. His response was **"that I was unable to meet with the Board until I attend a professional**

## Chapter 24 - The Largest Lessons Are Learned from the Largest Tragedies

**assessment program, and pay them their $90,000 fine"**. I examined the recent list of professional assessment programs provided to me by Jacqueline Johnson, and carefully researched them. I spoke with all four program directors, and as a result, I have come to this conclusion:

- The program at Drexel University has been canceled.
- The programs in Denver Colorado, San Diego, California, and in Harrisburg Pennsylvania, requires between $12,000 and $16,000 in payment for a two-day session for re-instatement. All have been discontinued as a result of the Covid19.

I eventually got back in touch with Dr. Leseig and reiterated the issues regarding these programs, and related to him that there ought to be a program in the state of New Jersey for physicians to be reinstated.
I was shocked by his answer: **"There are no programs at all in the state of New Jersey for professional reassessment."**

Following his statement, I said to him, that we certainly have many fine institutions in New Jersey, both in South Jersey, and in North Jersey. Why then is the **elitist** Board of Medical Examiners of the state of New Jersey unable to provide a simple program of professional reassessment for their physicians? Dr. Leseig then swallowed his tongue for a few seconds, **and was unable to answer my question in a reasonable manner.**

I stated to Dr. Leseig, the Board of Medical Examiners is there to protect the public, therefore, the state of New Jersey certainly should be able to produce a simple, two-day reassessment program for their physicians. I have never received any responsible answers to my questions from Dr Leseig.

The Board of Medical Examiners of the state of New Jersey is simply a **pathetic organization** who have been quick to assess significant fines on me, **an innocent physician,** representing their illegal activity, **perjury** and **tyranny**.

# "Due Process" Denied

They however, are unable to produce a program of reassessment for New Jersey physicians who **do represent the public good.**

I'd like to share a bit of my history with two of my New Jersey positions in my earlier years.

- In the summer of 1968, I received a scholarship from the state of New Jersey for a research program in the science building, in Trenton, between my first and second years of medical school.

- From 1972 through 1976, I was appointed New Jersey State Medical Examiner in the Department of Labor and Industry, Division of Worker's Compensation.

In both positions, I worked with **honest, intelligent**, attorneys and judges and chemistry PhD 's. They were terrific people, they knew their business well, and my experience was *excellent and transparent*.

**Further in my opinion, today, New Jersey is full of dishonest, disreputable hypocrites, with a monochromatic thought process, who possess a monopoly on illegitimate behavior sanctioned by the state of New Jersey, the county of Cape May, and the Board of Medical Examiners.**

In my candid opinion, these entities are staffed by *disgraceful, cynical, deceptive*, prosecutors and detectives and certain judges, whose *perception, and critical thinking process*, remains **clinically disturbed**. Furthermore, in my opinion, and with regard to my experience, these creatures function, and demonstrate, a **cognitive bias, devoid** of a **moral compass,** which is not only **corrupt, and subversive,** but **functionally inept,** and **completely dishonest.** They possess the ability, devoid of ethics, and common sense, to **weaponize** the justice system, and **criminalize the practice of medicine.**

# Chapter 24 - The Largest Lessons Are Learned from the Largest Tragedies

**Currently, in 2021, my medical license remains in Trenton, and the Board of Medical Examiners has refused to grant me a hearing, to enable me to return to the practice of medicine.**

I plan to continue to petition the various personalities at the Board of Medical Examiners, to provide me with a hearing before the newly appointed physicians and deputies at the Board, in an effort to resolve the lack of **"due process"**, by the **previous deviants**. There are now newly appointed deputy attorneys, and newly appointed physicians on the board who may ultimately understand the **unconstitutional injustices** rendered to me by the previous disgraceful DAGs and physician board members.

# Chapter 25

"I'm a kind person, I'm kind to everyone, but if you are unkind to me, then kindness is not what you'll remember me for."
- Al Capone

"May the Lord have mercy upon my enemies because I won't."
- General George Patton

I would be remiss if I did not speak to certain subjective, political, and social initiating factors regarding my arrest and prosecution in September of 2007. These initiating factors are based upon **facts, not hyperbole**, and are all true. Robert Taylor, had a history of improper prosecutions in Cape May Country outlined previously in this text. With my case, according to a confidential and reliable source, a colleague of mine, Taylor was given specific direction by Sandra Dick at the Board of Medical Examiners to arrest me.

I embarrassed Sandra Dick and certain D.A.G. Board attorneys in the late 1990's by writing a formal letter to the National Data Bank criticizing, and challenging DAG Dick and her " girlfriends" at the Board, regarding their false charge against me of a regulation that did not exist until several years later. **Sandra Dick** was embarrassed by my letter to the **National Data Bank** criticizing her and her *"girlfriends"*, on the BME who attempted a civil prosecution of me, in the late 1980's.

Chapter 25

Sandra Dick and certain deputies attempted to civilly prosecute me at the Administrative Law Court for a perceived breach of a **regulation, that did not exist in the 1980's** until several years later. This failed civil prosecution, and false charge at the BME, and at the Administrative Law Court, was dismissed by the presiding administrative law judge in 1995 as **completely false**. This civil prosecution represented nothing more than a **political stunt,** by DAG Sandra Dick and her DAG *"girlfriends"* at the Board, over which she had complete influence. Following the dismissal of this *spurious complaint,* Dick then orchestrated a **reprimand** by the Board in 1995. While a "reprimand" became a matter of record, it did not in any way affect my medical license to practice medicine, however, it was **completely unjust.**

This "reprimand" represented a political stunt, orchestrated by Sandra Dick, because she **failed** in her quest at the administrative law court, to her *grave disappointment and embarrassment.*

As a result of the Board's reprimand, I was very upset and then decided set the record straight. I wrote a full report to the **National Data Bank**, severely criticizing Sandra Dick and her DAG cohorts for their egregious charge, cognitive dissidence, deception and failed prosecution. Based upon the medical regulations, and the laws of the state of New Jersey, the Board's action by Sandra Dick was a **corrupt misrepresentation** of the BME regulations, in their attempt to discredit my practice of medicine.

My formal letter to the National Data Bank severely criticized Sandra Dick, and her "girlfriends" at the BME, in which I revealed all the facts of my case which began in 1985. *Sandra was incensed*, that a physician in New Jersey, would "call her out" for the **disgraceful**, and **evil creature** that she represents.

An additional episode that I'm certain upset Sandra Dick occurred in 2003 following the sanction of one of my colleagues, a licensed physician in Cape May County. Dr. John Napoleon was an accomplished physician in Cape May County, the medical examiner of the county for many years, and the medical director of the Cape May County prison, and of the Bayside State Prison in Cumberland county. Sandra Dick and her disgraceful Board of Medical Examiners revoked Dr Napoleon's license to practice medicine as a result of a perceived minor infraction of a BME regulation. Following this deplorable act by her and her Board, I as a friend and colleague, went to his defense, and petitioned our State Senator, Nicolas Asselta to intervene with the state's commission in an effort to restore Dr. Napoleon's medical licensure. I had several meetings with Senator Asselta during a period of approximately six months, however, the goal was never accomplished and Dr. Napoleon never returned to his medical practice.

## Now a short review:

Fast forward to 2005, while I have been a practicing physician since 1971, in emergency medicine, general internal medicine, physical medicine, pain management, and addiction medicine, treating thousands of patients. Robert Taylor, with **complete ignorance,** and in **conjunction with Sandra Dick, targeted my pain management practice.**

Robert Taylor was encouraged by Sandra Dick at the BME to have me arrested, one of only two pain management physicians in Cape May County in 2007. Taylor utilized completely **false data** in December of 2005 when he attempted his first "entrapment" procedure using *detective Landis* posing as a heroin addict. **This first "entrapment" episode, not only failed miserably, but it was also clear to detective Landis, and law enforcement, based upon his excellent report, that there was no history whatsoever of improper behavior on my part with regard to "pain management".** In 2005, Taylor was **ignorant** of the laws of the State of New Jersey, ( "State v Vaccaro" ), and obviously **ignorant** of the practice of pain management. In 2007 Taylor, Sandra Dick, and certain corrupt detectives, **George Hallett, Marie Hayes,** and assistant prosecutor Megan Hoerner, fabricated invalid and fraudulent statements which lead to my arrest. **Without "due process", Taylor initiated this second "objective due process entrapment" procedure against me, a capable and law abiding licensed physician.**

## Chapter 25

This second "objective due process entrapment" initiated in 2007 by Taylor and his corrupt underlings, in conspiracy with Sandra Dick, was initiated because at this time in our society, the practice of *pain management* was being **assaulted by law enforcement**.

Following an insufficient quality of thought process, and an *insufficient* and *inaccurate* body of evidence, Taylor and his minions, began this "objective due process entrapment" procedure against me. At my criminal trial in 2012, following five years of misery, the jury found my treatment of the two undercover females perfectly legal and conformed to all the laws of the state of New Jersey. *Remember,* **"State v Vaccaro" is the 1976 appellate published decision that governs the** *practice of medicine, pain management, and prescription products,* **in the state of New Jersey.**

Following my arrest in September of 2007 by Taylor, I was summoned by the other **conspirator**, Sandra Dick, at the BME, to appear for a hearing. I unfortunately was represented by an insufficient attorney, who had little or no experience with Sandra Dick, her cohorts, and certain henchmen physicians, who do Sandra Dick's bidding at the Board. My medical license was suspended in December of 2007, *without* **a criminal indictment**, **and** *certainly without* **any conviction, thereby terminating my ability to practice medicine as a physician, and to earn a living.**

To go a step further in my explanation, **and in my opinion**, most of the assistant prosecutors, and detectives in the Cape May County prosecutor's office, and *especially Taylor*, are democrats, who dislike successful, conservative republicans. **Taylor** was the Democratic Party chairman in Cape May County for a number of years, and targeted Dr. Costino, a conservative physician, and the president of the Cape May County Union League, a republican organization.

I'm certain that politics also played a significant role in targeting me and my medical practice of *pain management* and *addiction medicine*. Furthermore, and again, in my **candid opinion**, I feel certain, that the *narcissistic* Taylor, was extremely jealous of me personally, because I was able to purchase "preferred stock" in his Sun Bank. I purchased "preferred stock" in Sun Bank, through the efforts of one of my medical colleagues, Dr. Richard Renza. This fact, I'm certain, became a significant problem for Mr. Taylor, and also, in my opinion, for Raymond Batten, as both were principles and controlling board members of Sun Bank.

I do believe that these subjective issues in conjunction with the egregious activity between Taylor and Sandra Dick, **both democrats**, had a significant influence, along with the politics associated, and collectively, were the triggering mechanisms that not only contributed, but precipitated my illegal arrest followed by five years of corrupt activity by the creatures in the Cape May County Prosecutor's Office, the Board of Medical Examiners, and at the Administrative Law Court.

Furthermore, and in my opinion, I was **targeted** by the *narcissistic, and insufficient,* Taylor, assisted by certain corrupt assistant prosecutors, and detectives, in consort with Sandra Dick, at the BME, to suspended my medical license **without cause, and without indictment or conviction**. This **travesty of justice** was followed by the landslide of **legal tyranny,** in Superior court with Judge Raymond Batten, with the DEA, and postal system creatures, and at the Board of Medical Examiners, with corrupt DAGs, and certain physicians, **devoid of a moral compass, and hell bent to criminalize my practice of medicine.**

# *Cast of Characters*
## *( a.k.a. Cast of Creatures )*

In my professional opinion, these are my candid observations and descriptions of the pathetic creatures involved in my case:

### 1. Robert Taylor:
In my opinion...corrupt prosecutor of Cape May County, narcissitic, egomaniac with a personality disorder, and above all, ignorant of the law.

### 2. Tonya Anderson:
In my opinion...a Class II cop, Egg Harbor Township, NJ, with poor self-esteem, a liar and perjurer is her legacy.

### 3. George Hallett:
In my opinion...stupid and ignorant of the law, a moronic detective in Cape May County, a liar, confabulator, and perjurer.

### 4. Meghan Hoerner:
In my opinion... Assistant Prosecutor of Cape May County, ignorant of the law, with an insufficient intellect. She composed Anderson's second insufficient court certification, and caused multiple indictments with absolute prosecutorial misconduct, knowingly, willfully and maliciously.

### 5. Matthew Weintraub:
In my opinion...Assistant Prosecutor of Cape May County, also ignorant of the law but smart enough to leave the county of Cape May at just the right time.

### 6: Tina Kell: ( *The Drama Queen* )
In my opinion...Assistant Prosecutor of Cape May County, extremely narcissistic, and an egomaniac like her boss Taylor.

### 7. Dara Paley:
In my opinion... ...Assistant Prosecutor in Cape May County who unfortunately followed the moronic Taylor's instructions, but did nothing to correct the insufficiencies of this case.

## *Cast of Characters* continued
*( a.k.a. Cast of Creatures )*

### 8. Thomas Prevoznik:
In my opinion... DEA Supervisor, liar, confabulator, and perjurer, with false accusations, false narratives and insufficient knowledge of law in the state of New Jersey. A corrupt DEA personality who played a role in the alteration of my medical records.

### 9. Alex Sylvester:
In my opinion... Postal Inspector, liar, perjurer, who played a role in altering my medical records. Another corrupt creature.

### 10. Sandra Dick:
(a.k.a. Sandra Y. Ben-Asher)
*In my candid opinion...* Chief Deputy at the Board of Medical Examiners, the "Wicked Witch of the West". Corrupt, devoid of a moral compass, subversive and fundamentally dishonest.
She possessed the singular ability to generate enough abuse of power to steal my medical license.
She represents the state's MOST corrupt employee.

### 11. David Puteska:
In my opinion... Another Deputy at the Board, slave to Sandra Dick and performed all of her bidding. A prolific liar and principal intermediary in the conspiracy between Sandra Dick and Tonya Anderson. Puteska composed Tonya Anderson's first perjured certification.
He knew that it was false and insufficient.

### 12. William Roeder:
In my opinion.. Here's a guy who sits in his office all day, a paper pusher, the executive director of the Board of Medical Examiners and the one who has refused to respond to my multiple letters for reinstatement.
He and his staff have completely eliminated the record of my BME case secondary to its blatant corruption.

There were only two **excellent judges** in my case who were honest, and expressed their briefs as a matter of law and not politics. I thank both of them for their honesty and perseverance in the face of the political and legal tyranny that was prevalent in my case:
**Judge Bruce Gorman and Judge Albert Garofolo**

## Chapter 26 - Cast of Characters

Through the pernicious, deplorable, unethical, and corrupt justice system, the creatures of both the Cape May County Prosecutor's Office, and at the Board of Medical Examiners in Trenton, **CONSPIRED** utilizing their **abuse of power,** and the **force of legal tyranny** to destroy my life and my family, but failed. They did however create some destruction in my family, and destruction in the lives of hundreds of my **good, honest, supportive patients.**

The great Winston Churchill, the most significant intellect of the twentieth century said:

**"The truth is incontrovertible, malice may attack it, and ignorance may deride it, but in the end, there it is!!!"**

*"You could stay up all night and not think of that."*

Redundancy, in this text, was necessary to satisfy my anger with regard to the issues and personalities that I dealt with over the past thirteen years. If you got this far in the book, I thank you for your indulgence, and endurance in digesting the events of my last thirteen years.

**"It is out of the deepest depth that the highest must come to its height."**

- Thus spoke Zarathustra

# Chapter 27

"The Stoic proclaims the power of indifference reigns supreme."
- *Meditations,* by Marcus Aurelius

"Courage is not the absence of fear,
courage is the presence of fear,
but the fortitude to act."

**There is a universal truth, a universal principal of life, of morality, which must prevail within the milieu of the intellectual pygmies of the justice system class, to enable the trained physician to defeat this corrupt system.** As one who is objectively rational, and responsibly organized, I was blindsided by the corrupt and irresponsible action of law enforcement, who possess an ***extreme excess* of illegitimate power,** along with a **monochromatic thought process.**

To be a capable and prudent physician in this society today, one must be an individual, free and responsible, through acts of willful morality and scientific endeavor. The prudent physician must be relentless in questioning and rethinking those things that used to be taken for granted. One must reconsider everything, one must doubt everything.

As an "existentialist", and a trained physician, responsible for the lives of many patients through acts and decisions of *unselfishness, care, and concern* for their welfare and health, I was **devastated.**

# Chapter 27

A casual stroll through the **lunatic asylum** of Taylor's Cape May County Prosecutor's office, his assistants, and certain detectives, and the Board of Medical Examiners, with corrupt DAGs, and certain irresponsible physicians, **demonstrates that stupidity and ignorance, while prevalent, does not prove anything**.

The "war" was won on **logic, principal, and evidence**. I repeat, to be a capable and prudent physician in this society today one must be relentless in questioning and rethinking those things that *used to be taken for granted*:

- An honest and moral justice system
- An honest and moral Board of Medical Examiners

**In the face of the intellectual deficiencies of the characters, both in the prosecutor's office, and at the Board of Medical Examiners, a trained physician must possess the fortitude to defeat the ignorance of this enemy.**

The physician must overcome the slave mentality that we share as a result of the overburdening presence of the **corrupt justice system.** The physician must be *honest, noble and possess the courage* to face the reality of this corrupt system, and fight them on superior ground.

In my opinion, both the "Board of Assholes" in Trenton and "specific morons" in the Cape May County Prosecutor's Office, **resent the fame and fortune of the successful physician, as their only goal persists to reduce the physician down to their level of mediocrity.**

The *weaponized justice system* of Cape May County, and the *corrupt* Board of Medical Examiners in Trenton was energized based upon **unsupported, false and fraudulent data** initiated by the *defective and intellectually deficient* group of Cape May County detectives and prosecutors, and those defective creatures at the Board of Medical Examiners, mostly *devoid of a moral compass*.

**The prudent physician must be true to himself, he must be courageous, and ignore the contemptible element of the personalities in the prosecutor's office and the DAGs at the Board of Medical Examiners.**

# "Due Process" Denied

**Too many agencies possess an excess of power. You must face your enemy on superior ground, never shallow your defense against their framed ideology, follow an effective path and you will overcome their deficiencies. Most importantly, be true to yourself, and you will prevail!!!**

"The largest lessons are learned
from the largest tragedies."

"Being strong-minded and courageous allows you to
withstand the frightening power and corruption
of the justice system."

"No price is too high to pay for the privilege of
owning yourself."

**"What does not kill us makes us stronger."**
- Friedrich Wilhelm Nietzsche

# Postscript

The Cape May County prosecutor, Robert Taylor, created multiple criminal accusations and charges, the optics and kinetics of which were orchestrated through the political lens of his corrupt imagination. Taylor was completely ignorant of the medical, as well as the criminal justice laws and statutes of the state of New Jersey regarding the practice of medicine.

The superior court judge, his buddy Batten, was also completely ignorant of "State v Vaccaro," the controlling legal appellate decision, and authority regarding the practice of medicine principally the administration of Class I – II –III – IV – V controlled substances.

Additionally, the remaining morons in Taylor's prosecutor department were not only ignorant of the governing laws, and statutes outlined in this text, but fervently were able to alter the facts of my case, by altering the transcripts, eliminating certain words and statements within the transcripts, in addition to committing perjury under oath, as this was their primary mechanism in chief.

Taylor, along with his assistant prosecutor's and detectives, colluded with Sandra Dick at the Board of Medical Examiners to produce a fundamentally dishonest, subversive, and corrupt false narrative regarding my practice of medicine, in an effort to suspend my medical license. This suspension was accomplished as a vendetta by Sandra Dick and her cohorts in December of 2007.

# "Due Process" Denied

Historically, in February of 1998, her previous BME case against me was dismissed by the Administrative Law Judge Robert Miller. This same corrupt group of deputies lead by Sandra Dick formulated a fundamentally dishonest, corrupt, set of complaints against me based solely upon Sandra Dick's imagination of regulations that did not exist.

Sandra Dick was embarrassed at the office of Administrative Law civil court in 1998 but endeavored to retaliate against me which was accomplished by her and her cohorts in December of 2007 with the suspension of my medical license at the initial BME hearing. This suspension of my medical license was accomplished eliminating "due process" without a criminal indictment, and certainly without any conviction.

The behavior of Dick and her BME was unconscionable, dishonest, corrupt, unethical and tyrannical. The BME has no oversight therefore; these criminal liars can act with all of their abuse of power and get away with all of this essentially illegal activity without reprisal. Furthermore, they have such immunity, that they have become untouchable even after I have provided **absolute proof of their false narratives, lies, and perjury under oath**.

The final insult and disgrace of my case consists of unjust financial penalties assessed by both the Board of Medical Examiners, and separately, the State of New Jersey.

The BME penalty is **$90,000.**
The State of New Jersey penalty is **$100,000.**

To this day they still have complete control of my medical license.

The state has refused to give me an opportunity to address the new members of the Board of Medical Examiners either in conference, or at their general monthly meeting. They have demanded a $190,000 penalty to be paid which of course I am unable to accomplish.

# Postscript

**After five years in criminal court, from September of 2007 to November of 2012, in Cape May County, a jury of my peers who understood the disgrace of the Cape May County justice parade acquitted me of ALL 26 criminal charges. Since November of 2012 I have made multiple attempts to have my medical license returned to me with no relief in sight.**

This text that you have graciously read and understood, is my autobiography of the last fourteen years of my life through to the summer of 2021. Fortunately, I am still alive, in reasonably good health, have the love of my wife, children and grandchildren and await the next throw of the dice.

# Appendix

Pg. 264  Defense Witness List

Pg. 265  Misspelling of the name Artiz Exhibit C147

Pg. 266  2007 PDR - Physician's Desk Reference - pg 1131

Pg. 267  Signed Pain Management Agreement - Exhibit R-7, C165

Pg. 269  Response Letter from DEA

Pg. 270  First Signed Certification of Tonya Anderson

Pg. 272  Second Signed Certification Certification of Tonya Anderson

Pg. 274  Seaport Chiropractic (4pgs)

Pg. 278  Victim Notification forms for Dr. Costino

Pg. 280  Notification of the Release / Parole of R. Conyers

Pg. 281  Dr. Costino's Letter to BME Re: Reinstatement

Pg. 283  Civil Lawsuit - Dr. Costino vs Edwin Jacobs

Pg. 287  Civil Lawsuit - Dr. Costino vs Alan Lands

Pg. 295  1983 Civil Rights Lawsuit in Superior Court, Cape May County

Pg. 303  1983 Civil Rights Lawsuit in Federal Court, Camden, NJ

Pg. 319  Summary Judgment in my 1983 Civil Rights case : Anderson, George Hallett ands Little Egg Harbor Twp.

Pg. 320  The Order to Dismiss - Administrative Law Judge in February 1998 - Rejection of BME and Sandra Dick

"Due Process" Denied

# Defense Witness List
"State v John Costino"
October 2012 Trial

**Testimony of Character Witnesses for Consideration:**
Evidence of good character or reputation of an accused is always competent in the trial of a criminal action, and is entitled to be considered by you.

The jury should consider all of the relevant testimony, including that relating to the defendant's good character or reputation, and if, on such consideration, there exists a reasonable doubt of his guilt, even though that doubt may arise merely from his previous good repute, he is entitled to an acquittal.

James O'Donnell
Alfred Campbell
Aldo Palombo, Pharmacist
Fred Melroy, Pharmacist
Dr. Eileen Kelly
Dr. Robert Speer
Lionel Desrosiers
Ed Fox
Dominic Natale
Hon, James Cafiero
*Judge & Former Senator*

Mary D'Amico
John Bartleson, III
Hon. John Callinan
William Henfey
*Mayor of N. Wildwood*

James Bowen
Dennis McDonough
Donald Staffier

Roman Osadchuk
Slawka Osadchuk
Richard Francisconi
Sandra Diehl
Curt Kelly
Dr. Robert Beitman
Robert McCallion
Barry Gehring
Joseph Spuhler
Anthony Trivelis
Valerie Trivelis
Raymond McGrath
Robert Harkins, Sr.

Al Cremin
Charles LaRosa
Markus Karavan
Dr. Robert Maurer
Dr. Richard Renza
Dr. Robert Renza

Appendix

# Courtroom Evidence EXHIBIT C147

See below the deliberate MISSPELLING of the name Maggie Ortiz, (UC2) from the prosecutor's evidence log of patient files. Correct spelling of their undercover officer's name is Maggie ORTIZ *NOT* ARTIZ.

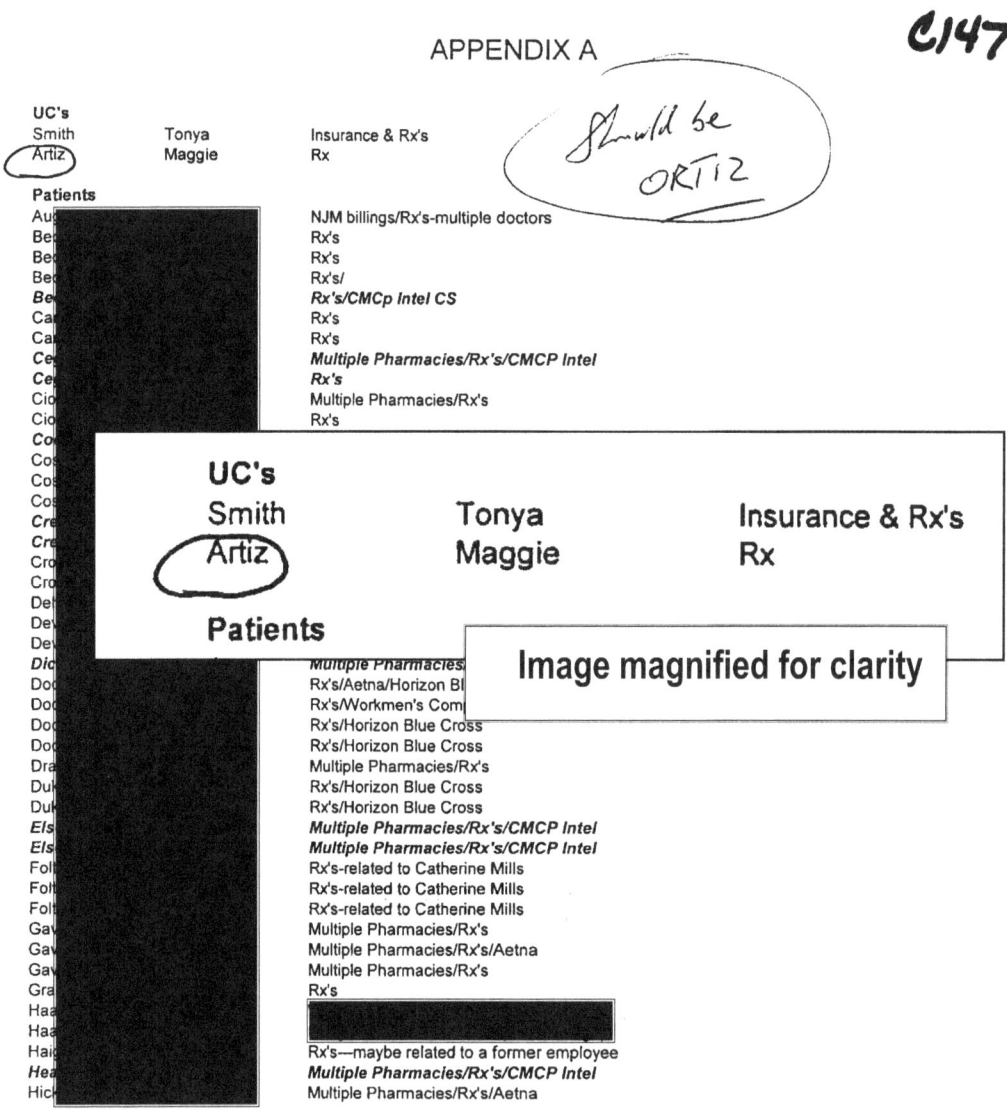

Patient names in **Exhibit C147** have been redacted for privacy

# "Due Process" Denied

## PDR - Physician's Desk Reference Pg. 1131

*Pg 1131*
*2007*
*PDR*

**PERCOCET®**
[perk' ō-sĕt]
(Oxycodone and Acetaminophen Tablets, USP)
℞ only

**DESCRIPTION**
Each tablet, for oral administration, contains oxycodone hydrochloride and acetaminophen in the following strengths:
Oxycodone Hydrochloride, USP 2.5 mg
Acetaminophen, USP 325 mg
2.5 mg oxycodone HCl is equivalent to 2.2409 mg of oxycodone.
Oxycodone Hydrochloride, USP 5 mg
Acetaminophen, USP 325 mg
5 mg oxycodone HCl is equivalent to 4.4815 mg of oxycodone.
Oxycodone Hydrochloride, USP 7.5 mg
Acetaminophen, USP 325 mg
7.5 mg oxycodone HCl is equivalent to 6.7228 mg of oxycodone.
Oxycodone Hydrochloride, USP 7.5 mg
Acetaminophen, USP 500 mg
7.5 mg oxycodone HCl is equivalent to 6.7228 mg of oxycodone.
Oxycodone Hydrochloride, USP 10 mg
Acetaminophen, USP 325 mg
10 mg oxycodone HCl is equivalent to 8.9637 mg of oxycodone.
Oxycodone Hydrochloride, USP 10 mg
Acetaminophen, USP 650 mg
10 mg oxycodone HCl is equivalent to 8.9637 mg of oxycodone.
All strengths of PERCOCET also contain the following inactive ingredients: Colloidal silicon dioxide, croscarmellose sodium, crospovidone, microcrystalline cellulose, povidone, pregelatinized starch, and stearic acid. In addition, the 2.5 mg/325 mg strength contains FD&C Red No. 40 Aluminum Lake and the 5 mg/325 mg strength contains FD&C Blue No. 1 Aluminum Lake. The 7.5 mg/325 mg strength and the 7.5 mg/500 mg strength contains FD&C Yellow No. 6 Aluminum Lake. The 10 mg/325 mg strength and the 10 mg/650 mg strength contains D&C Yellow No. 10 Aluminum Lake.
Acetaminophen, 4'-hydroxyacetanilide, is a non-opiate, non-salicylate analgesic and antipyretic which occurs as a white, odorless, crystalline powder, possessing a slightly bitter taste. The molecular formula for acetaminophen is $C_8H_9NO_2$ and the molecular weight is 151.17. It may be represented by the following structural formula:

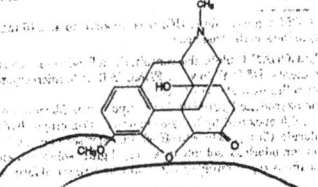

Oxycodone, 14-hydroxydihydrocodeinone, is a semisynthetic pure opioid agonist which occurs as a white, odorless, crystalline powder having a saline, bitter taste. The molecular formula for oxycodone hydrochloride is $C_{18}H_{21}NO_4 \cdot HCl$ and the molecular weight 351.83. It is derived from the opium alkaloid thebaine, and may be represented by the following structural formula:

**CLINICAL PHARMACOLOGY**
The principal ingredient, oxycodone, is a semisynthetic opioid analgesic with multiple actions qualitatively similar to those of morphine; the most prominent involves the central nervous system and organs composed of smooth muscle. The principal actions of therapeutic value of the oxycodone in PERCOCET are analgesia and sedation. Oxycodone is similar to codeine and methadone in that it retains at least one-half of its analgesic activity when administered orally.
Acetaminophen is a non-opiate, non-salicylate analgesic and antipyretic.

**INDICATIONS AND USAGE**
PERCOCET is indicated for the relief of moderate to moderately severe pain.

**CONTRAINDICATIONS**
PERCOCET should not be administered to patients who are hypersensitive to oxycodone, acetaminophen, or any other components of this product.

and it should be prescribed and administered with the same degree of caution appropriate to the use of other oral opioid-containing medications. Like other opioid-containing medications, PERCOCET is subject to the Federal Controlled Substances Act (Schedule II).

**PRECAUTIONS**
**General**
*Head Injury and Increased Intracranial Pressure:* The respiratory depressant effects of opioids and their capacity to elevate cerebrospinal fluid pressure may be markedly exaggerated in the presence of head injury, other intracranial lesions or a pre-existing increase in intracranial pressure. Furthermore, opioids produce adverse reactions which may obscure the clinical course of patients with head injuries.
*Acute Abdominal Conditions:* The administration of PERCOCET (Oxycodone and Acetaminophen Tablets, USP) or other opioids may obscure the diagnosis or clinical course in patients with acute abdominal conditions.
*Special Risk Patients:* PERCOCET should be given with caution to certain patients such as the elderly or debilitated, and those with severe impairment of hepatic or renal function, hypothyroidism, Addison's disease, and prostatic hypertrophy or urethral stricture.
**Information for Patients**
Oxycodone may impair the mental and/or physical abilities required for the performance of potentially hazardous tasks such as driving a car or operating machinery. The patient using PERCOCET should be cautioned accordingly.
**Drug Interactions**
Patients receiving other opioid analgesics, general anesthetics, phenothiazines, other tranquilizers, sedative-hypnotics or other CNS depressants (including alcohol) concomitantly with PERCOCET may exhibit an additive CNS depression. When such combined therapy is contemplated, the dose of one or both agents should be reduced. The concurrent use of anticholinergics with opioids may produce paralytic ileus.
**Usage in Pregnancy**
*Teratogenic Effects; Pregnancy Category C:* Animal reproductive studies have not been conducted with PERCOCET. It is also not known whether PERCOCET can cause fetal harm when administered to a pregnant woman or can affect reproductive capacity. PERCOCET should not be given to a pregnant woman unless in the judgment of the physician, the potential benefits outweigh the possible hazards.
*Nonteratogenic Effects:* Use of opioids during pregnancy may produce physical dependence in the neonate.
*Labor and Delivery:* As with all opioids, administration of PERCOCET to the mother shortly before delivery may result in some degree of respiratory depression in the newborn and the mother, especially if higher doses are used.
**Nursing Mothers**
It is not known whether PERCOCET is excreted in human milk. Because many drugs are excreted in human milk, caution should be exercised when PERCOCET is administered to a nursing woman.
**Pediatric Use**
Safety and effectiveness in pediatric patients have not been established.

**ADVERSE REACTIONS**
The most frequently observed adverse reactions include lightheadedness, dizziness, sedation, nausea and vomiting. These effects seem to be more prominent in ambulatory than in nonambulatory patients, and some of these adverse reactions may be alleviated if the patient lies down.
Other adverse reactions include euphoria, dysphoria, constipation, skin rash and pruritus. At higher doses, oxycodone has most of the disadvantages of morphine including respiratory depression.

**DRUG ABUSE AND DEPENDENCE**
PERCOCET (Oxycodone and Acetaminophen Tablets, USP) is a Schedule II controlled substance.
Oxycodone can produce drug dependence and has the potential for being abused (See WARNINGS).

**OVERDOSAGE**
**Acetaminophen**
*Signs and Symptoms:* In acute acetaminophen overdose, dose-dependent, potentially fatal hepatic necrosis is the most serious adverse effect. Renal tubular necrosis, hypoglycemic coma and thrombocytopenia may also occur. In adults, hepatic toxicity has rarely been reported with acute overdoses of less than 10 grams and fatalities with less than 15 grams. Importantly, young children seem to be more resistant than adults to the hepatotoxic effect of an acetaminophen overdose. Despite this, the measures outlined below should be initiated in any adult or child suspected of having ingested an acetaminophen overdose.
Early symptoms following a potentially hepatotoxic overdose may include: nausea, vomiting, diaphoresis and general malaise. Clinical and laboratory evidence of hepatic toxicity may not be apparent until 48 to 72 hours post-ingestion.

*Continued on next page*

*Consult 2007 PDR® supplements and future editions for revisions*

*Pharmacologic/Physiological Actions of oxycodone in Percocet are Analgesia + Sedation*

Appendix

## Courtroom EXHIBIT R-7 / C165
## Dr. Costino's Pain Management Agreement - 6/7/07

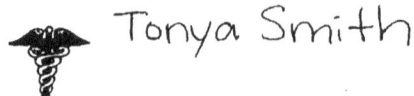

Tonya Smith

C165

John G. Costino, D.O., F.A.O.C.Rh., P.A.
404 Surf Avenue
North Wildwood, New Jersey, 08260-5897

Phone: (609) 522-8358 • Facsimile: (609) 729-8662 • Tax Id. 22-2089139

EXHIBIT R-7

### *Pain Management Agreement*

The purpose of this Agreement is to prevent misunderstandings about certain medicines you will be taking for pain management. This is to help both you and your doctor to comply with the law regarding controlled pharmaceuticals.

I understand that this Agreement is essential to the trust and confidence necessary in a doctor/patient relationship and that my doctor undertakes to treat me based on this Agreement.

I understand that if I break this Agreement, my doctor will stop prescribing these pain control medications.

In this case, my doctor will taper off the medicine over a period of several days, as necessary, to avoid withdrawal symptoms. Also, a drug-dependence treatment program may be recommended.

I will communicate fully with my doctor about the character and intensity of my pain, the affect of the pain on my daily life, and how well the medicine is helping to relieve the pain.

I will not use any illegal controlled substances, including marijuana, cocaine, etc.

I will not share, sell or trade my medication with anyone.

I will not attempt to obtain my controlled medicines, including opioid pain medicines, controlled stimulants, or anti anxiety medicines from any other doctor.

I will safeguard my pain medicine from loss or theft. Lost or stolen medicines will not be replaced.

Sports Medicine and Pain Management • Board Certified Quality Assurance and Utilization Review • Board Certified Forensic Examiner

"Due Process" Denied

## Courtroom EXHIBIT R-7
## Dr. Costino's Pain Management Agreement

**I agree** that refills of my prescriptions for pain medicine will be made only at the time of an office visit or during regular office hours. No refills will be available during evenings or on weekends.

**I agree** to use _Eckerd Pharmacies_ Pharmacy, located at _Atlantic City_, telephone number _____, for filling prescriptions for all my pain medicine.

Authorize the doctor and my pharmacy to cooperate fully with any city, state or federal law enforcement agency, including this state's Board of Pharmacy, in the investigation of any possible misuse, sale or other diversion of my pain medicine. I authorize my doctor to provide a copy of this Agreement to my pharmacy. I agree to waive any applicable privilege right of privacy or confidentiality with respect to these authorizations.

**I agree** that I will submit to a blood or urine test if requested by my doctor to determine my compliance with my program of pain control medicine.

**I agree** that I will use my medicine at a rate and that use of my medicine at a greater rate will result in my being without medication for a period of time.

**I will** bring all unused pain medicine to every office visit.

**I agree** to follow these guidelines that have been fully explained to me. All of my questions and concerns regarding treatment have been adequately answered. A copy of this document has been given to me.

This Agreement is entered into on this __7__ day of __June__, __2007__.

Patient Signature: _[signature]_

Physician Signature: _[signature]_

Witnessed by: _Dana Grumhausen_

Appendix

# Response from the DEA 2/22/2010

**U.S. Department of Justice**

**United States Attorney**
**District of New Jersey**

---

Camden Federal Building and U.S. Courthouse
401 Market Street, 4th Floor
P. O. Box 2098
Camden, New Jersey 08101-2098

PHONE: (856) 968-4926
FAX: (856) 968-4917

February 22, 2010

Jordan Zeitz, Esquire
38 Haddon Avenue
Haddonfield, NJ 08033

    Re:    Investigation of Dr. Costino

Dear Mr. Zeitz:

    It is my understanding that you, on behalf of Dr. Costino, recently served a subpoena on the Drug Enforcement Administration ("DEA") seeking copies of prescriptions that the DEA might have obtained in connection with a pharmacy audit that you advised me had been conducted. I contacted the DEA and was advised of the following. During the Costino investigation, the DEA obtained physician profiles for Dr. Costino from various pharmacies and corporations (like Target and Rite-Aid) that operate pharmacies. At no time was the DEA given, or did it obtain, any prescriptions underlying those profiles. Therefore, the DEA has nothing to give you in response to your subpoena.

    On a related matter, the DEA asked me to ask you whether Dr. Costino will be surrendering his DEA registration.

    Thank you for your attention and consideration.

                                 Very truly yours,

                                 PAUL J. FISHMAN
                               United States Attorney

                By:    HOWARD WIENER
                        Assistant U.S. Attorney

c:    Tom Prevoznik, DEA
      Meg Hoerner, Assistant Prosecutor

Costino1LTR.wpd

"Due Process" Denied

# Anderson's First Certification
## September 19, 2008
# Written by DAG Puteska and COMPLETELY false.

ANNE MILGRAM
ATTORNEY GENERAL OF NEW JERSEY
Division of Law
124 Halsey Street
P.O. Box 45029
Newark, New Jersey 07101

By: David M. Puteska
Deputy Attorney General
Tel. (973) 648-4742

STATE OF NEW JERSEY
DEPARTMENT OF LAW AND PUBLIC SAFETY
DIVISION OF CONSUMER AFFAIRS
STATE BOARD OF MEDICAL EXAMINERS
OAL DOCKET NO. BDSME 00736-2008S

| | |
|---|---|
| IN THE MATTER OF THE SUSPENSION OR REVOCATION OF THE LICENSE OF | Administrative Action |
| JOHN G. COSTINO, JR. D.O. LICENSE NO. 25MB02575800 | CERTIFICATION OF TONYA ANDERSON |
| TO PRACTICE MEDICINE AND SURGERY IN THE STATE OF NEW JERSEY | |

Tonya Anderson, certifies and states:

1. I am currently employed as a police office with the Little Egg Harbor Township Police Department. In 2007 I participated in an undercover investigation with the Cape May County Prosecutor's Office and Drug Enforcement Administration. During the investigation I posed as a patient for multiple visits to the medical office of Dr. John Costino. During these visits I utilized the name Tonya Smith. I have also been identified in the above-captioned matter as undercover number one or UC#1.

2. Pursuant to the order of the New Jersey State Board of Medical Examiners issued on September 10, 2008, I hereby certify that from the time period of April 12, 2006, thru and including

## Anderson's First Certification Page 2
### September 19, 2008

August 23, 2007, I did not have any medical problems related to the cervical spine, thoracic spine or lumbar spine.

    I hereby certify that the foregoing statements made by me are true. I am aware that if any of the foregoing statements made by me are willfully false, I am subject to punishment.

*Tonya Anderson*

Dated: September 19, 2008

"Due Process" Denied

# Anderson's Second Certification
July 20, 2009
Written by Asst. Pros. Megan Hoerner.
ONLY PARTIALLY TRUE 7/09

ROBERT L. TAYLOR, ESQUIRE
CAPE MAY COUNTY PROSECUTOR
DN 110 – CENTRAL MAIL ROOM
CAPE MAY COURT HOUSE, NJ 08210

| | |
|---|---|
| STATE OF NEW JERSEY,<br>Plaintiff. | SUPERIOR COURT OF NEW JERSEY<br>CRIMINAL – LAW DIVISION<br>CAPE MAY COUNTY<br>DOCKET NO. 07001173 |
| vs. | INDICTMENT NO. 08-08-00637-I |
| JOHN COSTINO,<br>Defendant. | CERTIFICATION OF<br>TONYA ANDERSON |

Tonya Anderson, certifies and states:

1) I am currently employed as a police officer with the Little Egg Harbor Police Department. In 2007, I participated in an undercover investigation with the Cape May County Prosecutor's Office and DEA. During the investigation, I posed as a patient for seven visits to the medical office of Dr. John Costino. During these visits I utilized the name Tonya Smith. I have also been identified in the above captioned matter as undercover number two or UC #1.

2) Pursuant to Judge Raymond Batten's Order dated May 5, 2009, I hereby certify that from the time period of August 23, 2005 thru and including August 23, 2007, I went to Seaport Chiropractic Center on one occasion.

3) I also hereby certify that during the aforementioned period in question, I saw Dr. William Glenn for annual physicals.

## Anderson's Second Certification Page 2
## July 20, 2009

I hereby certify that the foregoing statements made by me are true. I am aware that if any of the foregoing statements made by me are willfully false, I am subject to punishment.

Tonya Anderson

Dated: July 20th, 2009

"Due Process" Denied

## Seaport Chiropractic Center - Dr. O'Rourke's Office
## Patient Case History Forms for Tonya Anderson
## Date of visit - 7/26/07 page 1

02:09p                                                                          p.1

### Patient Case History

Name **Tonya Anderson**  Date **7/26/07**
Address ▓▓▓▓▓▓ City **LEH** State **NJ** Zip **08087**
Phone ▓▓▓▓▓▓ Work # ▓▓▓▓▓▓ Cell ▓▓▓▓▓▓
D.O.B ▓▓▓▓▓▓ Age ▓▓ M __ F ✓ Marital Status **m** Children ▓▓
SS# ▓▓▓▓▓▓ Spouses D.O.B. ▓▓▓▓▓▓ SS# ▓▓▓▓▓▓
Employer's Name and Address **LEH Police Dept. 665 Airlin Rd LEH**
Emergency Contact & Relationship ▓▓▓▓▓▓ Phone ▓▓▓▓▓▓
Spouses Employer and Address ▓▓▓ **Police Dept** ▓▓▓▓▓▓
Ins Primary ▓▓▓ ID# ▓▓▓ Secondary ▓▓▓ # ▓▓▓
Major Complaint **upper back, neck (R) shoulder pain**
Other Complaint —
What improves your condition? **?**
What worsens your condition? **sleep position**
Primary Care Physician and phone # **Dr. Glenn**
Have you had any medical care for this condition? ___ If so, what? ___
_____ Results _____
Is/Does your condition (Circle) Deteriorating Constant **Comes and goes**
Interfere with (**Sleep**) your work (**Daily Routine**) Other ___ Have you
had same/similar symptoms in the past? **yes** Explain **during + after**
**pregnancy**

Is there a family history of this condition **no** Have you had previous chiropractic care?
**yes** If so, where ___

How did you hear of us? **drive by**
List previous surgeries and dates: ▓▓▓▓▓▓ **1/99 + 2/07**

Medications currently taking **no**
_____

Do you take birth control pills ▓▓▓ What type ___ Are you HIV positive ▓▓▓
Do you have Breast Implants ▓▓▓
Person responsible for this account **self**

# Seaport Chiropractic Center - Dr. O'Rourke's Office
## 7/26/07 page 2

Jul 17 09 02:23p                                                                 p.1

# SEAPORT CHIROPRACTIC CENTER
### Joseph P. O'Rourke D.C.

Patient Name: Tonja Alderson  Age: ▓  B/P: /  Date: 7/26/07  Visit: /
Patient Complaint: (1) Shoulder (2)

**Objective Findings:** Paravertebral Muscle Spasms / Decreased Range of Motion / Inflammation / Normal Gait / Irregular Gait / Normal Ambulation / Impaired

| K1 | K2 | K3 | K4 |
|---|---|---|---|
| 98940 | 98941 | 98942 | 98943 |

Therapy: Hot UB/LB — Cold UB/LB 97010 — Muscle Stim. UB/LB 97014 — Ultrasound UB/LB 97035

---

Review / Changes Since last Visit: _____  Date: __/__/__  Visit: ____

**Objective Findings:** Paravertebral Muscle Spasms / Decreased Range of Motion / Inflammation / Normal Gait / Irregular Gait / Normal Ambulation / Impaired

---

Review / Changes Since last Visit: _____  Date: __/__/__  Visit: ____

**Objective Findings:** Paravertebral Muscle Spasms / Decreased Range of Motion / Inflammation / Normal Gait / Irregular Gait / Normal Ambulation / Impaired

"Due Process" Denied

## Seaport Chiropractic Center - Dr. O'Rourke's Office
## 7/26/07 page 3

Jul 17 09 02:09p                                                         p.2

Please check the appropriate space for any of the following symptoms, which you now have or have had previously. We need all the facts about your health before we can accept your case.

| | |
|---|---|
| __Arthritis | __Gallbladder Trouble |
| __Bursitis | __Hemorrhoids |
| __Foot Trouble | __Pain over Stomach |
| __Hernia | __Excessive Menstrual Flow |
| ✓ Low Back Pain | __Sore Throat |
| ✓ Neck Pain/ Stiffness | __Asthma |
| ✓ Pain between shoulders | __High Blood Pressure |
| __Headaches | __Low Blood Pressure |
| __Loss of Sleep | __Kidney/Infection/Stone |
| ✓ Sciatica | __Painful Menstruation |
| __Spinal Curvature | __Vaginal Discharge |
| __Swollen Joints | __Cramps/Backache |
| __Allergy | __Sinus Infection |
| __Fatigue | __Hot Flashes |
| __Dizziness | __Irregular Cycle |
| __Loss of Weight | __Painful Urination |
| __Nervousness/ Depression | __Prostate Trouble |
| __Constipation | __Diarrhea |

Pain or Numbness in:

| | | | |
|---|---|---|---|
| ✓ Shoulders | __Arms | __Hands | __Hips |
| __Legs | __Knees | __Feet | |

Check the following conditions you have had:

| | | | |
|---|---|---|---|
| __Alcoholism | __Diphtheria | __Influenza | __Pneumonia |
| __Anemia | __Eczema | __Lumbago | __Polio |
| __Appendicitis | __Emphysema | __Lymes Disease | __Rheumatic Fever |
| __Arteriosclerosis | __Epilepsy | __Malaria | __Scarlet Fever |
| __Arthritis | __Fever Blisters | __Measles | __Stroke |
| __Cancer | __Goiter | __Miscarriage | __Tuberculosis |
| __Chorea | __Gout | __Multiple Sclerosis | __Typhoid Fever |
| __Cold Sores | __Heart Disease | __Mumps | __Ulcers |
| __Diabetes | __Hepatitis | __Pleurisy | __Venereal Disease |
| __Other (Explain)_____ | | | |

Date of Last: X-rays_____ Blood Test_____ Urinalysis_____ Spinal Tap_____

**NOTICE TO OUR NEW PATIENTS**
CHIROPRACTIC SERVICES PROVIDED IN OUR OFFICE ARE PAYABLE ON THE DAY SERVICES ARE RENDERED UNLESS OTHER ARRANGEMENTS ARE MADE WITH THE DOCTOR.

**INSURANCE CASES**
1. Assignments of Insurance benefits will be accepted upon proper verification of coverage and at the discretion of this office.
2. Patients are personally responsible for all charges.
3. We will prepare necessary reports to help collect your benefits if an assignment is not taken.
4. By signing below you give us the authority to bill your insurance company directly.

Patient's Signature _____ Insured's Signature _____

# Seaport Chiropractic Center - Dr. O'Rourke's Office
## 7/26/07 page 4

Jul 17 09 02:11p

NAME: Tonja Anderson  DATE: 7/24/2007

(B)  K1  K2  (K3)  K4  (M)  (N)  (Q)  R  Other: _____

- Headache 784.0
- Subluxation Head Region 739.0
- Subluxation Cervical Region (739.1)
- Displacement IVD Cervical 722.0
- Cervical Sprain/Strain 847.0
- Cervicalgia (723.1)
- Cervical Brachial Syndrome 723.3
- Reversed Cervical Lordosis 737.0
- Torticollis 723.5
- Thoracic Neuritis 724.4
- Subluxation Thoracic Region (739.2)

- Thoracic Spine Pain (724.1)
- Thoracic Sprain/Strain 847.1
- Thoracic Outlet Syndrome 723.3
- Displacement IVD Thoracic 722.11
- Subluxation Lumbar Region 739.3
- Lumbago 724.2
- Lumbar Muscle Spasm 728.85
- Lumbar Sprain/Strain 847.2
- Facet Syndrome 724.8
- Lumbosacral Neuritis 724.4
- Sciatic Neuralgia 724.3

- Displacement IVD Lumbar 722.10
- Degenerative IVD Syn 722.52
- Bursitis of Hip 726.5
- Supraspinatus Tend 840.6
- Bursitis of Shoulder 726.10
- Shoulder Sprain/Strain 840.9
- Medial Epicondylitis 726.31
- Lateral Epicondylitis 726.32
- Myositis (unspecified) 729.1
- Spondylolisthesis 738.4
- Other: _____

History of Illness _____

George's _____  Adson's _____  DeKleyn's _____

DATE DX          TREATMENT PLAN

"Due Process" Denied

## 1st Victim Notification Form Addressed to Dr. John Costino - 5/14/07

OFFICE OF THE PROSECUTOR
COUNTY OF CAPE MAY
DN-110 CENTRAL MAIL ROOM
11 JUSTICE WAY
CAPE MAY COURTHOUSE NJ 08210-0000
FAX: 609-465-1347
609-465-1135

JOHN COSTINO, MD
404 SURF AVENUE
NORTH WILDWOOD NJ 082600000

OFFICE OF VICTIM-WITNESS ADVOCACY
MAY 14, 2007
PROSECUTOR FILE #: 07-000452

STATE VS. AMENHAUSER

DEAR JOHN COSTINO, MD

THE OFFICE OF VICTIM-WITNESS ADVOCACY HAS BEEN NOTIFIED THAT YOU HAVE BEEN A VICTIM OF A CRIME. OUR UNIT PROVIDES SERVICES AND OFFERS ASSISTANCE TO VICTIMS AND WITNESSES.

WE WILL PROVIDE YOU WITH INFORMATION ABOUT THE STATUS OF YOUR CASE AND ARE AVAILABLE TO ANSWER ANY QUESTIONS YOU MAY HAVE ABOUT THE CRIMINAL JUSTICE PROCESS. WE WILL HELP YOU FILE A CLAIM WITH THE VIOLENT CRIMES COMPENSATION BOARD FOR REIMBURSEMENT OF MEDICAL EXPENSES AND LOSS OF WAGES, IF ANY. IF ANY OF YOUR PROPERTY WAS TAKEN, WE CAN ASSIST YOU IN SECURING ITS RETURN OR OBTAINING RESTITUTION. IF YOU FEEL YOU ARE IN NEED OF COUNSELING DUE TO THE INCIDENT, WE CAN REFER YOU TO THE APPROPRIATE AGENCIES.

AS A VICTIM, YOU HAVE THE RIGHT TO SUBMIT A WRITTEN STATEMENT TO THE PROSECUTOR EXPLAINING THE IMPACT THIS CRIME HAS HAD ON YOUR LIFE OR THE LIVES OF YOUR FAMILY MEMBERS. IF YOU WISH TO SUBMIT A STATEMENT, KINDLY COMPLETE AND RETURN THE ENCLOSED FORM IN ACCORDANCE WITH THE INSTRUCTIONS ON IT. IF YOU NEED ASSISTANCE IN PREPARING THE FORM, PLEASE CALL OUR OFFICE.

IF YOU CHANGE YOUR ADDRESS OR TELEPHONE NUMBER, PLEASE NOTIFY US IMMEDIATELY. IF WE CAN BE OF ASSISTANCE TO YOU OR IF YOU HAVE ANY QUESTIONS, DO NOT HESITATE TO CONTACT US AT 609-465-1163.

VERY TRULY YOURS,

ROBERT L TAYLOR
COUNTY PROSECUTOR

*Claire McArdle*
CLAIRE MCARDLE
VICTIM-WITNESS COORDINATOR

Appendix

## 2nd Victim Notification Form Addressed to Dr. John Costino - 6/20/09

OFFICE OF THE PROSECUTOR
COUNTY OF CAPE MAY
DN-110 CENTRAL MAIL ROOM
11 JUSTICE WAY
CAPE MAY COURTHOUSE NJ 08210-0000
FAX: 609-465-1347
609-465-1135

JOHN COSTINO, MD  OFFICE OF VICTIM-WITNESS ADVOCACY
404 SURF AVENUE  JUNE 20, 2009
NORTH WILDWOOD NJ 082600000  PROSECUTOR FILE #: 07-000445
  INDICTMENT #: 09-06-00431-I

STATE VS. AMENHAUSER, CONYERS
RE: DANNA M AMENHAUSER → got Probation only.

DEAR JOHN COSTINO, MD

PLEASE BE ADVISED THAT ON JULY 09, 2009 AT 09:00 AM. THE ABOVE NAMED DEFENDANT IS TENTATIVELY SCHEDULED TO APPEAR BEFORE THE HONORABLE JUDGE RAYMOND A. BATTEN FOR A STATUS CONFERENCE. ALTHOUGH YOU ARE NOT REQUIRED TO APPEAR, IT IS YOUR RIGHT BY LAW TO HAVE INPUT AND TO BE INFORMED OF PRE-TRIAL MATTERS. SINCE COURT PROCEEDINGS ARE OFTEN POSTPONED OR RESCHEDULED, PLEASE CALL THE NUMBER BELOW TO VERIFY DATE AND TIME.

AS A RESULT OF A STATUS CONFERENCE, THE PROSECUTOR'S OFFICE MAY ENTER INTO A NEGOTIATED PLEA AGREEMENT. IF YOU WISH TO OBTAIN AN EXPLANATION OF THE TERMS OF ANY SUCH AGREEMENT, THE REASONS FOR THE AGREEMENT, OR IF YOU HAVE ANY OTHER QUESTIONS, PLEASE CALL THE OFFICE OF VICTIM-WITNESS ADVOCACY AT 609-465-1163.

VERY TRULY YOURS,

ROBERT L TAYLOR
COUNTY PROSECUTOR

*Claire McArdle*

CLAIRE MCARDLE
VICTIM-WITNESS COORDINATOR

6B

"Due Process" Denied

## Parole Hearing Notification Form - 9/4/09
## Notifying Victim of the Release of Ryan Conyers

**OFFICE OF THE PROSECUTOR**
**COUNTY OF CAPE MAY**

J. DAVID MEYER
*First Assistant Prosecutor*

JAMES E. RYBICKI
*Chief of County Detectives*

ROBERT L. TAYLOR
*COUNTY PROSECUTOR*

4 Moore Road, DN-110
CAPE MAY COURT HOUSE
NEW JERSEY 08210-1654

Phone: (609) 465-1135
Fax: (609) 465-1347

September 4, 2009

Dr. John Costino
404 Surf Avenue
North Wildwood, NJ 08260

RE:    Pros. File #: 07000445
          Indictment #: 07-07-00446A
          State vs. Conyers, Ryan

Dear Dr. John Costino:

Please be advised that the above named defendant will be considered for parole during the month of October 2009.

Prior to his/her release, a Parole hearing will be conducted to determine the possible parole release of the above named inmate. Any comments relevant for consideration by the Parole Board should be submitted by September 24, 2009 to:

          New Jersey State Parole Board
          Victim Services Unit
          CN-862
          Trenton, NJ 08210

Should you have any questions concerning this matter or questions regarding the status of this case, please do not hesitate to contact the office of Victim-Witness Advocacy at (609)- 465-1163.

Sincerely,

Kelly M. Johnson
Victim-Witness Advocate

# Letter to the NJ Board of Medical Examiners with regard to the Reinstatement of Dr Costino's Medical License

Jacqueline Johnson
New Jersey Board of Medical Examiners
Division of Consumer Affairs
P.O. Box 183
Trenton, New Jersey 08608


Dear Jacqueline:

Regarding the reinstatement of my medical license, after speaking to you and Dr. Lesig I like to give you the following information:

1) The Drexel Medicine Physician Re-entry Course is no longer available as a result of the current bankruptcy of Hahnemann University

2) The Center for Personalized Education for Physicians (CPEP) in Denver, Colorado is a 3 day program the cost of which is $10,000 plus expenses For a total cost of between $12,000 and $13,000.

3) The Comprehensive Health Professional Assessment Program at University of California at San Diego Medical Center in San Diego, California is a 3 day program the cost of which is between $10,000 and $12,000 plus expenses, which brings the total cost to approximately $14,000.

4) The "Lifeguard" Program is a 3 day program in Harrisburg, Pennsylvania the cost of which, stated clearly in their documents, is between $10,000 and $16,000 plus expenses

Enclosed please find copies of my IRS returns for the past 4 years as requested.

I have been unemployed for the past 12 years. My wife and I have been existing on borrowed money and certain assets which have now been exhausted. As I have explained to you in the recent past, I am essentially broke and need to return to gainful employment as a physician.

I have spent a great deal of time researching the various physician evaluation sites given to me by your office. The fees and expenses of the various 4 programs outlined above representing a 2 or 3 day evaluation are both exorbitant and unconscionable. I am unable to sustain these cost

"Due Process" Denied

# Letter to the NJ Board of Medical Examiners with regard to the Reinstatement of Dr Costino's Medical License

structures for the 4 various programs. Furthermore it is difficult to understand why the state of New Jersey does not provide reasonable access for medical assessment for physician re-entry for qualified physicians to return to medical practice.

I have exhausted all venues, and financial assets at this point in time in an effort to comply to the demands of the Board of Medical Examiners (BME).

I respectfully request either a reasonable solution for my re-instatement or an eye to eye meeting with representatives of the BME to solve this problem as soon as possible. I need to return to gainful employment!!!

Very truly yours,

John G. Costino, D.O.

cc: Dr. Lesig, Medical Director BME
William Roeder, Executive Director BME

Appendix

# Civil Lawsuit : 9-17-2012
# Dr. Costino vs Edwin Jacobs

| | |
|---|---|
| STANLEY B. CHEIKEN, ESQUIRE<br>Identification No. 62106<br>101 Greenwood Avenue, Suite 400<br>Jenkintown, PA 19046<br>(215) 572-8600 | ASSESSMENT OF DAMAGES HEARING:<br>____ IS ____ NOT REQUIRED<br>____ JURY OF 12 PERSONS<br>____ NON-JURY ____ ARBITRATION |
| JOHN G. COSTINO, Jr., D.O.<br>404 Surf Avenue<br>North Wildwood, NJ 08260, | : IN THE COURT OF COMMON PLEAS<br>: OF PHILADELPHIA COUNTY<br>: |
| Plaintiff, | : **CIVIL ACTION** |
| -vs.- | : |
| EDWIN J. JACOBS, Jr., ESQUIRE<br>1125 Pacific Avenue<br>Atlantic City, NJ 08401 | : JUNE TERM, 2014<br>: No. 01124<br>: |
| Defendant. | : |

### COMPLAINT - CIVIL ACTION

Plaintiff, John G. Costino, Jr., D.O., by and through undersigned counsel, hereby brings this Complaint against defendant Edwin J. Jacobs, Jr., Esquire, and avers as follows:

1. Plaintiff John G. Costino, Jr., D.O. (hereinafter "Dr. Costino") is an adult individual and a citizen of the State of New Jersey, residing therein at the address set forth in the caption.

2. Defendant Edwin J. Jacobs, Jr., Esquire (hereinafter "Jacobs") is an adult individual and a citizen of the State of New Jersey with an office for the transaction of business located at the address set forth in the caption. At all relevant times, Jacobs has regularly transacted business as an attorney at law admitted pro hac vice in the United States District Court

"Due Process" Denied

## Civil Lawsuit -
## Dr. Costino vs Edwin Jacobs

for the Eastern District of Pennsylvania located in the City and County of Philadelphia.

3. Dr. Costino first became licensed to practice osteopathic medicine in the State of New Jersey in May 1972.

4. For more than 35 years, Dr. Costino maintained a local practice specializing in pain management and geriatric medicine.

5. In September 2007, criminal charges were filed against Dr. Costino for improper distribution of controlled substances and health insurance fraud.

6. Dr. Costino retained defendant Jacobs as his attorney to defend the criminal charges.

7. Although defendant Jacobs had never previously represented Dr. Costino, defendant Jacobs failed to communicate in writing to Dr. Costino the scope and terms of his legal representation of Dr. Costino.

8. In November 2007, the Attorney General's Office notified defendant Jacobs that it intended to seek a suspension of Dr. Costino's license to practice medicine by the State Board of Medical Examiners unless Dr. Costino agreed to temporary suspension.

9. At that time, defendant Jacobs represented to Dr. Costino that he was well versed and experienced in the representation of physicians in matters before the State Board of Medical Examiners.

10. In reliance upon defendant Jacobs' representations, Dr. Costino engaged defendant Jacobs as his attorney to represent him before the State Board of Medical Examiners.

11. Defendant Jacobs failed to communicate in writing to Dr. Costino the scope and

# Appendix

## Civil Lawsuit -
## Dr. Costino vs Edwin Jacobs

terms of his representation of Dr. Costino in the State Board of Medical Examiners.

12. Defendant Jacobs served as Dr. Costino's legal counsel at the hearing before the State Board of Medical Examiners in December 2007.

13. On December 20, 2007, the State Board of Medical Examiners entered an order temporarily suspending Dr. Costino's license to practice medicine.

14. Defendant Jacobs failed to advise Dr. Costino of his right to seek leave to appeal the suspension order to the New Jersey Superior Court, Appellate Division.

15. Defendant Jacobs failed to preserve Dr. Costino's appellate rights by seeking leave to file an appeal with the New Jersey Superior Court, Appellate Division.

16. In late June 2008, Dr. Costino hired Glenn A. Zeitz, Esquire to represent him.

17. Ultimately, Dr. Costino was acquitted of all criminal charges.

### COUNT I
### PROFESSIONAL NEGLIGENCE

18. All previous paragraphs are incorporated as though fully set forth herein.

19. As set forth above, there existed an attorney-client relationship between defendant Jacobs and Dr. Costino.

20. As a result of the attorney-client relationship, defendant Jacobs had a duty to represent Dr. Costino with the reasonable care, skill, and diligence possessed and exercised by an ordinary attorney in similar circumstances.

21. Defendant Jacobs failed to exercise reasonable care, skill and diligence by failing to advise Dr. Costino of his legal right to seek to appeal the suspension order and/or by filing the

## Civil Lawsuit -
## Dr. Costino vs Edwin Jacobs

paperwork necessary to timely appeal the suspension order.

22. As a result of said defendant Jacobs' professional negligence, Dr. Costino's appellate rights were lost and he was unable to appeal from the temporary suspension of his license to practice medicine.

23. By virtue of defendant Jacobs' professional negligence, Dr. Costino has suffered substantial financial harm including, *inter alia*, that he was unable to practice medicine during the period of his temporary suspension.

WHEREFORE, plaintiff John G. Costino, Jr., D.O. demands judgment in his favor and against defendant Edwin J. Jacobs, Jr., Esquire in an amount in excess of $50,000, together with costs of suit.

Date: September 17, 2014

STANLEY B. CHEIKEN, ESQUIRE

Jenkintown Plaza – Suite 400
101 Greenwood Avenue
Jenkintown, PA 19046
(215) 572-8600

*Attorney for Plaintiff*

Appendix

## Civil Lawsuit
## Dr. Costino vs Alan Lands

HERCULES PAPPAS, ESQUIRE
Attorney for Defendant
hpappas@legalhelm.com
Helm Legal Services LLC
333 East Lancaster Avenue STE 140
Wynnewood, PA 19096
215.568.4316

| | |
|---|---|
| JOHN G. COSTINO, <br> PLAINTIFF, <br><br> V. <br><br> ALAN M. LANDS, <br> DEFENDANT | SUPERIOR COURT OF NEW JERSEY <br> LAW DIVISION <br> CAMDEN COUNTY <br> DOCKET NO.: CAM-L- 3673-13 <br><br> CIVIL ACTION <br><br> COMPLAINT AND JURY DEMAND |

Plaintiff, John G. Costino, resides in North Wildwood, New Jersey, County of Cape May, State of New Jersey, by way of Complaint against the Defendant, Alan M. Lands, hereby alleges and states:

### FACTS COMMON TO ALL COUNTS

1. Plaintiff, Dr. John G. Costino, was at all times relevant hereto a longtime resident of North Wildwood, New Jersey, County of Cape May, State of New Jersey.

2. Dr. Costino is a doctor who was licensed to practice medicine for over 35 years prior events in 2007 resulting in the suspension of his medical license.

3. Defendant, Alan M. Lands, is an individual, residing at 1021 South Main Street, Pleasantville, Atlantic County, State of New Jersey.

## Civil Lawsuit
## Dr. Costino vs Alan Lands

4. On June 1, 2005, the Defendant sent to the State Board of Medical Examiners a complaint against Plaintiff. Complaint contained false accusations, alleging that Plaintiff billed Rita Sheridan for medical treatment which was never rendered. Mr. Lands indicated the Plaintiff committed insurance billing fraud.

5. In June 2005 and January 2006, Mr. Lands filed another complaint with the NJ Office of Insurance Fraud Prevention alleging fraudulent billing practices.

6. The Office of Insurance Fraud Prevention investigates billing submitted to insurance companies for reimbursement. No insurance companies were involved in this investigation.

7. As a result of the mentioned false accusations Defendant was investigated by the New Jersey Department of Law and Public Safety, Division of Criminal Justice, and by civil investigators.

8. In the report dated January 16, 2006, criminal investigator wrote he interviewed Alan Lands and Rita Sheridan about the matter. Mr. Lands, falsely and with malice intent, reiterated that Dr. Costino fraudulently billed for services he did not render. Mrs. Sheridan told investigators she had Mr. Lands handle this matter directly and did not have any information about the ongoing complaints with Office of Insurance Fraud Prevention.

9. As of January 17, 2006, finding no insurance billing irregularity, the Office of Insurance Fraud Prevention closed its investigation in the matter.

10. On May 21, 2007, Alan Lands arranged a meeting with Cape May County Assistant Prosecutor Meg Hoerner; US Drug Enforcement Agency Investigator Tom Prevoznik,

Appendix

## Civil Lawsuit
## Dr. Costino vs Alan Lands

16. Alan Lands knew in June 2007 that the insurance fraud claims were investigated and unsupported in fact or law. Moreover, he knew these facts had no rational relationship to the Cape May County Prosecutor's Office, US Drug Enforcement Agency, US Postal Inspector or National Insurance Crime Bureau. Nor ultimately, to Detective Hallet's investigation of distribution of controlled substances.

17. Criminal proceedings against Plaintiff continued from 2007 through 2012. At a trial held in said court in November 2012, the jury found the Plaintiff not guilty on all charges, and the case was therefore finally determined in Plaintiff's favor.

### COUNT ONE
### FALSE COMPLAINTS OF UNPROFESSIONAL CONDUCT
### (MALICIOUS PROSECUTION)

18. Plaintiff repeats and incorporates all averments made in the previous paragraphs as if the same were set forth at length herein.

19. Plaintiff's license to practice medicine was revoked in December 2007 by the State Board of Medical Examiners and the revocation was a result of Defendant's complaint and his acts of instigating criminal proceedings against Plaintiff.

20. Defendant did not and could not have personal knowledge about any falsely claimed incidents. Defendants acted without probable cause in making false statements against Plaintiff, because the Defendant did not honestly and reasonably believe that there were grounds for the action due to the absence of facts or any evidence establishing any wrongdoing on the part of Plaintiff.

## Civil Lawsuit
## Dr. Costino vs Alan Lands

21. Defendant knew that the accusations were false but continued to make them throughout the course of criminal and disciplinary proceedings against Plaintiff.

22. Accusatory statements were made by the Defendant with reckless disregard to the truth. The accusations were made absent probable cause, in in bad faith, maliciously and with clear intent to harm the Plaintiff.

23. The mentioned acts by the Defendant constitute malicious prosecution under New Jersey law.

24. Malicious prosecution acts by the Defendant stem from the acrimonious dispute between Plaintiff and Defendant regarding a medical bill in a civil slip-and-fall case. Mentioned case was settled by the Defendant, where Plaintiff performed treatment of the Rita Sheridan, a party to the case represented by the Defendant. In that case Plaintiff obtained a written assurance that the medical bill will be paid, then the Defendant refused to pay the bill amount upon settlement of the case, and both parties could not reach an agreement to settle the bill. The case was slip-and-fall case on November 27, 2001, where Plaintiff treated mentioned patient in 2001-2002.

25. Malicious prosecution by the Defendant was based on nothing more than the personal desire to get even and harm Plaintiff by improper means.

26. As a result of malicious prosecution by the Defendant, Plaintiff suffered great interference with his liberty and property. As a direct and proximate result of Defendant's willful and knowing presentation of false facts and consequent criminal and disciplinary

# Appendix

## Civil Lawsuit
## Dr. Costino vs Alan Lands

proceedings against Plaintiff, Plaintiff lost his career, livelihood, reputation and ability to practice medicine for a prolonged period of time.

27. Plaintiff lost significant number of his patients to other medical providers.

28. Plaintiff was injured, suffered in his business and reputation, and was otherwise damaged.

29. As a direct and proximate result of the malicious prosecution of the Defendant, Alan Lands, Plaintiff, John Costino, was caused to retain defense counsel and further endure mental pain and anguish as well as humiliation, incapacitating him from pursuing his usual activities. Defendant's acts have severely damaged Plaintiff monetarily.

30. As a result of malicious prosecution by the Defendant, Plaintiff suffered loss of his medical practice, livelihood and incurred expenses in legal and other fees in the amount of at least $10 million dollars, defending his liberty, property, reputation and ability to practice medicine.

31. Making false accusations constituted malicious prosecution on the part of the Defendant against Plaintiff, and his conduct, being willful, wanton and malicious, warrants punitive damages.

32. Plaintiff requests special damages as may be shown and for general compensatory damages in tort as may be fixed by the jury, punitive damages as may be assessed by the jury, and for costs, disbursements and reasonable attorney fees incurred as a result of defending this action.

## Civil Lawsuit
## Dr. Costino vs Alan Lands

WHEREFORE, Plaintiff, Dr. John G Costino, hereby demands judgment against the Defendant, Alan M. Lands, for all compensatory damages, interest, punitive damages, attorney's fees and costs of suit, and such other and further relief recoverable by law, as the court may deem proper.

### COUNT TWO
### TORTIOUS INTERFERENCE WITH PROSPECTIVE ECONOMIC ADVANTAGE

33. Plaintiff repeats and incorporates all averments made in the previous count as if the same were set forth at length herein.

34. False statements and deliberate and calculated acts made by the Defendant predictably resulted in interference with the prospective economic advantage of Plaintiff. By instigating criminal prosecution and disciplinary proceedings, Defendant achieved desired consequences, including the complete loss of ability by Plaintiff to practice medicine for a prolonged time and loss of Plaintiff's patients.

35. Plaintiff had had an established, known, successful and respectable private medical practice. Plaintiff had reasonable expectation of continuing this successful medical business, and he had protectable property rights to revenues and profits.

36. Defendant intentionally, knowingly and maliciously instigated criminal prosecution of the Plaintiff without any reasonable factual justification for his acts and statements. Defendant's statements and acts had no other basis than Defendant's desire to cause damages to Plaintiff's medical practice in order to achieve personal revenge and emotional satisfaction from seeing Plaintiff and his family suffer economically and psychologically.

# Civil Lawsuit
## Dr. Costino vs Alan Lands

37. Defendant's false statements and acts were instrumental in the development of a criminal prosecution against Plaintiff and in resulting revocation of his license by the Board of Medicine. If the Defendant would not instigate and encourage criminal prosecution by knowingly making false statements, Plaintiff would be able to keep receiving economic benefit from practicing medicine.

38. Defendant's actions resulted in that not only Plaintiff's current patients left, but also in that Plaintiff could not acquire new patients because prospective patients could not be served by Plaintiff's in the absence of license to practice medicine.

39. Defendant's actions also resulted in that Plaintiff's business reputation is damaged so that many prospective patients will never use Plaintiff's services.

40. Loss of ability to practice medicine resulted in Plaintiff loosing stream of revenues and profits from his previously very successful, known and respectable medical practice.

41. As a direct and proximate result of the intentional interference with economic prospects of the Defendant, Alan Lands, Plaintiff, John Costino, was caused to retain defense counsel and further endure mental pain and anguish as well as humiliation, incapacitating him from pursuing his usual activities and has severely damaged him monetarily.

42. Defendant by his acts and false statements brought permanent economic damage to Plaintiff's ability to practice medicine after Plaintiff's license had been suspended and in the years to come.

"Due Process" Denied

## Summons for Alan Lands
### September 6, 2013

HERCULES PAPPAS, ESQUIRE
Attorney for Defendant
hpappas@legalhelm.com
Helm Legal Services LLC
333 East Lancaster Avenue STE 140
Wynnewood, PA 19096
215.568.4316

Attorney for Plaintiff

JOHN G. COSTINO,
    Plaintiff,

v.

ALAN M. LANDS,
    Defendant

SUPERIOR COURT OF NEW JERSEY
LAW DIVISION
CAMDEN COUNTY
DOCKET NO.: CAM-L- 3673-13

CIVIL ACTION

Summons

From The State of New Jersey To The Defendant(s) Named Above:

    The plaintiff, named above, has filed a lawsuit against you in the Superior Court of New Jersey. The complaint attached to this summons states the basis for this lawsuit. If you dispute this complaint, you or your attorney must file a written answer or motion and proof of service with the deputy clerk of the Superior Court in the county listed above within 35 days from the date you received this summons, not counting the date you received it. (The address of each deputy clerk of the Superior Court is provided.) If the complaint is one in foreclosure, then you must file your written answer or motion and proof of service with the Clerk of the Superior Court, Hughes Justice Complex, P.O. Box 971, Trenton, NJ 08625-0971. A filing fee payable to the Treasurer, State of New Jersey and a completed Case Information Statement (available from the deputy clerk of the Superior Court) must accompany your answer or motion when it is filed. You must also send a copy of your answer or motion to plaintiff's attorney whose name and address appear above, or to plaintiff, if no attorney is named above. A telephone call will not protect your rights; you must file and serve a written answer or motion (with fee of $135.00 and completed Case Information Statement) if you want the court to hear your defense.

    If you do not file and serve a written answer or motion within 35 days, the court may enter a judgment against you for the relief plaintiff demands, plus interest and costs of suit. If judgment is entered against you, the Sheriff may seize your money, wages or property to pay all or part of the judgment.

    If you cannot afford an attorney, you may call the Legal Services office in the county where you live or the Legal Services of New Jersey Statewide Hotline at 1-888-LSNJ-LAW (1-888-576-5529). A list of these offices is provided. If you do not have an attorney and are not eligible for free legal assistance, you may obtain a referral to an attorney by calling one of the Lawyer Referral Services. A list of these numbers is also provided.

/s/ Jennifer M. Perez
Jennifer M. Perez
Clerk of the Superior Court

DATED: September 6, 2013

Name of Defendant: Alan M. Lands
Address for Service:

Appendix

# 1983 Civil Rights Lawsuit in Superior Court, Cape May County

Hercules Pappas, Esquire
18 King's Highway West
Haddonfield, NJ 08033
Tel: (856) 222-9991
Fax: (856) 222-9994
hpappas@legalhelm.com

Attorney for Plaintiffs

| | |
|---|---|
| JOHN J. COSTINO AND BARBARA HAAS A/K/A BARBARA COSTINO<br><br>Plaintiff,<br><br>V.<br><br>CAPE MAY COUNTY PROSECUTOR, ROBERT TAYLOR, individually and in his official capacity, CAPE MAY COUNTY ASSISTANT PROSECUTOR MATTHEW WEINTRAUB, individually and in his official capacity, CAPE MAY COUNTY ASSISTANT PROSECUTOR TINA KELL, individually and in her official capacity, CAPE MAY COUNTY DETECTIVE TRICIA LYNN KALITA, individually and in her official capacity, CAPE MAY COUNTY DETECTIVE PAUL WORRELL, individually and in his official capacity, CAPE MAY COUNTY, municipality, CAPE MAY COUNTY, DEFENDANT JOHN DOES 1-100,<br><br>DEFENDANTS. | SUPERIOR COURT OF NEW JERSEY CAPE MAY COUNTY LAW DIVISION<br><br>DOCKET NO.:<br><br>CIVIL ACTION<br><br>**Complaint and Jury Demand** |

Plaintiffs by way of Complaint against defendants say as follows:

## FACTS COMMON TO ALL COUNTS

1. Dr. John G. Costino and Barabara Haas, Plaintiffs, were at all times relevant hereto, longtime residents and taxpayers in the North Wildwood, Cape May County New Jersey. Plaintiff Dr. John Costino was a doctor for over 30 years, treating patients at his general

## 1983 Civil Rights Lawsuit in Superior Court, Cape May County

practice in North Wildwood and providing other medical and rehabilitation services to the general public. Plaintiff Barbara Haas is a New Jersey Registered Nurse providing medical services to the long time patients of Dr. Costino. Plaintiffs are and were concerned and active members of their communities and Plaintiff Haas had never experienced a negative encounter with law enforcement nor committed any crimes or offenses for which they could be subjected to arrest or prosecution.

2. In September 2007, Plaintiff Dr. John G. Costino was arrested and charged with indictable offenses under the Criminal Code of the State of New Jersey, stemming from his ownership, operation and practice of his medical business located in North Wildwood NJ. Following a lengthy criminal trial process lasting over 5 years, a jury expeditiously found Dr. Costino not guilty of all charges in November 2012.

3. In the midst of an ongoing criminal prosecution of Dr. Costino, in 2009, Plaintiff Barbara Haas a/k/a Barbara Costino (Haas), together with Dr. Costino, were charged with health care fraud and conspiracy stemming from there employment, association, and/or affiliation with the practice of Dr. John G. Costino D.O. P.A.

4. Upon information and belief, defendants Cape May County Prosecutor Robert Taylor, Cape May County, All Defendant Prosecutors, Cape May County Detective Tricia Lynn Kalita and other defendants then conspired and collaborated to maliciously prosecute plaintiffs and violate their civil rights by initiating, directing and participating in and in the filing of a contrived investigation which revealed no wrong doing by either plaintiff, but which had as a purpose to pretextually justify two successive legally and factually defective prosecutions, which defendants knew wholly lacked probable cause because of all of plaintiffs' actions were legal, open and authorized, all of which action have severely and devastatingly damaged the plaintiffs, who have valuable business relationships and ties to the community at large with whom with defendants shared and operated their business for the sole purpose of maintaining the sustenance, support, and assistance for themselves, their family, their agents and their employees alike.

5. The Plaintiffs were compelled to appear at a time which was inconvenient and processed and fingerprinted like criminals. The Plaintiffs were detained and held against their will for an unreasonable period of time while they were processed and fingerprinted.

6. Plaintiffs were forced and required to answer to and defend against the charges that were falsely obtained by the Defendants.

7. The criminal prosecution was initiated by the signing of a complaint in the Superior of New Jersey by the defendants.

# Appendix

## 1983 Civil Rights Lawsuit in Superior Court, Cape May County

8. Any probable cause affidavit submitted to the Superior Court of New Jersey was false, established no probable cause to charge Plaintiffs
9. Said Defendant, and other defendants, acted with malice and their purpose was not to bring the Plaintiffs to justice but to enhance their own careers or for some other personal or other purpose unrelated to the administration of justice.
10. The prosecution against the plaintiffs ended in not one but two dismissals of the indictments and, as a result of the actions of the Defendants, plaintiffs were deprived of their liberty.
11. Defendants herein maliciously and falsely prosecuted the Plaintiffs presented false, inaccurate and erroneous information to the Court(s), and otherwise caused an indictment to be issued and pursued a prosecution of charges based upon facts and evidence they knew to be false and in reckless disregard for any investigation into the truthful facts.
12. Defendants deliberately failed to inform the acting Judge(s) and grand jurors of the falsity of that information and of any relevant exculpatory evidence in favor of the Plaintiffs.
13. Defendants signed a complaint against the Plaintiffs charging them with indictable offenses under the Criminal Code of the State of New Jersey. The complaint herein was made with malice.
14. On December 17, 2009, the Honorable Raymond A. Batten, J.S.C. dismissed the indictment.
15. On August 25, 2010, Defendants caused new charges to be initiated against the Plaintiffs based upon further false and erroneous information and facts.
16. On March 22, 2011, the Honorable Raymond A. Batten, J.S.C. in dismissing this second indictment concluded:

    "How in America can an indictment returned substantially predicated upon facts not accurate be permitted to stand" and "this indictment was an indictment based upon that factual inaccuracy and no one in this Court's view, at least, should be required to stand trial based upon inaccurate tracks (sic), however developed before the Grand Jury... .But this, to this Court is not, not a close call. And that's my decision."

17. Plaintiffs had to retain and compensate legal counsel to defend themselves against the charges falsely made and/or caused to be made by the Defendants.
18. Plaintiffs have lost their careers, their livelihood and their chance to secure any gainful employment in the future as a result of the Defendants willful and knowingly false acts as outlined above and further in this Complaint, as alleged.

## 1983 Civil Rights Lawsuit in Superior Court, Cape May County

### COUNT ONE
### MALICIOUS PROSECUTION

19. Plaintiffs incorporate every paragraph of this complaint into every other paragraph of this complaint as if fully set forth therein.

20. On July 28, 2009, defendants unlawfully obtained an Indictment against plaintiffs, No. 09-07-00584 which charged them with Health Care Fraud and Conspiracy. The Court dismissed this indictment on 12/17/2009. In the face of a dismissal following plaintiffs' Motion to Dismiss same for, *inter alia*, lack of probable cause and unethical conduct, defendants voluntarily participated in conduct and a course of action to again charge the Plaintiffs August 25, 2010, Indictment number 10-08-591-I.

21. The second round of charges were likewise dismissed March 22, 2011 by The Honorable Raymond A. Batten, J.S.C. as to both plaintiffs due to a complete lack of evidence and an incorrect presentation of erroneous facts to the Grand Jury in order to secure the indictment.

22. Defendant Prosecutor Robert Taylor, acting individually, and in his official capacity, and in conspiracy with the other defendants, manipulated, misrepresented, and otherwise misdirected evidence, knowing full well that it was not and could never be supported by probable cause because plaintiffs committed no crime nor any illegal or illicit acts.

23. The second indictment proves that defendants were acting with malice because it alleged facts and legal conclusions and/or theory which were completely different than the first failed indictment.

24. Defendants committed these acts and offenses upon the Plaintiffs regardless of the ethical, legal or other implications for the purpose of attacking, harassing, or harming the plaintiffs for their own personal gain and/or interests.

25. Defendant Prosecutor Taylor's abuse of office, in conjunction with the conspiracy and collaboration with the other defendants, was proven when the second unsupported indictment was dismissed by Judge Batten on March 22, 2011.

26. Defendants knew, at all relevant times hereto, that there was no probable cause or other lawful basis to initiate and continue a criminal prosecution against plaintiffs, but did nonetheless maliciously prosecute plaintiffs causing them to suffer severe damages and injuries, in order to attack plaintiffs for Defendants' own political, social or personal gain or for any other reason inconsistent with the administration of justice.

# Appendix

## 1983 Civil Rights Lawsuit in Superior Court, Cape May County

27. As a result of Defendants' actions as aforesaid, Plaintiffs were seriously damaged, both financially and emotionally and will continue to suffer damage for an indefinite period of time into the future.

WHEREFORE, plaintiffs demand judgment against all jointly, severally and individually, as follows:

Compensatory damages;

Punitive damages;

Attorney's fees, interest and costs of suit; and

Any other relief which the Court deems equitable and just.

### COUNT TWO
### VIOLATION OF PLAINTIFFS' CIVIL RIGHTS
### N.J.S.A. 10:6-1, ET SEQ.

28. Plaintiffs incorporate every paragraph of this complaint into every other paragraph of this complaint as if fully set forth therein.
29. Defendants collaborated and conspired to and actually did violate the civil rights of plaintiffs by, including, but not limited to, abridging their right to be free from improper arrest and prosecution, specifically Article 1, Paragraph 7 of the New Jersey Constitution, and by requiring them to present themselves in Superior Court on multiple occasions for fear and threat of arrest based solely upon manufactured indictments which were maliciously initiated and fraudulently obtained by all defendants, who knew they had no probable cause to do so.
30. As a result of Defendants' actions as aforesaid, Plaintiffs were seriously damaged, both financially and emotionally and will continue to suffer damage for an indefinite period of time into the future.

WHEREFORE, plaintiffs demand judgment against all jointly, severally and individually, as follows:

Compensatory damages;

Punitive damages;

Attorney's fees, interest and costs of suit; and

Any other relief which the Court deems equitable and just.

## 1983 Civil Rights Lawsuit in Superior Court, Cape May County

### COUNT THREE
### ABUSE OF PROCESS

31. Plaintiffs incorporate every paragraph of this complaint into every other paragraph of this complaint as if fully set forth therein.
32. As a result of the wrongful and intentional actions of the defendant as described above, an indictment against the Plaintiffs was issued.
33. Based upon this false and misleading information, a complaint was signed and issued charging the Plaintiffs with offenses under the Criminal Code of the State of New Jersey.
34. Said complaint was obtained by means of a false Affidavit, which some or all of Defendants knew to be false.
35. Defendants improperly used and/or abused the process to facilitate and execute their improper purposes of unlawfully detaining, charging and indicting the Plaintiffs.
36. As a result of Defendants' actions as aforesaid, Plaintiffs were seriously damaged, both financially and emotionally and will continue to suffer damage for an indefinite period of time into the future.

WHEREFORE, plaintiffs demand judgment against all jointly, severally and individually, as follows:

Compensatory damages;

Punitive damages;

Attorney's fees, interest and costs of suit; and

Any other relief which the Court deems equitable and just.

### COUNT FOUR
### EMOTIONAL DISTRESS

37. Plaintiffs incorporate every paragraph of this complaint into every other paragraph of this complaint as if fully set forth therein.
38. The Plaintiffs prior to the initiation of the charges and subsequent indictment(s) by Defendants, were successful, upstanding, and contributing members of the community. They were highly respected citizens.

# 1983 Civil Rights Lawsuit in Superior Court, Cape May County

39. As a result of the outrageous conduct of the Defendants, the Plaintiffs reputation in the medical community, as well as the community at large, was demeaned, lessened, impugned and, as a result, they lost their medical practice, employment, and subsequent ability to earn a living.
40. As a result of the consequences of the actions of Defendants, the Plaintiffs suffered emotional distress, which had a debilitating and devastating effect upon them, causing them emotional and physical pain and damage.
41. As a result of Defendants' actions as aforesaid, Plaintiffs were seriously damaged, both financially and emotionally and will continue to suffer damage for an indefinite period of time into the future.

WHEREFORE, plaintiffs demand judgment against all jointly, severally and individually, as follows:

Compensatory damages;

Punitive damages;

Attorney's fees, interest and costs of suit; and

Any other relief which the Court deems equitable and just.

## COUNT FIVE
## FAILURE TO TRAIN, SUPERVISE, DISCIPLINE, OR ASSIGN

42. Plaintiffs incorporate every paragraph of this complaint into every other paragraph of this complaint as if fully set forth therein.
43. At all times relevant to this complaint, any and/or all Defendants were aware of, had knowledge of, condoned, encouraged, and/or failed to deter or to stop the above-described pattern, history and custom of other acting defendants, thereby violating the civil rights of citizens within the boundaries of the Cape May County and the rights of the Plaintiffs in particular.
44. All defendants acting solely or in concert negligently failed to properly supervise, discipline, train, or otherwise sanction assistant district attorney, county detectives, police officers, investigators, sergeants, lieutenants and/or or other individuals or officers who violated the rights of citizens, including the rights of plaintiffs, thus encouraging, acquiescing and condoning the actions of the remaining defendants to engage in the unlawful and actionable conduct described above.

## 1983 Civil Rights Lawsuit in Superior Court, Cape May County

45. Defendants, at all relevant times, had an official custom of knowledge or deliberate indifference that caused the constitutional violations.
46. All defendants acting solely or in concert as a further matter of public policy and practice failed to properly train its investigators, prosecutors, police officers, and other agents acting in their official capacity, individually and on said Defendants' behalf and at said Defendants' direction and authority, including remaining defendants, with respect to the constitutional, statutory and departmental limits of their authority.
47. At all times herein mentioned, all defendants were acting as the agents, servants, and/or employees of the defendant Cape May County.
48. All defendants were on actual notice of the need to train, supervise, discipline or terminate its defendant officers, investigators or agents prior to the incident in question as other similar incidents may have occurred in the past.
49. All Defendants intentionally, recklessly and/or negligently as a matter of policy and practice, failed to properly supervise, discipline, train, or otherwise sanction police officers, sergeants, lieutenants and other agents who violated the rights of individuals, including the rights of these plaintiffs, thus encouraging, acquiescing the remaining defendants to engage in the unlawful and actionable conduct described above.
50. All Defendants as a further matter of public policy and practice failed to properly train its police officers, investigators, prosecutors, and/or other agents, including remaining defendants with respect to the constitutional, statutory and departmental limits of their authority.
51. At all times herein mentioned, defendants were acting as the agents, servants, and/or employees of the defendants which was under the supervision, management or control of defendants and therefore their acts are attributable to each defendant.
52. Defendants were on actual notice of the need to train, supervise, discipline or terminate its defendant officers prior to the incident in question as other similar incidents may have occurred in the past.
53. As a result of Defendants' actions as aforesaid, Plaintiffs were seriously damaged, both financially and emotionally and will continue to suffer damage for an indefinite period of time into the future.

WHEREFORE, plaintiffs demand judgment against all jointly, severally and individually, as follows:

    a. Compensatory damages;

Appendix

# 1983 Federal Court Civil Rights Lawsuit, Camden, NJ

**IN THE UNITED STATES DISTRICT COURT**
**FOR THE DISTRICT OF NEW JERSEY**

| | | |
|---|---|---|
| JOHN G. COSTINO, | : | CIVIL ACTION |
| Plaintiff, | : | |
| v. | : | No. 14-CV-06940 (JHR)-JS |
| POLICE OFFICER TONYA ANDERSON, SPECIAL AGENT MARGARITA ABBATTISCIANNI, CAPE MAY COUNTY ASSISTANT PROSECUTOR MEGHAN HOERNER, CAPE MAY COUNTY ASSISTANT PROSECUTOR MATTHEW D. WEINTRAUB, CAPE MAY COUNTY ASSISTANT PROSECUTOR TINA KELL, DETECTIVE GEORGE HALLETT, LIEUTENANT DETECTIVE LYNN FRAME, CAPE MAY COUNTY PROSECUTOR ROBERT L. TAYLOR, CAPE MAY COUNTY, LITTLE EGG HARBOR TOWNSHIP | : | JURY TRIAL DEMANDED |
| Defendants. | : | |

## COMPLAINT

Plaintiff John G. Costino, by and through undersigned counsel, hereby brings this action and avers as follows:

### PARTIES

1. Plaintiff John G. Costino ("Costino") is an adult individual residing in North Wildwood, Cape May County, New Jersey.

2. Defendant Tonya Anderson, at all times relevant hereto, was a Police Officer in the Little Egg Harbor Township Police Department.

3. Defendant George Hallett, at all times relevant hereto, was a Detective in the Cape May County Prosecutor' Office.

# "Due Process" Denied

## 1983 Federal Court Civil Rights Lawsuit, Camden, NJ

4. Defendant Lynn Frame, at all times relevant hereto, was a Lieutenant Detective in the Cape May County Prosecutor's Office.

5. Defendant Meghan Hoerner, at all times relevant hereto, was a Cape May County Assistant Prosecutor.

6. Defendant Matthew D. Weintraub, at all times relevant hereto, was a Cape May County Assistant Prosecutor.

7. Defendant Tina Kell, at all times relevant hereto, was a Cape May County Assistant Prosecutor.

8. Defendant Margarita Abbattiscianni, at all times relevant hereto, was a Special Agent in the Drug Enforcement Administration.

9. Defendant Robert L. Taylor, at all times relevant hereto, was a Cape May County Prosecutor.

10. Defendants Anderson, Hallett, Frame, Kell, Hoerner, Weintraub, Abbattiscianni, and Taylor shall be referred to herein collectively as Individual Defendants.

11. Defendant Cape May County, at all times relevant hereto, was a county of the State of New Jersey.

12. Defendant Little Egg Harbor Township, at all times relevant hereto, was a Township and a municipality of the State of New Jersey.

13. Defendants Cape May County and Little Egg Harbor Township shall be referred to herein collectively as Government Defendants.

Appendix

## 1983 Federal Court Civil Rights Lawsuit, Camden, NJ

23. Costino's medical practice apparently came under the scrutiny of the Cape May County Prosecutor's office in 2005, as a result of a statistical report identifying Costino as prescribing excessive amounts of addictive pain medications.

24. The fact that Costino was prescribing a significant amount of addictive pain medications was readily understandable to any investigative authority performing a reasonable investigation for two reasons:

    a. A substantial portion of his practice was dedicated to pain management patients and to the treatment of patients addicted to opioids; and

    b. On three occasions in 2004 and 2005, prescription pads were stolen from Costino's office and used illegally to obtain addictive pain medications. On each such occasion, Costino reported these thefts and the perpetrators were prosecuted by the authorities.

25. Thus, the Cape May County Prosecutor's office had actual knowledge of the reason why an excessive amount of addictive pain medication prescriptions may have appeared to have been prescribed by Costino.

26. Nevertheless, in December 2005, the Cape May County Prosecutor's office, apparently determined to investigate the alleged excessive amount of addictive pain medication prescriptions written by Costino, sent an undercover detective to Costino's office, posing as a heroin addict. The detective, Agent Landis, attempted obtain a prescription for pain medication. Costino refused to prescribe the medication because the patient presented as a heroin addict. Instead, Costino urged the patient to enter the Suboxone program for treatment of the heroin addiction. After his undercover assignment concluded, Agent Landis wrote a report that was favorable to Costino, there being no evidence to support any allegation that Costino improperly prescribed medication.

"Due Process" Denied

## 1983 Federal Court Civil Rights Lawsuit, Camden, NJ

27. In 2007, despite a complete and utter lack of probable cause, Individual Defendants determined to maliciously prosecute Costino in violation of his civil rights by initiating, directing and participating in a contrived criminal investigation.

28. In furtherance of said criminal investigation without probable cause, on April 12, 2007, defendant Tonya Anderson, wired with a recording device, sought treatment from Costino. She posed as an exotic dancer, who had been taking Percocet for pain without a valid prescription. She asked to establish herself as a patient of Costino's practice and to obtain a lawful prescription for Percocet. Costino took a history and performed a physical examination on defendant Anderson. Costino diagnosed defendant Anderson with acute and chronic strain and sprain of the thoracolumbar spine, primarily based upon her complaints relative to the physical demands of dancing on a stage for eight hours per night. She signed Costino's pain management agreement and left the office with a valid prescription for 30 Percocet pills.

29. On August 3, 2007, defendant Margarita Abbattiscianni, another undercover officer, also sought treatment from Costino, also posing as an exotic dancer. Abbattiscianni complained of pain and difficulty with sleeping as a result of her job keeping her up sometimes until 6:00 am. She also left the office with a valid prescription for 30 Percocet pills.

30. Defendants Anderson and Abbattiscianni treated with Costino on several occasions in the 2007, each time posing undercover as exotic dancers whose rigorous provision made their pain symptoms appear to justify the lawful use of Percocet as treatment.

31. Costino's treatment of defendants Anderson and Abbattiscianni was at all times reasonable, appropriate and based upon his professional judgment.

32. Nevertheless, Individual Defendants sought and obtained an Indictment against Costino charging him with drug related offenses relating to the unlawful distribution of controlled substances.

33. In procuring the indictment, and later a superseding indictment alleging unlawful distribution of drugs and health insurance fraud, Individual Defendants concealed exculpatory

# Appendix

## 1983 Federal Court Civil Rights Lawsuit, Camden, NJ

evidence from the Grand Jury and from Costino, knowingly procured and relied upon false certifications and testimony, and procured the alteration of evidence. The conduct of Individual Defendants was intended to support a prosecution for which they knew did not exist probable cause.

34. In September 2007, approximately 25 law enforcement officers stormed Costino's office, placed him in handcuffs, and seized records from his medical practice. At that time, Costino was arrested and taken into police custody. There he remained until he was able to post $100,000 bail.

35. Individual Defendants provided false and misleading evidence to the State of New Jersey Board of Medical Examiners resulting in Costino being falsely accused of professional misconduct and in the revocation of his medical license.

36. Costino was required to defend himself against the criminal charges and the administrative action in the Board of Medical Examiners at great expense, all while having been driven out of business by Defendants' unlawful conduct.

37. After an ordeal lasting more than 5 years, the criminal charges were finally tried before the Honorable Raymond A. Batten in the Superior Court of Cape May County.

38. Costino testified on his own behalf.

39. After deliberating less than two hours, on November 8, 2012, the jury returned a verdict in favor of Costino and he was acquitted of all criminal charges.

## COUNT I
### 42 U.S.C. § 1983
### MALICIOUS PROSECUTION IN VIOLATION OF THE 4TH AND 14TH AMENDMENTS
(Against Individual Defendants)

40. Costino incorporates all other paragraphs of this Complaint as if fully set forth herein.

## 1983 Federal Court Civil Rights Lawsuit, Camden, NJ

41. 42 U.S.C. § 1983 provides that:

> Every person, who under color of any statute, ordinance, regulation, custom or usage of any state or territory or the District of Columbia subjects or causes to be subjected any citizen of the United States or other person within the jurisdiction thereof to the deprivation of any rights, privileges or immunities secured by the constitution and law shall be liable to the party injured in an action at law, suit in equity, or other appropriate proceeding for redress....

42. Costino is a citizen of the United States and all of the Individual Defendants are persons for purposes of 42 U.S.C. § 1983.

43. The Individual Defendants, at all times relevant hereto, were acting under the color of state law and their acts and omissions were conducted within the scope of their official duties or employment.

44. At the time of the complained of events, Costino had the clearly established constitutional right to be free from malicious prosecution without probable cause under the Fourth Amendment and in violation of due process under the Fourteenth Amendment.

45. Individual Defendants knew or should have known of these rights at the time of the complained of conduct as they were clearly established at that time.

46. Individual Defendants violated Costino's Fourth and Fourteenth Amendment rights to be free from malicious prosecution without probable cause and without due process by working in concert to secure false charges against him, resulting in his arrest, confinement and prosecution.

47. Individual Defendants engaged in the conduct described by this Complaint willfully, maliciously, in bad faith, and in reckless disregard of Costino's federally protected constitutional rights.

48. The procurement of prosecution against Costino by Individual Defendants was

malicious, shocking, and objectively unreasonable in the light of the circumstances.

49. The criminal proceedings terminated in Costino's favor when, after less than two hours of deliberation, a Cape May County jury returned a verdict acquitting him of all charges contained in the indictment.

50. The acts and omissions of Individual Defendants as aforesaid deprived Costino of his constitutional and statutory rights and caused him other damages.

51. Individual Defendants, at all times relevant hereto, were acting pursuant to municipal/county custom, policy, decision, ordinance, regulation, widespread habit, usage, or practice in their actions pertaining to Costino.

52. As a proximate result of Individual Defendants' unlawful conduct, Costino has suffered financial losses, the loss of his medical license, lost earnings and earning capacity, harm to his reputation, emotional harm, and other damages and losses entitling him to compensatory and special damages.

53. Costino is further entitled to attorney's fees and costs pursuant to 42 U.S.C. §1988.

54. Costino is entitled to punitive damages against each of the Individual Defendants under 42 U.S.C. § 1983, in that the actions of each of Individual Defendants were taken maliciously, willfully and with a reckless or wanton disregard of the constitutional rights of Costino.

## COUNT II
## 42 U.S.C. § 1983
### DELIBERATELY INDIFFERENT POLICIES, PRACTICES, CUSTOMS, TRAINING, AND SUPERVISION IN VIOLATION OF THE 4TH AND 14TH AMENDMENTS
(Against Government Defendants)

55. Costino incorporates all other paragraphs of this Complaint as if fully set forth

herein.

56. The Government Defendants developed and maintained policies, procedures, customs, and/or practices exhibiting deliberate indifference to the constitutional rights of citizens, which were moving forces behind and proximately caused the violations of Costino's constitutional rights as aforesaid.

57. The Government Defendants have created and tolerated an atmosphere of lawlessness, and have developed and maintained long-standing, department-wide customs, law enforcement related policies, procedures, customs, practices, and/or failed to properly train and/or supervise their employees in a manner amounting to deliberate indifference to the constitutional rights of Costino and of the public.

58. The deliberately indifferent training and supervision provided by the Government Defendants resulted from a conscious or deliberate choice to follow a course of action from among various alternatives available to them and were moving forces in the constitutional injuries suffered by Costino.

59. As a direct result of the Government Defendants' unlawful conduct, Costino has suffered harm as aforesaid.

## COUNT III
### N.J.S.A.10:6-1, et seq.
### MALICIOUS PROSECUTION IN VIOLATION OF NEW JERSEY CIVIL RIGHTS ACT
(Against All Defendants)

60. Costino incorporates all other paragraphs of this Complaint as if fully set forth herein.

61. The conduct of Defendants as aforesaid constitutes malicious prosecution in violation of Costino's civil rights as secure by the Constitution and laws of the State New Jersey.

Appendix

## 1983 Federal Court Civil Rights Lawsuit, Camden, NJ

62. The conduct of Defendants as aforesaid constitutes a violation of the New Jersey Civil Rights Act.

63. As a result of said conduct, Costino has suffered harm as aforesaid.

### COUNT IV
### MALICIOUS PROSECUTION
### (Against All Defendants)

64. Costino incorporates all other paragraphs of this Complaint as if fully set forth herein.

65. The conduct of Defendants as aforesaid constitutes common law malicious prosecution.

66. As a result of said conduct, Costino has suffered harm as aforesaid.

67. The conduct of Defendants further violates N.J.S.A 2A:47A-1, thereby entitling Costino to an award of punitive damages against Individual Defendants.

### PRAYER FOR RELIEF

Plaintiff John G. Costino prays that this Honorable Court enter judgment in his favor and against each of the Defendants and grant:

a. compensatory damages for Costino's lost earnings and earning capacity, expenses incurred in the defense of the criminal charges, damage to his reputation, emotional distress, embarrassment, humiliation, and loss of life's pleasures

## 1983 Federal Court Civil Rights Lawsuit, Camden, NJ

    b.    special damages for the harm to Costino's liberty occasioned by his arrest, confinement and bail conditions, as well as for the loss of his medical practice and the long-term positive relationships he enjoyed with his patients, staff and professional colleagues.

    c.    punitive damages on all claims allowed by law against Individual Defendants and in an amount to be determined at trial; and

    d.    attorneys' fees and the costs associated with this action under 42 U.S.C. § 1988.


Date: November 11, 2014        /s/ Stanley B. Cheiken, Esquire (SC1060)
                                          STANLEY B. CHEIKEN, ESQUIRE

                                          2500 McClellan Avenue
                                          Suite 120
                                          Pennsauken, NJ 08109
                                          (856) 486-2110

                                          *Attorney for Plaintiff*

Appendix

## 1983 Federal Court Civil Rights Lawsuit, Camden, NJ

Case 1:14-cv-06940-JHR-JS   Document 67   Filed 03/02/18   Page 26 of 27 PageID: 1547

The doctrine of qualified immunity protects government officials "from liability for civil damages insofar as their conduct does not violate clearly established statutory or constitutional rights of which a reasonable person would have known." *Harlow v. Fitzgerald*, 457 U.S. 800, 818, 102 S.Ct. 2727, 73 L.Ed.2d 396 (1982). "Qualified immunity balances two important interests-the need to hold public officials accountable when they exercise power irresponsibly and the need to shield officials from harassment, distraction, and liability when they perform their duties reasonably." *Pearson v. Callahan*, 555 U.S. 223, 129 S.Ct. 808, 815, 172 L.Ed.2d 565 (2009).

"Qualified immunity . . . gives government officials breathing room to make reasonable but mistaken judgments, and protects all but the plainly incompetent or those who knowingly violate the law." *Fiore v. City of Bethlehem*, 510 F. App'x 215, 219–20 (3d Cir.2013). Qualified immunity attaches if the official can demonstrate his or her conduct was "objectively reasonable." *Badalamenti v. Borough of Westville*, 2014 WL 4798617, at *8 (D.N.J. Sept. 26, 2014)(citing *Harlow*, 457 U.S. at 818).

Here, as set forth in detail in the previous section, Defendant Hallett's conduct was not objectively reasonable. To the contrary, he was intentionally deceptive and malicious in communicating the alleged details of Costino's conduct, resulting in the indictment.

Based upon these facts, Defendant Hallett cannot escape liability by contending that he acted in an objectively reasonable fashion. To the contrary, because the evidence supports a conclusion that he knowingly violated Costino's rights, his defense of qualified immunity fails.

"Due Process" Denied

## 1983 Federal Court Civil Rights Lawsuit, Camden, NJ

Case 1:14-cv-06940-JHR-JS   Document 67   Filed 03/02/18   Page 27 of 27 PageID: 1

### IV. CONCLUSION

For all of the foregoing reasons, plaintiff John G. Costino respectfully requests this Honorable Court to deny Defendant Hallett's Motion for Summary Judgment.

Respectfully submitted,

Date: March 2, 2018

/s/ Stanley B. Cheiken, Esquire (SC1060)
STANLEY B. CHEIKEN, ESQUIRE

101 Greenwood Avenue
Suite 400
Jenkintown, PA 19046
(856) 486-2110
*Attorney for Plaintiff*

(5) the party against whom the doctrine is asserted was a party to or in privity with a party to the earlier proceeding.

*Olivieri v. Y.M.F. Carpet, Inc.*, 186 N.J. 511, 521-522 (2006); *In re Estate of Dawson*, 136 N.J. 1, 20 (1994).

Since collateral estoppel is an equitable doctrine, "it should only be applied when fairness requires." *Pivnick v. Beck*, 326 N.J. Super. 474, 486 (App. Div. 1999), aff'd, 165 N.J. 670 (2000). Factors disfavoring application of collateral estoppel include: the party against whom preclusion was sought could not have obtained review of the judgment in the initial action; the quality or extensiveness of the procedures in the two actions were different; it was not foreseeable at the time of the initial action that the issue would arise in subsequent litigation; and the party sought to be precluded did not have an adequate opportunity to obtain a full and fair adjudication in the first action. *Pivnick*, 326 N.J. Super., at 486.

Defendant Anderson contends that issue preclusion should be based upon either of two separate matters that preceded the instant case: 1) the state court criminal proceedings; and/or 2) the license revocation proceeding. However, neither of these prior proceedings were of the nature that would entitle Defendant Anderson to utilize issue preclusion as a bar to Costino's claims in this case.

First, the state court criminal proceedings were not fully and fairly litigated to a judgment against Costino on the issue at hand. Indeed, Costino was acquitted of all criminal charges and his acquittal was never appealed by the State of New Jersey. Thus, Costino never had an opportunity (much less an incentive) to appeal the trial court's decision on his motion to suppress evidence.

Moreover, there was a significant difference between the issues presented in the suppression hearing and in the instant case. In the suppression hearing, the trial court was asked to determine whether the prosecution had probable cause to seize certain evidence. Here, on the other hand, the issue is whether two law enforcement officers, Defendants Anderson and Hallett, had probable cause to pursue charges against Costino. The unique question before this Court is whether Defendants' maliciously misled prosecutors by falsifying evidence and failing to disclose exculpatory evidence. See, *Thomas*, 2018 WL 684836 *6 (an officer is liable if he "fails to disclose exculpatory evidence to prosecutors, makes false or misleading reports to the prosecutor, omits material information from the reports, or otherwise interferes with the prosecutor's ability to exercise independent judgment in deciding whether to prosecute.") This issue was never before the state trial court in Costino's criminal proceedings and it would be manifestly unjust to preclude Costino from litigating it in this Court.

Second, the license revocation proceedings did not present the same issues for determination as those before this Court. Indeed, in the license revocation proceeding, an administrative action, the issue of whether there was probable cause to charge Costino with a crime was not raised. In fact, even if it had been raised, it would be an irrelevant issue. That proceeding merely addressed the issue of whether Costino had violated state medical board regulations, and thus, was subject to discipline. Of course, a practitioner can be held subject to administrative discipline without engaging in behavior that gives rise to criminal charges. The State Board of Medicine was not asked to determine, and did not determine, whether Defendants Anderson and Hallett had probable cause for their actions. Thus, that administrative action cannot provide a valid basis for the application of issue preclusion.

# 1983 Federal Court Civil Rights Lawsuit, Camden, NJ

Moreover, the Section 1983 case cited by Defendant Anderson is not applicable. In *Allen v. McCurry*, 449 U.S. 90, 101 S.Ct. 411 (1980), the Supreme Court held that collateral estoppel barred a subsequent Section 1983 action under circumstance where the identical issue was fully and fairly litigated in the state court criminal proceedings. In contrast to this case, in *Allen*, there was a conviction and the Section 1983 plaintiff had a full and fair opportunity to challenge the conviction on appeal, which included a final and binding decision by the appellate court that there existed probable cause for the relevant search and seizure. *Allen*, 449 U.S. at 91.

Here, there is no such final and binding adjudication against Costino. For these reasons, claim preclusion is no to Costino's Section 1983 claim.

### E. The New Jersey Civil Rights Act Claim Is Also Viable

Defendant Anderson also seeks the dismissal of Costino's claim under the New Jersey Civil Rights Act claim which is asserted under *N.J.S.A.* 10:6-1 *et seq*. As Defendant Anderson readily concedes, courts construe the New Jersey Civil Rights Act in "nearly identical" terms to that of its federal counterpart, Section 1983. *Chapman v. State of New Jersey*, 2009 WL 263488, at *3 (D.N.J.), citing, *Newport v. Fact Concerts*, 453 U.S. 247, 259-61 (1981). Thus, when presented with both federal and New Jersey civil rights claims, the courts do not address their merits separately. *Chen v. Newark Public Schools*, 2009 WL 3756872, at *4 (D.N.J.).

Defendant Anderson offers no separate analysis for Costino's New Jersey Civil Rights Act claim. Thus, there is nothing additional for the Court to consider. Costino's state law claim is viable for precisely the reasons that his Section 1983 claim withstands the instant Motion for Summary Judgment.

## 1983 Federal Court Civil Rights Lawsuit, Camden, NJ

Case 1:14-cv-06940-JHR-JS   Document 66   Filed 03/02/18   Page 50 of 50 PageID: 1220

### IV. CONCLUSION

For all of the foregoing reasons, plaintiff John G. Costino respectfully requests this Honorable Court to deny Defendant Anderson's Motion for Summary Judgment.

Respectfully submitted,

Date: March 2, 2018

/s/ Stanley B. Cheiken, Esquire (SC1060)
STANLEY B. CHEIKEN, ESQUIRE

101 Greenwood Avenue
Suite 400
Jenkintown, PA 19046
(856) 486-2110
*Attorney for Plaintiff*

Appendix

# Federal Judge Rodriguez granted Summary Judgment in my 1983 Civil Rights case to the defendants: Tonya Anderson, George Hallett ands Little Egg Harbor Twp.

UNITED STATES DISTRICT COURT
DISTRICT OF NEW JERSEY

| | | |
|---|---|---|
| JOHN G. COSTINO, | : | Hon. Joseph H. Rodriguez |
| Plaintiff, | : | Civil Action No. 14-6940 |
| v. | : | ORDER |
| POLICE OFFICER TONYA ANDERSON, et al., | : | |
| Defendants. | : | |

This matter having come before the Court on motions for summary judgment pursuant to Fed. R. Civ. P. 56 filed by the remaining Defendants; and

The Court having reviewed the submissions and having decided the matter based on the briefs pursuant to Fed. R. Civ. P. 78(b);

For the reasons in this Court's accompanying Opinion,

IT IS ORDERED this 26th day of September, 2018 that the motions for summary judgment filed by Defendants Little Egg Harbor Township and its Police Officer Tonya Anderson [Doc. 63] and Cape May County Prosecutor's Office Detective George Hallett [Doc. 64] are hereby GRANTED.

/s/ Joseph H. Rodriguez
JOSEPH H. RODRIGUEZ
U.S.D.J.

"Due Process" Denied

# The Order to Dismiss - Decision of the Administrative Law Judge (Judge Miller) in February 24, 1998  -Pg 1
## Rejection of BME and Sandra Dick

OAL DKT. NO. BDS 10628-94

It is well settled that the burden of proof in most administrative law cases is upon the agency. *Atkinson v. Parsekian*, 37 *N.J.* 143, 179 (1962); *In re Polk, supra*, 90 *N.J.* 550. On this issue, as on the first issue discussed above, complainant has been unable to carry its burden.

### CONCLUSIONS AND ORDER

For the reasons expressed above, I **CONCLUDE** that the complaint against respondent should be **DISMISSED**. It so **ORDERED**.

I hereby **FILE** my initial decision with the **BOARD OF MEDICAL EXAMINERS** for consideration.

This recommended decision may be adopted, modified or rejected by the **BOARD OF MEDICAL EXAMINERS**, which by law is authorized to make a final decision in this matter. If the Board of Medical Examiners does not adopt, modify or reject this decision within forty-five (45) days and unless such time limit is otherwise extended, this recommended decision shall become a final decision in accordance with *N.J.S.A.* 52:14B-10.

# Appendix

## The Order to Dismiss - Decision of the Administrative Law Judge (Judge Miller) in February 24, 1998   -Pg 2
## Rejection of BME and Sandra Dick

OAL DKT. NO. BDS 10628-94

Within thirteen (13) days from the date on which this recommended decision was mailed to the parties, any party may file written exceptions with the **EXECUTIVE DIRECTOR OF THE BOARD OF MEDICAL EXAMINERS, 140 East Front Street, 2nd Floor, Trenton, New Jersey 08608**, marked "Attention: Exceptions." A copy of any exceptions must be sent to the judge and to the other parties.

_February 24, 1998_
DATE

**ROBERT S. MILLER**, ALJ

Receipt Acknowledged:

DATE

BOARD OF MEDICAL EXAMINERS

Mailed To Parties:

DATE

OFFICE OF ADMINISTRATIVE LAW

tmp

www.ingramcontent.com/pod-product-compliance
Lightning Source LLC
Chambersburg PA
CBHW082103220526
45472CB00009B/2029